THE COMPLETE ILLUSTRATED GUIDE TO
BEADING
& MAKING JEWELRY

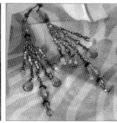

THE COMPLETE ILLUSTRATED GUIDE TO
BEADING
& MAKING JEWELRY

A PRACTICAL VISUAL HANDBOOK OF TRADITIONAL & CONTEMPORARY
TECHNIQUES, INCLUDING 175 CREATIVE PROJECTS SHOWN STEP BY STEP

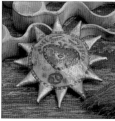

MORE THAN 1700 STUNNING PHOTOGRAPHS SHOW EVERY INSTRUCTIONAL
STAGE AND EACH INSPIRATIONAL PIECE **ANN KAY & LUCINDA GANDERTON**

HERMES
HOUSE

Contents

Introduction 6

BEADWORK HISTORY AND
TECHNIQUES 10
History 12
Gallery 16
Beads 20
Equipment 22
Materials 24
Basic Techniques 26

BEAD JEWELLERY 34
Venetian Necklace 36
Pearl and Crystal Necklace 38
Beaded Charm Bracelet 40
Cascade Earrings 42
Chinese-style Necklace 44
Cord-beaded Bracelet 46
Libran Earrings 48
Beaded Hatpins 49
Woven Bracelet 50
Victorian Earrings and Brooch 52
Butterfly Brooch 53
Off-loom Mesh Bracelet 54
Spiral Bracelets 56
Crystal Butterfly 58
Pearl Hair Comb 60
Wrapped Earrings 62
Loom-woven Choker 64
French Beading Corsage 66

BEADED ACCESSORIES 68
Monogrammed Bag 70
Bead-encrusted Frames 72
Beaded Wire Candlesticks 74
Bead-trimmed Voile Jug Covers 76
Little Fringed Bag 78
Beaded Buttons 80
Silver Chain Belt 83
Giant Bead Cord-pulls 84
Table Decoration Set 87
Spiral Chandelier 90

Bead Candle-holder 92
Child's Slippers 94
Heart-shaped Bag 96
Glittering Trinket Box 98
Devoré Scarf 100
Christmas Beadwork Decorations 102
Chunky Bead Tie-backs 104
Beaded Wall Sconce 106
Glittering Bead Spheres 108
Strawberry Pincushion 110
Silken Key Tassels 112
Edwardian-style Pincushion 114
Beaded Boat Tapestry 116
Woven Bead Trim 118
Beaded Tassels 120
Sequin and Bead Frame 122
Lacy Bottle Collars 124
Needlepoint Photograph Album 126
Flowery Frame 128
Waterfall Screen 131

DECORATIVE HOME FURNISHINGS 134
Glittering Window Decoration 136
Simple Door Curtain 138
Beaded Throw 140
Bead Window Hanging 142
Bead-encrusted Appliqué Flower 144
Velvet Bolster Cushion 146
Fringed Lampshade 148
Chunky Beaded Lampshade 150
Bead Pendant Light 152
Bead-fringed Cushions 154
Beaded Cushion Trims 157
Fish Mosaic Splashback 160

MACHINE EMBROIDERY 162
History 164
Gallery 166
Materials 168
Equipment 170
Basic Techniques 172
Sparkling Starfish Brooch 178

Heart Hatpin 180
Blazer Badge 182
Embroidered Sun Hatpin 184
Horse Brooch 185
Harlequin Bracelet 188
"Diamond" Earrings 190
Glittering Hair Comb 192
Beaded Necklace 194
Iridescent Earrings and Pendant 196

FELT, RAGS AND LEATHER 198
History 200
Gallery 202
Feltwork Materials 204
Feltwork Equipment 205
Feltwork Techniques 206
Lace Collar 208
Felt Bead Necklace 210
Felt Bracelet 212
Felt Flower Brooch 214
Felt Hat 216
Appliquéd Purse 218
Marbled Earrings 220
Acorn Buttons 222
Ragwork Materials and
   Equipment 224
Ragwork Techniques 225
Domino Hairslide and Earrings 226
Hooked Hair Accessories 228
Geometric Hairband 230
Wrapped Jewellery 232
Textured Brooch and Ring 234
Hooked Hat 236
Textured Shoulder Bag 238
Leatherwork Materials and
   Equipment 240
Leatherwork Techniques 241
Oak-leaf Purse 242
Floral Headband and Brooch 245
Oak-leaf Hair Clasp and Buttons 246
Leather Chain Belt 248
Suede Tassels 250

Coin Purse 252
Sewing Purse 254
Shopping Bag 257

RIBBONWORK HISTORY AND
TECHNIQUES 260
History 262
Gallery 264
Equipment 267
Types of Ribbon 268
Basic Techniques 270
Basic Stitching Techniques 274

RIBBONWORK ACCESSORIES 276
Ballet Shoes 278
Luxurious Giftwrapping 280
Rosy Lampshade 282
Gift Boxes 284
Bathroom Set 286
Ribbon-embroidered Bag 288
Embroidered Basket 290
Ribbon Table Mats 292
Sunflower-motif Jacket 294
Ribbon Jewellery 296
Tartan Ribbon Roses 298
Ribbon-rose Coat Hangers 300
Ribbon Hat Box 303
Lavender Bottles 306
Decorative Heart 307
Ribbon Christmas Decorations 308
Classic Evening Purse 311
Ribbon Evening Bag 314
Woven Ribbon Folder 316
Roll-up Needlework Case 318
Flower and Ribbon Headdress 320
Woven Ribbon Waistcoat 323

RIBBONWORK FURNISHINGS 326
Pillowcase Edgings 328
Ribbon Door Curtain 330
Golden Braid Cushion 332
Ribbon-decorated Throw 334
Striped Ribbon Cushion 336
Ribbon Lantern 338

Satin and Velvet Ribbon Shade 340
Ribbon Tassel Tie-back 342
Appliquéd Ribbon Café Curtain 345
Deckchair Cover 348
Basket-weave Cushion 350
Woven Ribbon Headboard 352
Ribbon-embroidered Baby Pillow 354

ENAMELLING AND METALWORK 356
History 358
Gallery 360
Enamelling Materials 362
Enamelling Equipment 363
Enamelling Techniques 364
Bird Lapel Pin 368
Multicoloured Buttons 370
Gold Foil Beads 372
Reptilian Ring 374
Striped Necklace 377
Plique-à-jour Earrings 380
Banded Ring 382
Fishy Cufflinks 384
Stargazer Earrings 386
Pet Brooch 388
Flower Pendant 390
Shield Earrings 392
Wave Brooch 395
Cloisonné Earrings 398
Cloisonné Brooch 400
Triangular Pendant 403
Metal and Wirework Materials 406
Metal and Wirework Equipment 407
Wirework Techniques 408
Metalwork Techniques 409
Pocket Clips 410
Furry Flower Necklace 411
Painted Tin Brooch 412
Spider's Web Brooch 414
Tinware Jewel Box 416

CLAY AND SHELLS 418
History 420
Gallery 422
Clay Materials 424

Clay Equipment 425
Polymer Clay Techniques 426
Spider Buttons 429
Abstract Hair Clasp 430
Burnished Bronze Necklace 432
Egyptian Bangle 434
Shimmering Earrings 436
Composite Beads 439
Orange-slice Earrings 442
Modelling Clay Techniques 443
Moulded Star Earrings 444
Florentine Boxes 446
Sun and Moon Earrings 449
Shells 450
Shell Techniques 452
Snail-shell Buttons 453
Cockle-shell Necklace 454
Seashell Jewellery Box 455
Valentine's Locket 456

PAPER, CARD AND WOOD 458
History 460
Gallery 462
Paper and Card Materials 464
Paper and Card Equipment 465
Paper and Card Techniques 466
Star-sign Brooch 469
Mirrored Trinket Box 470
Fruity Bracelet 472
Presentation Box 474
Rolled-paper Beads 476
Winged Cupid Brooch 478
Decoupage Roses Box 480
Sun and Moon Badges 483
Woodwork Materials and
    Equipment 484
Woodwork Techniques 485
Sunflower Badge 486
Shooting Star Badge 488
Crab Jewel Box 490

Templates 492
Index 504
Acknowledgements 510

Introduction

Everyone loves jewellery, whether to wear or to give, and it seems to satisfy a basic human need for personal adornment, style and possession. Many of the oldest artefacts found by archaeologists have been personal ornaments, and all over the world jewellery has always been just as significant for its meaning as for its intrinsic beauty and worth. It's a universal symbol of wealth, power, love and desire. Yet the word "jewel" is derived from a Latin word for plaything, and jewellery can certainly also be a source of pleasure and amusement. While you might keep family heirlooms such as pearls and diamonds in the bank, the pieces you choose to wear

every day have a different kind of value – they're a daily delight and a perfect way to express your personality, especially if you've made them. This book takes a look at the art of making jewellery, as well as adorning and bejewelling a multitude of home accessories to add colour, texture, femininity and personal style to your home environment.

You'll find here plenty of easy, undemanding projects that require minimal equipment, as well as guidance on developing specialist skills such as bead weaving, enamelling and metalwork. There are some surprising and original ideas for turning materials such as ribbon, paper and felt into characterful jewellery, transformed with paint and gilding. You can even discover how to create glittering filigree confections using your sewing machine.

Beads and ribbons in particular, in all their many and varied forms, have never been more fashionable, or more sought after, than they are today. On the catwalk, in sophisticated interior stores, in bijou boutiques and even in some toy shops, an ever-increasing amount of beaded or be-ribboned jewellery and accessories is to be found, and specialist suppliers now stock a vast and enticing array of materials for making your own original creations.

As we embark on a new century, contemporary craftworkers are looking back to the traditional techniques of previous generations, but reinterpreting and reworking them into something new and original. Bead weaving, for example, has been practised by Native Americans for centuries, but was also all the rage with Victorian ladies, who made intricate strips of beadwork on their wooden looms. Similarly, bead- or ribbon-embellished lampshades were a favourite design detail in Art Nouveau room schemes. Beautiful accessories and decorative objects inspired by many of these styles can be found here, along with contemporary new looks and ideas using newly available materials.

This book is full of imaginative and exciting ideas from leading designers, with chapters covering bead jewellery; beaded accessories; beaded home furnishings; machine embroidery; felt, rags and leather; ribbonwork accessories; ribbonwork furnishings; enamelling and metalwork; clay and shells; and paper, card and wood.

Each section also has an informative introduction, a basic history and gallery of work by contemporary craft artists. Each includes all the basic techniques, materials, tools and equipment required. The step-by-step instructions are straightforward and the make up of each project is clearly illustrated. The ●●● symbol indicates how com-

plex a project is. One ● means the project is easy and a

beginner could tackle it with ease. Projects with ●●●

indicate that a more advanced level of skill is required.

Whether you are a complete beginner or an experi-

enced crafter you are bound to find something to make

for yourself, or as a special present. The ornamental qualities of many of the ideas

presented here are irresistible. They will add glamour, colour, sparkle and texture to

your work, and the creative possibilities are endless.

Jewellery Fittings

To make your own jewellery, you need a variety of fittings, such as necklace clasps, brooch
pins, chains, metal pendant "blanks" that
you can infill with enamel, and earring wires.
The term "findings" is the name given to the
many different parts used to fasten or link
jewellery. The commonest findings are jump
rings, the small metal rings used in all kinds of ways to link different parts of
jewellery items.

If you become very adept at metalwork, you might choose to make the most
of these things yourself, but in the meantime certain craft stores, and some
jewellery stores, sell an enormous range of fittings to make jewellery-making
easy. You can also obtain fittings from the many companies selling them to the
trade; most of these operate mail order schemes and have accessible websites.

Beadwork History
and Techniques

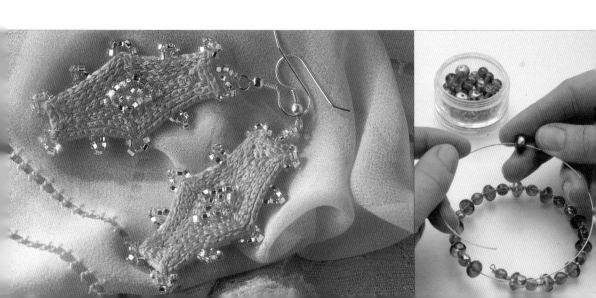

The appeal of beads has many aspects and their history holds far more than their use as purely decorative objects. They have been used as currency, worn as status symbols and regarded as talismans imbued with mystical powers. Collectors appreciate the skill involved in the creation and manufacture of the myriad types available, while craft designers enjoy their weight and shimmering qualities as well as the richness and depth they add to any creation.

Historically, the role of beads in society has not been as mere ornaments; across the world they have had great cultural significance as artefacts that reflect economic, religious and social conditions.

History

In the earliest societies, beads were used as currency, and in Africa, even in modern times for the Zulu people and the Ndbele-speaking people, beads are still a symbol of wealth and status. Men and women still wear necklaces, head bands, belts, bangles and anklets made from narrow lengths of bead-weaving and beaded, wrapped rope, worn with skins and fur. Women of different status are distinguished by heavily beaded girdles, aprons, cloaks and hats. Young women send colour- and pattern-coded messages in bead-work to their lovers when they are far from home.

In Europe, during the 15th century, beads became an important trading currency. Explorers to the Americas used them as gifts to the indigenous peoples to initiate friendship and trust. As trade grew between the Native Americans and European merchants, beads and steel needles were

exchanged mainly for skins. The imported glass beads soon replaced locally made bone and shell beads, which had been applied to hides with moosehair and porcupine quills. The Native North American Indians in particular adopted the fluid floral

Above: These highly decorated Native American beaded moccasins use the tiny beads that European traders first brought to the American continent. These glass beads were known as "trade" or "pony" beads, and were used as a form of currency. The North American Indians took to them with enthusiasm and integrated them into their existing artistic traditions.

Left: An example of the traditional bead-work of the Zulu people. Work like this acts as a statement of wealth and status for whoever wears it.

Right: The richly worked dress of this Elizabethan woman is encrusted with beads, and proclaims her position in England's highest social echelons.

styles of the foreigners and assimilated them with traditional patterns to make beautiful and distinctive moccasins, pipe bags and skirts.

Commercially manufactured beads were first introduced to Africa in the 15th century by Asians and Europeans. Caravan routes carried the easily portable currency deep into the continent. Merchants traded their glass beads for ivory, skins and even slaves. The more valuable and rare beads quickly became prized possessions, indicators of the wealth and status of the wearer. Such was the social significance of certain beads that only the upper strata of society was allowed to wear them. The etiquette of beads highlighted other differences apart from social hierarchy. Particular combinations and patterns, as well as the exact position of a given piece, identified the married and the unmarried, the young and the old. Furthermore, these differences reflected the personal achievements and the birthplace or village of an individual. Certain elaborately beaded costumes took on special significance and could be worn only by participants during ceremonial performances, weddings and initiation rites.

In medieval England, the wearing of beads and embroidery had a ceremonial function. The first manufactured beads were made from expensive raw materials, such as precious and semi-precious stones. They were available only to the nobility and the Church. Professional embroiderers embellished rich fabrics during the first great period of excellence in English embroidery, the "Opus Anglicum". Drilled pearls and coral were applied with metallic threads to make elaborate and heavy ecclesiastical vestments. These garments must have been a wondrous sight as they sparkled and gleamed in the candle-lit churches. The beads used were so valuable that, when Henry VIII seized the wealth of the Catholic Church during the Reformation in the 16th century, the prized beads were removed and some were then embroidered on to the extravagant costumes of the Tudor nobility. This ushered in a second period of superior craftsmanship. Travelling needlewomen created fabulously rich costumes, which were stiff with embroidery and heavy with pearls, spangles, sequins and corals. These gloriously impractical outfits indicated the importance of the

wearer and rendered them virtually helpless, needing a coterie of servants to dress them.

In the middle of the 17th century, young ladies were encouraged to practise and display their needle and beadworking skills by producing textile jewel boxes as part of their "education". They used a technique now known as stumpwork in which three-dimensional or padded embroidery is worked with silk thread and wool yarn and embellished with small glass beads, spangles and mica. These wonderful caskets feature houses, their elaborately dressed inhabitants and landscape gardens, a particular 17th-century preoccupation. These gardens were crammed with exotic flowers, plants and trees, sometimes three-dimensional, and worked with beads threaded on wire and bent into shape. The bizarre proportions of the features indicate that they were not observed, but copied from illustrations.

During the 19th century, embroidery and beadwork became popular hobbies among upper- and middle-class ladies. These gentle pursuits were employment enough for privileged

Above: A typical example of the complex beadwork produced in Europe in the 17th century by women of leisure. This one shows Adam and Eve surrounded by animals from the Garden of Eden, while, top right, Abraham prepares to sacrifice Isaac and, bottom right, Cain murders his brother, Abel.

women who did not have to work, and the results demonstrated not only the status of the women but also the qualities of femininity, patience and diligence that were then considered desirable. Victorian ladies also made delicate three-dimensional pieces, such as butterflies, flowers and

Left: Throughout the nineteenth century, women of the leisured classes in Europe demonstrated their skill, patience and application by producing works of embroidery. Beadwork became more and more extravagant as ladies displayed their skills and creativity.

insects, by threading beads on to wire. They arranged the finished structures as a display under a glass dome or used them to make corsages, tiaras and combs for themselves and as gifts for friends and family.

A passion emerged for using scraps of rich fabrics recycled from favourite dresses to make abstract or "crazy" patchworks. These extravagant quilts were scattered liberally with embroidery stitches, ribbons, buttons, glass beads and sequins.

Beadwork was not just the preserve of women, however – sailors at sea laboured over tokens of affection for their loved ones at home. They made patchwork pincushions using scraps of wool fabric from uniforms and stuffed with sawdust, and spelt out sentimental messages of love and remembrance in beads and sequins threaded on to pins and pressed firmly into the cushion.

The most important craft, however, was Berlinwork, or canvas covered with tent or cross stitch worked in wool yarn. This craze swept across Europe and America, its popularity based upon the ease with which it could be worked.

To take advantage of such a huge market, manufacturers produced thousands of patterns and different-coloured threads and wools. Some patterns featured beadwork. Tiny brass or more often glass beads were stitched in place of yarn to give a shimmery surface to the piece. Different tones were used to give a mottled effect, known as "grisaille work". Homes were filled with bags, tea cosies, covers, bed-spreads, slippers, cushions and fire-

screens, all the results of the labours of women.

Throughout the latter half of the 19th century there was a fashion for heavily beaded bodices on evening dresses using jet and black glass beads, and small bags embellished with fringes and tassels.

During the 1920s, women's lives changed rapidly, as they celebrated the end of the Great War, voted for the first time and began to enter the workplace. Fashions reflected this new-found freedom. Narrow, low-waisted dresses dripped with rows of fringes of sequins, bugle, drop and glass beads. The shorter styles of dress allowed much greater freedom of movement and the swinging fringes were designed to dazzle while dancing the new jazz-age dances. The popularity of beadwork declined with the onset of the Second World War, as rationing meant that clothes became simpler and more austere. In recent years, however, beaded fashions and crafts have had a tremendous revival.

Today, beads are produced in great numbers and variety. The incredible choice on the market allows contemporary designers and craft artists to explore fully the integral beauty and creative possibilities of beads.

Above: This diaphanous silk georgette evening dress, from the 1920s, uses delicate beadwork to create a shimmering, stunning effect, in the drop-waisted, show-stopping fashion of the time. Although it is quite ornate, a garment such as this was far easier to wear than the boned, corseted gowns of previous decades. The beaded necklace is a classic accessory of the Roaring Twenties.

Below: A lovely beading detail of a floral pattern from a woman's dress c.1925–27

Beadwork is a centuries-old craft with a rich history. Today, designers and craftspeople are drawn to the medium for its decorative qualities, and these examples of contemporary work illustrate its versatility.

Gallery

Beadwork can be made from all types of materials, from the reassuringly traditional to the unexpectedly modern, and is just as likely to be found embellishing haute couture garments in a smart boutique as on the shelves of a craft shop. Fashionable jewellery and accessories have always made full use of glass and semi-precious beads, which are more popular than ever: there are now many shops devoted to accessories, many of which feature beadwork – scarves, bags, necklaces and earrings. Home accessories such as striking wire-wrapped candlesticks, candle jars and dramatic flower vases can now be seen in smart interior stores, along with fringed lampshades,

Below: BROOCH AND EARRINGS
The heart-shaped brooch and matching earrings are made from rich velvet fabric worked with gold machine embroidery and finished with bugle beads.
ISABEL STANLEY

Right: CANDLESTICK
This elegant candlestick has a metal base and is embellished with beads strung on wire and wrapped along the shaft.
LIBERTY

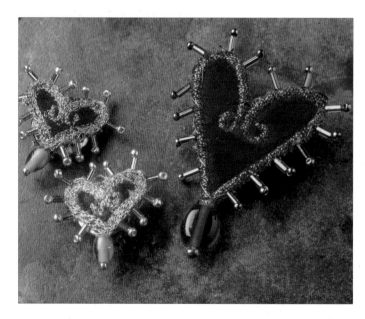

embroidered cushion covers and beaded picture frames. Most of these items are factory made, but there are many individual makers who are creating and exhibiting exquisite one-off items. Look out for their work at local art galleries and specialist craft fairs, and be inspired by the diversity of their ideas and inspirations, as beadwork takes yet another leap in its history.

Below: BEADED FLOWERS
These decorative beaded flowers are made from crystal chips, garnets and a variety of small and bugle beads, by working out from the centre of the flower and gradually building up the wired petals. The flowers can be pinned or sewn on to garments or headgear as fashionable trims. JANICE MARR

Right: ROCAILLES AND PEARLY DISCS
If circumstances do not allow you to dress from head to foot in sequins and pearls, then console yourself by adding strategic detail with strips of hand-stitched gold and pearlized beads. A taste of delicious luxury, this needle-woven panel would work well on a favourite dress or an evening bag. KAREN SPURGIN

Below: BEADED CANDLE JAR
Small red beads glow like jewels and allow the warm candlelight to show through the wire structure of this beaded candle jar. In any project that exposes beads to heat, care should be taken to use materials that are neither hazardous nor likely to melt in the heat of a flame. LIBERTY

Opposite: BEADED FRUIT
Scraps of duchesse satin and antique velvet have been beaded with cup sequins, small beads and crystal chips. For "feel appeal" they have been filled with lentils, like little bean bags. The stems are made of twisted jewellery wire and beads, some shaped like leaves.
KAREN SPURGIN

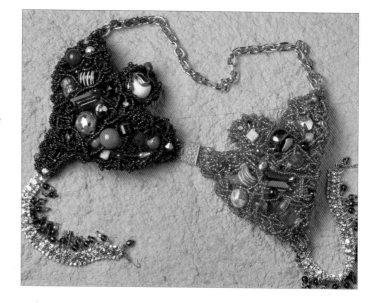

Right: BEADED BUSTIER
This stunning piece was worked on a wire base with beads woven in and out of the basic shape. DIANA LAURIE

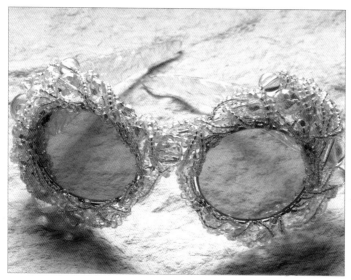

Above: SILVER FRAMES
Beads are woven in and out of a wire frame for these glamorous glasses. Old necklaces found on market stalls are a good source of beads with distinctive character. DIANA LAURIE

Right: DECORATIVE DISCS
Details such as these decorative discs turn a basic fabric into something for a special occasion. KAREN SPURGIN

An enormous range of beads can be found at specialist suppliers, in a variety of styles and shapes, in materials ranging from enamel and glass to wood or semi-precious stones.

Beads

Bugle beads

These narrow glass tubes, available in many sizes, are particularly effective when used in contrast with small glass beads.

Cloisonné

These intricate enamel beads are made in China. The metal bead is covered with wire outlines, which are filled in with coloured enamels.

Crystals

Usually cut glass, these beads have a faceted surface and are available in different shapes such as hearts and diamonds. Use beeswax to protect the beading thread from their sharp edges.

Drop beads

Shaped like teardrops, with a hole at the top, these are normally used to finish a strand.

Lampwork beads

Made in India, these are decorated with molten glass trailed in intricate patterns. Some lampwork beads have a central core of silver foil, which is visible through the coloured glass.

Metal beads

These beads often have sophisticated shapes and are made of either brass or copper and may be plated with silver or gold. They are most often used in jewellery to separate larger beads or at the end of a string.

Millefiori (thousand flowers)

Long rods of coloured glass are fused together then sliced into mosaic-like cross-sections. These beads are now also available in plastic.

Natural materials

Beads made from nuts, seeds, shells, mother-of-pearl and bone are regarded as potent talismans in some countries. Soft wooden beads are more suited to jewellery than embroidery.

Pearl beads

Artificial pearl beads with a pearlized finish come in colours, white and ivory.

Pottery beads

Ceramic beads were originally made by inserting a wooden stick through the clay shapes. During firing, the stick burnt away to leave a hole.

Rocailles

These small, slightly flattened glass beads are very popular. Many varieties, such as opaque, transparent, metallic and iridescent, are available. The hole may be lined with iridescent or opaque colour, gold or silver.

Semi-precious stones

Stones such as amber, turquoise, coral and jade are expensive, but artificial imitations are also available.

Sequins

Flat plastic shapes with one or two holes, are available in different colours and finishes. Originally sequins were made from sheets of gold and silver.

Small glass beads

Also known as seeds, these are used in many beading projects. The are spherical, but, like flatter rocailles, they come in many varieties. They are sometimes sold pre-strung, ready to transfer to a needle.

Venetian glass beads

These highly decorative beads are from one of the world's most famous beadmaking centres.

Wound beads

Molten glass is wound around a rotating metal rod to create swirling striped patterns.

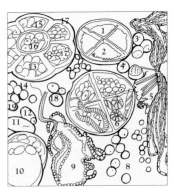

1 Rocailles; 2 Small glass beads; 3 Venetian beads; 4 Millefiori; 5 Bugle beads; 6 Bone beads; 7 Sequins; 8 Drop beads; 9 Pre-strung beads; 10 Found objects; 11 Lampwork beads; 12 Wound bead; 13 Artificial pearls; 14 Crystals; 15 Semi-precious stones; 16 Pottery beads (traditional Chinese design); 17 Metal beads; 18 Amber: 19 Cloisonné.

Beadwork is an ideal small-scale hobby as it requires very few specialist tools. Basic equipment such as scissors and needles will probably already be close to hand in the sewing basket or around the home.

Equipment

Bead loom

This small loom is specially designed for beadwork. The warp threads are fitted between metal springs and wound around wooden rollers.

Beading needles

These fine, long needles are available in various sizes and can be used to thread several beads at a time. To thread beads with large holes, you can also use sewing needles.

Beeswax

This is used to run along the beading thread to increase its strength and prevent it from snagging. It is particularly useful when using faceted beads.

Craft (utility) knife

A strong knife is needed to cut out card. Use with a cutting mat for safety.

Drawing pins (thumb tacks)

These are used to pin strands of beads on to a pin board.

Dressmaker's pins

These are used to pin fabric before tacking (basting) or slip stitching.

Embroidery hoop

Two tightly fitting rings hold fabric taut. Plastic hoops are recommended for use under a sewing-machine.

Embroidery scissors

These small, sharp scissors are used to cut and trim thread and fabric.

Fabric marker

The marks made with this specialized pen fade on contact with air or water.

Graph paper

This is used to measure and check the length of fringes and tassels.

Metal scissors

Use sturdy metal scissors to crack damaged beads and remove them from a string.

Needles

Some sewing needles, called "sharps", may be small enough to pass through beads. Leather needles, with triangular points, are used to stitch beads to tough material such as leather.

Paintbrush

This is used to apply fabric paint in some projects.

Palettes

When working on a project that invoves a number of small beads, it is useful to decant the beads into white china palettes, available from most artists' suppliers.

Pin board

Fringing or macramé work should be pinned out on a board to achieve accurate results. It is important that the board is large enough to accommodate the whole design. Small pieces of work can be pinned out on an ironing board.

Ruler

This is an essential tool for accurate measuring. A metal-edged ruler is the most suitable, though not essential, for these projects.

Tape measure

Use instead of a ruler for measuring larger pieces of fabric and any kind of curved surface.

Tweezers

These are very useful for picking up individual beads, especially small ones and sequins.

Wire cutters and round-nosed (snub-nosed) pliers

These are essential for bending and cutting wire.

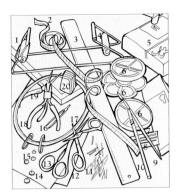

1 Pin board; 2 Tape measure; 3 Ruler; 4 Bead loom; 5 Sewing-machine; 6 Palettes; 7 Needles; 8 Beading needles; 9 Paintbrush; 10 Fabric marker; 11 Pins; 12 Embroidery scissors; 13 Metal scissors; 14 Graph paper; 15 Drawing pins; 16 Tweezers; 17 Embroidery hoop; 18 Wire cutters; 19 Round-nosed (snub-nosed) jewellery pliers; 20 Beeswax.

Apart from the beads themselves, only a few other materials are needed for beadwork, depending on the project. All of these can be purchased from specialist craft stores.

Materials

Beading thread

Use a strong, smooth polyester or one of the many threads designed especially for beadwork.

Beading wire

This is available in gold, copper and silver, and in many diameter sizes: 0.4mm and 0.6mm are the most useful.

Bookbinding fabric

This closely woven cotton fabric has a paper backing that can be glued. It is available from bookbinding suppliers.

Brass screw binders

These are used to hold sheets of paper together to make a book.

Buttons

Mix buttons with beads for extra decorative effect.

Cord

Beads can be wrapped around a core of three-ply cord, available from furnishing suppliers and haberdashers.

Cotton spheres

These are made of compressed cotton fibres and come in various shapes and sizes. They are usually available from specialist trimmings and beading suppliers.

Cover buttons

Sold in kit form in haberdashery departments, cover buttons consist of two pieces: a top, over which the fabric is pulled, and an underside with shank attached.

Embroidery threads (floss)

These include perlé cotton (a high-sheen 2-ply thread), stranded embroidery thread (separate the 5-ply strands for fine work) and machine embroidery threads. They are available in a full range of colours, including metallics.

Fabric paints

Water-based, non-toxic paints that are fixed by ironing are recommended.

Felt-tipped pen

This is useful for marking outlines and is also used for drawing decorative patterns for beadwork.

Fishing twine

For heavy beads, such as glass, fishing twine is recommended. It is stronger than polyester thread but more difficult to work with.

Floss thread

This fibrous thread has a silk-like sheen. Use it to cover wire stems.

Fusible bonding web

Ironed on to the back of appliqué fabric, this bonds it to the background fabric before stitching.

Interfacing

Normally used as a fabric stiffener, this also makes a good background fabric for beadwork.

Jewellery findings

Hatpins, earring wires, clasps, brooch backs, jump rings and other findings are available from beadwork suppliers.

Lil pins

Shorter than dressmaker's pins, these are ideal for pin-beading.

Ribbon

Silk, satin and velvet ribbons can all be used to embellish beadwork.

Tape

Fringes are stitched to fabric tape before being inserted into seams or rolled into tassels.

Tapestry canvas and wool (yarn)

This stiff, grid-like canvas is available in various weave sizes. Stitch over it with colourful, matt tapestry wools.

1 Tapestry wool; 2 Cord; 3 Beading thread; 4 Tape; 5 Ribbon; 6 Fabric paint; 7 Fabric paint; 8 Cotton spheres; 9 Fishing twine; 10 Floss thread; 11 Beading wire; 12 Jewellery findings; 13 Lil pins; 14 Brass screw bindings; 15 Bookbinding fabric; 16 Buttons; 17 Cover buttons.

When learning any new skill, it is worth taking time to master the basics before progressing to more complex techniques. Start with a straightforward project like stringing beads or making a short fringe.

Basic Techniques

Bead Picot

Use a tape measure and fabric marker to mark even points. Thread a needle, insert it into the fabric at one end of the picot and secure with a knot. Pass the needle through a large bead, followed by a small bead – the small bead will prevent the large one slipping off. Push both beads as far as possible up the needle then pass the needle back through the large bead. Make a stitch in the fabric to the next marked point.

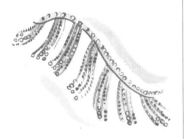

Long Fringe

1 Cut a piece of thread four times the length of the strand desired. Thread both ends through a needle. Insert into the fabric and knot. Pass the needle through the thread loop and pull taut.

3 Pass the needle through the second to last bead. Check that no thread is visible. Make a fastening-off stitch between the third and fourth beads from the end then continue up the string of beads, making fastening-off stitches every four beads.

2 Mark the length of the fringe on graph paper and place next to the thread. Thread on the required number of beads, pushing them up as far as possible.

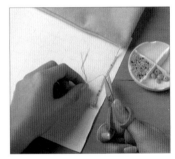

4 Pull the strand gently to remove kinks in the thread, then trim the thread close to the beads.

Short Fringe

This is worked with a continuous length of thread. Mark the length desired on graph paper. Insert the needle in the fabric and secure the thread with a knot. Thread on the required number of beads, pushing them up as far as possible. Pass the needle through the second to last bead, then back up the full length of the string. Insert the needle back into the fabric and bring it out at the next point on the fringe.

Pointed Fringe

Thread a needle, insert in the fabric and secure with a knot. Thread on a bugle bead, a small glass bead and another bugle. Push the beads up as far as possible to form points, then insert the needle at the next point along.

Drop Fringe

Thread a needle, insert in the fabric and secure with a knot. Thread on a small glass bead, a drop bead and another small glass bead. Push the beads up as far as possible, then insert the needle at the next point along.

Lattice Fringe

1 This pretty open diamond fringe uses long bugle beads, and can be made to any depth. It is worked on to a length of narrow petersham ribbon so that it can then be sewn on to a lampshade, bag or other accessory. Make a series of pencil marks along one edge of the ribbon, 1cm/½in apart.

2 Thread a beading needle with a long, strong thread and fasten it on at the first mark. Thread one small, one large and one small rocaille, then a bugle, a large rocaille, a second bugle, a large rocaille, a third bugle, a large rocaille and three small rocailles. Take the needle back through the last large rocaille and add a bugle, a large rocaille and another bugle.

3 Go back through the first single large rocaille of the first strand and add another bugle, a small rocaille, a large rocaille and another small rocaille. Take the needle through the edge of the ribbon at the next pencil mark, then come back through the first two beads. Add a small rocaille, a bugle, a large rocaille and another bugle, then go through the second single large rocaille of the last strand. Continue in this way to the end.

Looped Fringe

Mark points at even intervals with a fabric marker. Thread a needle, insert into the fabric at the first point and secure with a knot. Thread on enough beads to give the desired size of loop, pushing them up as far as possible. Insert the needle back at the same point to form a loop, then insert the needle at the next point along.

Looped Fringe with Stems

Before making a loop, thread on the required number of beads for the stem, then add the beads for the loop. Pass the needle back through the stem, then insert at the next point along.

Needle-woven Beading

Here a continuous thread runs through rounds of beads, with a second round fitting between pairs of the first, joined to the first by interweaving. The following instructions are for a three-dimensional object. For a two-dimensional design, work rows instead of rounds.

1 For round 1, thread on the required number of beads, tie around the neck of the bottle and knot the ends.

2 For round 2, pass the needle through the first bead of round 1, then thread the first bead of round 2 between the first and second beads. Pass the needle through the third bead of round 1. Continue until the design is complete.

Couching

Pre-strung beads are laid down on fabric to create or embellish the lines of the design, then stitched over (couched down) with thread to secure. Add a second thread of beads on top for extra texture.

Scallops

Mark points at even intervals. Thread a needle, insert it into the fabric at the first point and secure with a knot. Thread on enough beads to give the desired length of scallop, pushing them up as far as possible, then insert the needle back in at the next point.

Bead Weaving

Bead weaving is a fascinating and easy-to-learn technique, with roots in Native American craftwork. It is used to make long strips of beadwork with intricate patterns, following charted designs in which each coloured square represents a bead. The weaving is worked on a simple loom: a wire frame that holds the vertical warp threads and keeps them under tension. The horizontal threads, or weft, that carry the beads are worked across the warp. Use long beading needles for weaving: these are fine enough to pass through the smallest beads but tend to snap easily, so keep spares to hand.

1 The warp threads run along the length of the design. They should all be the same length: the length of the finished piece of weaving, plus 25cm/10in. You will require one more warp thread than the number of beads across the design, i.e. for a 15-bead design you need 16 threads. Measure and cut the threads and tie them together at one end with an over hand knot. Knot the other end.

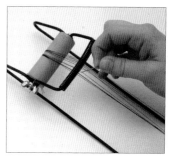

2 Divide the threads in half to form two bundles. There is a pin in the centre of each spool: slip one knot over the first of these. Slip the second knot over the other pin. Loosen the wing nut and turn the spool towards you until the threads are taut. Spread the first threads out over the wire separator so that each one lies in the groove between two coils.

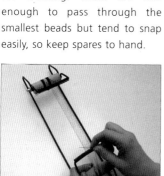

3 You may find it helpful to pick up and separate each thread with a needle. Separate the threads at the other end, ensuring that they all lie parallel. Tighten the wing nuts to maintain the tension.

4 Position the loom so that the shorter end of the warp is facing towards you. Cut a 60cm/24in length of nymo and thread it through a beading needle. Knot the long end to the bottom of the first thread on the left, leaving a loose tail of 5cm/2in.

5 The patterns for most bead weaving projects are given as coloured squares on a grid. Each of these squares represents a single bead in a different colour. For the first row of the pattern, use the point of the needle to pick up a bead to match each square, working from left to right.

Wire Beading

Wire brings a third dimension to beadwork, enabling you to make more sculptural forms. It is made from many different metals, from pure silver and brass to flexible alloys, which are often plated in bright colours. The diameter of all wire is given as the gauge (g): the smaller the 'g' number the thicker it is, from 10g up to fine 40g. Use 20g for making jewellery and 24g for wrapped techniques and flowers.

Bead Chains

Individually wired beads can be linked together to make attractive necklaces or set between lengths of chain – a good way to show off just a few expensive beads. Use 20g wire and round-nosed (snub-nosed) pliers to make the loops and flat-nosed pliers to join them together. Make a loop at the end of a short length of wire, as shown on page 32. Thread on the beads, then clip the wire to 6mm/¼in. Bend this end into a second loop, ensuring that it curls in the opposite direction to the first.

1 Wire up the next beads, leaving the second loop partly open. Join the loop on to the first bead, then close it with flat-nosed pliers. Repeat until you have the required length, then add a fastener to each end.

2 Joining the beads with lengths of chain gives a pretty, flexible look to the finished piece. Cut the chain into equal-sized lengths, each with an odd number of links, then use the wired beads to join the chains together.

Wrapping

Use this technique to embellish plain bangles and headbands. Thread small beads on to fine wire and secure the end by twisting around the foundation. Slide the beads down and wrap the wire so that the rows of beads lie close together. Finish off by twisting the loose end with flat-nosed pliers.

Memory Wire

This industrial-strength coiled wire retains its shape even when stretched. It comes in three diameters for chokers, bracelets and rings. Cut it with heavy-duty wire cutters and use round-nosed pliers to make a loop at one end. Thread on the beads, then secure the end with another loop.

Tiger Tail

This strong wire is coated with a layer of plastic in a range of bright colours. It works well with crimp beads, which can be used to secure feature beads at intervals along its length to make floating necklaces and bracelets. Use flat-nosed pliers to squeeze the crimp beads into place.

Bead Flowers These exquisite flowers have been made for centuries and were particularly popular on the Venetian glass-making island of Murano. Long-lasting and naturalistic, they were used to create garlands, posies and tiaras. Use small rocailles or short bugles threaded on fine wire. The same basic method, which is surprisingly easy to master, can be used to make leaves and petals of any size.

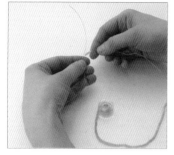

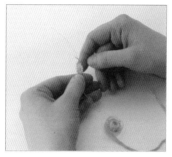

1 Thread the beads on to a reel of fine, flexible wire. Bend the last 15cm/6in into a loop and, leaving about 7cm/2¾in free at the end, twist the remaining wire loosely to make the stem. Slide the first five beads down the wire so they lie above the twist.

2 Wrap the working wire behind and in front of the loose end. Count off seven beads and hold them to the left of the centre beads. Take the wire once around the top of the stem below the beads, count off another seven, and bring it up to the right.

3 Wrap the wire once around the loose wire, just above the top bead. Make another round in the same way with nine beads on the left and eleven on the right. Continue adding more rounds until the petal is the required size, adding another two beads on each side as you work.

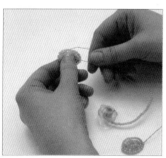

4 Finish off by bending both wires back down behind the beads. Twist all four strands together to complete the stem, and clip with wire cutters. Make another four petals in the same way and curve them gently between finger and thumb to give a natural shape.

5 To make the bead stamen centre, thread ten gold beads 30cm/12in along the wire. Pass the loose end back through the first seven beads, then repeat this seven times. Twist the loose ends together and clip them.

6 Hold the first petal up against the stamens and keep it in place by wrapping wire tightly around the top of the stem. Add the other petals, arranging them evenly around the centre core. Conceal the wires by binding the stalk with florist's tape (stem wrap).

Using Findings   Findings are the metal pins, clasps and loops that will transform your beads into items of jewellery. They come in a range of finishes to suit all styles from classically elegant to ruggedly ethnic.

Jump Rings

1 These wire circles are used to join fasteners to necklaces and earrings to stud posts, to link chains and droppers and to make earrings. Open sideways with a gentle twisting action, using pliers if necessary: forcing them from the centre will distort the shape.

2 For an earring, thread on dropper beads and an ear hook. Close the ring by twisting it in the opposite direction so the two ends touch again. Thicker rings may require pliers to open and close them but softer, small jump rings can be carefully opened by hand.

Triangles

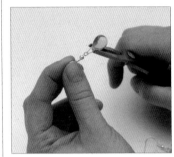

Teardrop beads have a hole at the narrow point, rather than through the centre, and are fixed to other findings with triangular links. Use pliers to open the space, slip over the top of the bead and gently squeeze the triangle shut with flat-nosed pliers.

Head Pins

1 Head pins are for making bead drops or simple earrings. If the holes in the beads are too wide, thread on a small, matching bead first. Add more beads until there is 6mm/¼in of wire left.

2 Bend into a loop with round-nosed (snub-nosed) pliers. Just before the loop is complete, bend the wire back to centre the loop above the pin. Thread on a dropper and ear hook and complete the loop.

Eye Pins

These pins have a small loop at the end for small charms and droppers. Open and close the loop with pliers. Make the top loop at a right angle so the charm will face forward.

Shell Calotte

Make a knot (two or three if the thread is fine) close to the end of the thread. Seal with glue. When dry, trim to 2mm/¹⁄₁₂in. Hold the calotte over the knot and squeeze it shut with pliers. At the other end, knot the thread close to the last bead, clip the end and fix a calotte over the knot.

Crab Claw

These functional, spring-loaded fasteners are joined on to a calotte with a jump ring. They come in several sizes: the smaller the beads, the smaller the crab claw should be. Fix a second jump ring to the other calotte to complete the fastening.

Hook and Eye Fastener

This fastener, which has a hollow tube at each end, is designed for use with leather thong or thick cord. Trim the cord to the required length and put a spot of superglue on the end. Insert the end into one part of the fastener and gently squeeze with pliers. Repeat at the other end.

Spacers and Bars

For multi-stranded bracelets or necklaces, the rows of beads are kept apart with these special findings, which accommodate anything from two to seven threads.

1 Tie the end of each strand securely to one of the loops on the spacer and pass the thread through the holes in a bar as you add the beads.

2 Space the bars at regular intervals – a bracelet will require two – and fasten the thread to a second spacer. For a necklace, you will need to increase the number of beads in each row so that it lies flat on the chest when worn.

Making Necklaces and Bracelets

Depending on its length, a string of threaded beads can be made into a bracelet, choker or necklace. Very long necklaces of 100cm/40in can be slipped over the head, but anything shorter will need a fastening of some kind. Each end of the thread is finished with a metal knot cover called a calotte: a small, hinged metal ball with an opening at one end and a loop at the other. The fastening is joined to the small loops.

Bead Jewellery

From necklaces and tiaras to belts and buttons, beadwork in all its many forms can now be found decorating the most glamorous outfits. International designers have always been inspired by the colour, patterns and textures that beads can create, and have used them to enhance their collections, as jewellery and on trimmings or accessories. The projects and ideas on the following pages make best use of the variety of beads now widely available.

Show off a few precious glass beads, like these exquisitely decorated Venetian lampwork beads, by joining them with multiple strands of smaller, more inexpensive rocailles in matching shades.

Venetian Necklace

1 Thread the needle with 1m/1yd of thread and tie a bead to the end. Thread on the following beads: one lilac, 25 bronze, one green, two bronze, two green, one red, three green, one red, one lilac, one Venetian, one lilac, one red, three green, one red, two green, two bronze, one green. Repeat this sequence six times. End with 25 bronze and a lilac.

2 Cut another 1m/40in length of thread, thread through the needle and tie around the anchor bead as before. Pass the needle through the first lilac bead then thread on 25 bronze, one green, two bronze, two green, one red and three green. Pass the needle through the red, lilac, Venetian, lilac and red beads. Repeat this sequence six times, ending with 25 bronze beads and passing the needle through the lilac bead.

3 Make another three strands in the same way. Knot the threads at each end, then attach a brass crimping bead over each knot with pliers.

4 Attach a jump ring to each crimping bead and thread the fastener through them.

Gleaming freshwater pearls and faceted crystals in feminine shades of pink and cream come together in this graceful necklace. They are threaded on fine tiger tail wire, which is almost invisible when worn.

Pearl and Crystal Necklace

you will need

180cm/2yd tiger tail wire

Wire cutters

Selection of freshwater pearls and crystal beads in various shades and sizes

Silver crimp beads

Flat-nosed pliers

2 silver shell calottes

10 small silver jump rings

Silver head pin

Crab-claw fastener

1 Cut the tiger tail into three 60cm/ 24in lengths with the wire cutters. Thread a pearl at the centre of one length and add a crystal and a crimp bead at each side. Squeeze the crimp beads with the tip of the flat-nosed pliers to hold them in place.

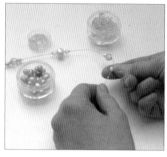

2 Fix a crimp bead 3cm/1¼in along and thread on a pearl, a crystal and another pearl. Secure with a second crimp bead. Continue adding groups of evenly spaced beads along each end of the wire.

3 Thread the second wire with alternate single pearls and crystals, at the same intervals, each one held in place with two crimp beads.

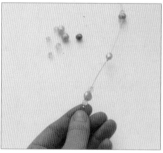

4 Add beads to the third length of wire at the same intervals, alternating the single beads with groups of three beads.

5 Lay the three strands flat and adjust them so that the beads lie within the spaces on the other wires. Thread each group of three loose ends through both a calotte and a crimp bead.

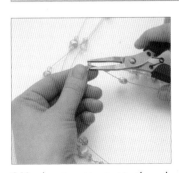

6 Use the wire cutters to trim the ends of the tiger tail very close to the crimp bead. Slide up the calotte and close it with pliers so that the ends are completely concealed.

7 Join the jump rings to make a chain. Thread two beads on to the head pin and bend the end into a loop. Add this to the chain, then fix the other end to one of the calottes.

8 Open the last jump ring by twisting it sideways with pliers and slip on the crab claw fastener. Pass the ring through the second calotte and close with pliers.

The bead droppers that hang from this pretty charm bracelet are made from an eclectic selection of pearl, iridescent glass and faceted crystal beads, in shades of amethyst and silver.

Beaded Charm Bracelet

you will need

Silver chain link bracelet

Selection of pearl, crystal and glass beads

Silver rondelles

2.5cm/1in silver head pins

A few rocailles in matching colours

Round-nosed (snub-nosed) pliers

Silver jump rings

Silver charms

Flat-nosed pliers

1 Make a dropper for every other chain link of the bracelet by threading a large bead, a rondelle and a small bead on to a head pin. Use a rocaille first, as a stopper, if the first bead has a narrow hole.

2 Bend the end of the wire into a loop using the round-nosed pliers. Gently ease the wire between the jaws to make a smooth curve, then just before you complete the ring, bend the wire at a right angle to make a question mark shape. Close the loop.

3 Add a jump ring to the top of the first dropper. Open up the ring by gently twisting the two halves apart with a sideways movement, using the flat-nosed pliers. Slip one end through the wire loop.

4 Slot the open jump ring on to the second chain link and squeeze it closed with flat-nosed pliers. Add the other droppers on to every other link along the bracelet.

5 Use a jump ring to attach a silver charm to the first empty link. To complete the bracelet, fix the remaining charms to the other links.

These bohemian earrings are made from a combination of bronze-effect wire and topaz-coloured glass beads, which give them a rich, vintage look. Try silver findings and foil-lined beads for a very different effect.

Cascade Earrings

you will need

30cm/6in chain

Wire cutters

2 small, 4 medium and 4 large oval crystal drops

12 jump rings

Medium-gauge wire

32 small bicone crystals

6 spacer beads

2 pear-shaped crystal beads

Pair of ear hooks

2 oval crystal beads

Round-nosed (snub-nosed) pliers

1 Make both earrings in the same way. Cut two lengths of chain, each of three links. Join these on to the medium crystal drops with jump rings. Cut two five-link pieces and join to the large drops in the same way.

2 For the centre dropper, make a loop at the end of a 5cm/2in piece of wire and fix on a small crystal drop. Thread on a bicone, a spacer and the pear-shaped bead, followed by another spacer. Clip the end and bend into a loop with the round-nosed pliers.

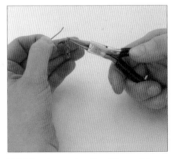

3 Make five beaded wires, each with three bicones and a loop at each end. Use a five-link chain to join one wire to the dropper. Add a seven-link length to the other end. Join the other wires to the crystal chains. Join three-link chains to the medium drops and five-link chains to the large.

4 Thread all five chains through a jump ring in the following order: medium drop, large drop, centre dropper, large drop and medium drop.

5 Make the earring head by making a loop at the bottom of a short length of wire. Add a spacer bead, an oval crystal and a bicone. Trim the other end and bend into a loop. Thread on an earring backing before closing the loop. Thread the jump ring on the other end and close.

The inspiration and starting point for this necklace was the unusual filigree pendant at the centre. The beads are strung on a core of thread, covered with naturally spiralling blanket stitch.

Chinese-style Necklace

you will need

2m/80in 2-ply silk thread

Scissors

Tape measure

Drawing pins (thumb tacks)

Pin board

4m/160in fine silk thread

2 large-eyed sewing needles

6 bone beads

2 round amber beads

2 round lampwork beads
with foil inserts

4 precious stone beads

3 lampwork discs with
foil insert

2 large amber beads

1 large Chinese pendant

1 clasp

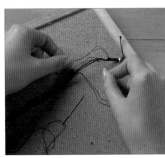

1 To make the first side, cut 1m/40in of 2-ply silk thread, fold it in half and pin the midpoint to the board. Cut two 2m/80in lengths of fine silk thread. Thread each on to a needle and knot the ends so the thread is doubled. Slip both knots over the pin. Lay one length alongside the 2-ply silk and use the other needle to blanket stitch over the threads for 12cm/5in.

2 Separate out the strands of the 2-ply silk and, using the two needles, work blanket stitch for 2cm/1in down each strand. Thread a bone bead on to one strand and a round amber bead on to the other. Tie double knots just below the beads to secure them in place. Use one strand of fine silk to work buttonhole stitch over all the strands for another 15mm/⅝in.

3 Add on a round lampwork bead and knot all the threads below the bead. Work buttonhole stitch over all the strands for 15mm/⅝in, then work as two strands for 15mm/⅝in. Thread a stone bead on each strand and knot.

4 Work two strands for 15mm/⅝in, then one strand for 1cm/½in. Add a disc, knot and work one strand for 1cm/½in. Add a bone, amber and a bone bead and knot. Make the second side, thread all ends through and knot.

5 Thread all the ends through the third disc. Knot them securely and pass the threads back up through the pendant and trim. Unpin the piece, and sew half of the clasp to each end.

This deceptively simple technique, in which beads are wound around a cord, is very popular among the Zulu people of South Africa, who are some of the most skilled and prolific beaders in the world.

Cord-beaded Bracelet

you will need

Thick cord

Scissors

Sewing thread

Fabric paint, to match beads

Paintbrush

Beading needle

Matching beading thread

Small glass beads

Button, diameter to match cord

1 Cut a length of cord to fit around your wrist. Bind both ends tightly with sewing thread to prevent them unravelling. Paint the cord with fabric paint so that it is the same colour as the beads. Leave to dry.

2 Thread the needle and fasten to one end of the cord. Thread on 20 beads, holding the thread taut and pushing the beads together. Wind the beads around the cord, make a couple of stitches then pass the needle back through the last few beads. Repeat along the length of the cord.

3 To finish off the ends of the cord, thread on a few beads and make a stitch across each blunt end. Make several more stitches to cover the ends completely.

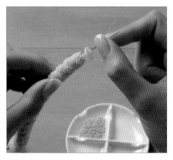

4 Make a beaded loop at one end of the cord (see Basic Techniques). At the other end, thread on three beads then pass the needle through the button. Thread on two more beads, pass the needle back through the button and make several stitches to finish off.

These delicate gold wire earrings are in the form of tiny sets of scales, the star sign of Libra, and are filled with green and blue beads. Thread the same number of beads in each so they will balance perfectly.

Libran Earrings

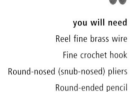

you will need

Reel fine brass wire

Fine crochet hook

Round-nosed (snub-nosed) pliers

Round-ended pencil

Selection of small blue and green glass beads

4 jump rings

2 split rings

Pair earring posts with loops

0.8mm/¹⁄₃₀in brass wire

Pair butterfly backs

Wire cutters

1 With the fine wire, crochet four round shapes 1cm/½in across. On the last round make three 2cm/¾in equally spaced loops with the pliers. Leave a long end of wire. Twist the loops.

2 Mould each round into a dome shape with the pencil. Thread equal numbers of beads on to each loose end of wire and secure them in each basket. Do not trim the wire yet.

3 With pliers, attach a jump ring and split ring to each. Cut two 4.5cm/1¾in lengths of thicket wire. Twist a loop in the centre of each, then bend each end into two loops to hang the baskets from. Attach the centre loop to the split ring using another jump ring. Thread the long end of wire on a basket through the top of the twisted loops and attach to the bar. Repeat with the other baskets. Trim.

Ornate hatpins were once an indispensable accessory, used to secure the wide-brimmed headgear worn by fashionable Edwardian ladies. These contemporary versions can be pinned, brooch-style, to the lapel.

Beaded Hatpins

you will need
Decorative and diamanté beads
Hatpin bases with safety ends
Glue gun or impact adhesive
Lengths of 6mm/¼in-wide ribbon
in several colours
Matching sewing thread

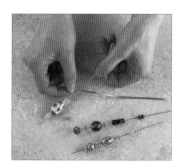

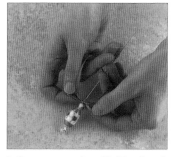

1 Choose a selection of beads in matching or complementary colours and in various shapes and sizes. Pick out a small bead to put on to the pin first to prevent the others slipping off. Smear the shaft of the pin with a very thin coat of glue, then add on the other beads.

2 Streamers can be added by threading a length of narrow ribbon between the beads. Tie into a bow and secure with a few stitches.

3 Make tiny roses from the ribbons, following the instructions on page 271. Sew the ends firmly and trim, before gluing the roses between the beads for a flowered effect.

The geometric pattern and pearlized ice-cream colours of this woven bracelet are inspired by the jazz age designs of the Art Deco movement. Each bead is represented by one square on the chart.

Woven Bracelet

you will need
Bead loom
Beading thread
Scissors
Beading needle
Small glass beads in light green, pink, grey and purple
Adhesive tape
Wool lining fabric
Sewing needle
Sewing thread
3 buttons with shanks

1 Following the instructions on page 29, thread the loom with a 75cm/30in warp of 21 threads. Thread a beading needle with a long thread and tie the end to the far-left warp thread, 2cm/¾in from the rollers. Following the pattern at the back of the book, thread on the first 20 beads.

2 Push them up into the spaces between the warp threads with the forefinger. Pass the needle back through the beads in the opposite direction, above the warp, and pull up. Thread on the next 20 beads and continue weaving to the last row of the chart.

3 Finish by passing the needle back through several rows, knotting and trimming the thread. Stick a length of adhesive tape over the warp threads at each end. Cut the threads.

4 Cut a piece of wool lining to the same size as the weaving. Tuck under the threads and place the weave on top of the lining. Join together with slip stitch.

5 At one end of the bracelet, stitch on three evenly spaced buttons. At the other end, make three beaded loops large enough to fit over the buttons.

We are accustomed to thinking of Victorian colour schemes as dark and sombre, but this jewellery set was reproduced from vivid original pieces, found in a local costume museum.

Victorian Earrings and Brooch

●●●

you will need
Thin card (stock)
Pencil
Craft (utility) knife
Fabric marker
30cm/12in square cream cotton fabric
Dressmaking scissors
Embroidery hoop
Needle
Stranded cotton in pink and green
Tiny crystal beads
30cm/12in square iron-on interfacing
30cm/12in square satin lining
Sewing thread
Beading needle
Brooch pin
2 earring hooks

1 Trace the brooch template on to thin card and cut out. Draw around it on to the centre of the cream fabric and mount in a hoop. Starting at the outer edge and using three strands of green cotton, work four rows of chain stitch. Work the next three rows in pink, then four more in green. Fill in the remaining space with beads.

2 Iron the interfacing on to the lining and draw on the brooch shape. Cut out, leaving a 1cm/½in seam allowance all round. Trim the corners, snip the curves and turn in the edges.

3 Slip stitch the backing in place. Sew a loop of five beads on to each point of the brooch, using a double thread, and finish off securely. Sew on the brooch clip.

4 Make the earrings in the same way, but add extra loops of beads in between the points. At the top of the earrings, thread on four beads and an earring hook and bring the thread back through the beads before finishing off securely.

Unmistakably Victorian in style, this butterfly would look most elegant on a simple evening dress. It could also be pinned to a belt or even adapted as a hair ornament for a special occasion.

Butterfly Brooch

you will need

Thin card (stock)

Pencil

Craft (utility) knife

Fabric marker

20cm/8in square close-woven fabric, black

Embroidery hoop

Beading needle

Black sewing thread

Large round iridescent beads, small long black beads and small round black beads

Scissors

20cm/8in square felt, black

Mounting (mat) board

Metal ruler

Double-sided tape

Brooch fastening

1 Transfer the butterfly template on to card and cut out. Draw round it on the centre of the black fabric and mount in an embroidery hoop. Thread a needle with black thread and knot both ends together to make a double length.

2 Sew on the large iridescent beads individually to make the eyes and wing highlights. Use the small long beads to stitch around the outline and then fill in the background with small round beads.

3 Cut out the butterfly, leaving a 6mm/¼in border. Remember to snip into the curves. Cut the shape of the butterfly from felt and mounting (mat) board. Score down each side of the "body" on the mounting board and turn over. Cut bits of double-sided tape to fit round the edges.

4 Stretch the beaded fabric on to the mounting board shape. Glue the felt shape on to the back of the brooch. Allow to dry before sewing the bead feelers on to the head and the brooch fastening on to the back. Gently bend the wings forward.

An easily learnt off-loom technique has been used to create this pretty diamond-shaped woven bracelet in delicate shades of lilac and purple: use beads with a silver core for a glittering effect.

Off-loom Mesh Bracelet

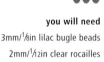

you will need

3mm/⅛in lilac bugle beads

2mm/1/12in clear rocailles

3mm/⅛in purple rocailles

Beading needle or size

10 sewing needle

Fine beading thread

2 6mm/½in round beads

Scissors

1 Thread the needle with 2m/80in of thread and knot the two ends together. Make a slip knot 15cm/6in from the end. Thread on four large rocailles, then seven bugles with small rocailles between them. Add another four large rocailles and a bugle, and take the needle back through the last small rocaille.

2 Add a bugle bead then go through the second rocaille to the left. Thread on a bugle, a small rocaille and another bugle and take the needle through the second small rocaille to the left. Repeat this sequence twice, taking the needle through the first of the large rocailles on the left, on the second action.

3 Add three large rocailles and a bugle, then go through the first rocaille to the right. Thread on a bugle, a small rocaille and a bugle.

4 Pass the needle through the second rocaille to the right. Repeat this sequence, taking the needle through the first large rocaille at the end of the row. Thread on another three small rocailles and a bugle.

5 Take the needle through the first rocaille to the left. Continue weaving in this way until the cuff fits snugly around your wrist. Tie on additional lengths of thread with a reef knot, positioned close to the last bead of a row. Leave the ends loose.

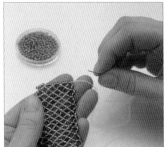

6 To finish off the end, thread on three large rocailles and take the needle through the next small rocaille. Thread on two large rocailles and go through the next small rocaille, Repeat this sequence twice, taking the needle through the first large rocaille at the end of the row.

7 Weave the needle back through the beads so it comes out through the final rocaille bead. Add three large beads, a large round bead and a large rocaille. Take the needle back through the large bead and three rocailles, then weave through to the second small rocaille along. Make another stalk in the same way and finish off securely.

8 At the other end, undo the slip knot and add large rocailles. Weave the needle through to the first rocaille and thread enough rocaille beads to make a loop to slip over the large bead. Add one more rocaille, then go back through the first rocaille and make another loop next to the next but one rocaille. Weave in any loose ends.

These sinuous bracelets are made using a simple off-loom weave known as peyote stitch. Once you have mastered the technique, the creative possibilities and colour variations are endless.

Spiral Bracelets

● ● ●

you will need

Nymo or quilting thread to match beads

Scissors

Beading needle or size 10 sewing needle

Rocailles in metallic green and red and green stripes

2 bell caps

2 2.5mm/⅛in silver beads

Small jump ring

Crab-claw fastener

1 Thread a 2m/2yd length of thread through the needle. Thread on nine green beads and tie them into a loop with a reef knot, 25cm/10in from the end. Hold the end of the thread between finger and thumb.

2 To make the first round, add a striped bead, then skip one bead and take the needle through the next bead. Thread on a green bead, skip one bead and pass the needle through the next bead.

3 To complete the round, add a striped bead and pass the needle through the next but one bead, then thread on a green bead, skip one green bead and go through the next bead. You will now have a flat, four-pointed star shape.

4 Start the next round by threading on a striped bead and taking the needle through the next striped bead to the right. Add a green bead and take the needle through the next green bead. Repeat this twice more and pull the thread up tightly so that the beads begin to form a cylinder.

5 When the thread runs out, join on another length with a reef knot. Use the point of the needle to position the knot so that it sits close to the last bead, then continue weaving, leaving the ends trailing on the outside of the cylinder. Taper the end with three beads between the next two beads. Repeat until you reach the required length, with space for the fastening.

6 Thread the needle once again through the last four beads. Bring it out through the centre of the cylinder and add a bell cap, a large silver bead and the jump ring. Go back through the findings five times, then fasten off.

7 Re-thread the needle at the other end, then complete in the same way, adding the fastener after the silver bead. Darn in the loose threads by taking them back through the weave for 2.5cm/1in and trim the ends.

8 To make striped patterns, work rounds of beads in a single contrasting colour or use three colours in one round to vary the width of the stripes. A bracelet made in a single colour is also very effective.

A delicate butterfly made entirely of wired beads, to perch on a favourite hat, a hair clip or a bag – just make sure that there are no projecting wire ends before you wear it.

Crystal Butterfly

●●●●

you will need

30cm/12in medium-gauge silver wire

3mm/$\frac{1}{8}$in faceted pale lilac oval beads

6mm/$\frac{1}{4}$in faceted oval beads in blue and lilac

Flat-nosed pliers

Reel of floristry wire

Wire cutters

Silver rocailles

2 15mm/$\frac{5}{8}$in heart-shaped blue beads

2 8mm/$\frac{1}{3}$in heart-shaped blue beads

4 4mm/$\frac{1}{6}$in round green beads

8mm/$\frac{1}{3}$in round green bead

4 8mm/$\frac{1}{3}$in bicone green beads

Round-nosed (snub-nosed) pliers

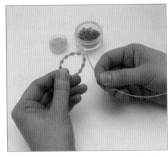

1 Make a small loop at one end of the silver wire, then thread on 12 small pale lilac beads interspersed with 11 large blue faceted beads. Pass the loose end of the wire through the loop, pull it up tightly to make the butterfly's upper wing shape and then bend it outwards.

2 Thread on eight more small beads interspersed with seven large lilac beads. Bend the wire into a loop for the lower wing and pass the end through the loop. Wrap the wire tightly once more through the loop, clip the end and bend it over with the flat-nosed pliers.

3 Fix a 30cm/6in length of floristry wire to the wire frame of the upper wing, just above the fifth large blue bead. Thread on a large lilac, a silver rocaille, a large heart, another rocaille, a large lilac bead and another rocaille. Finish off the wire at the bottom edge, just above the first large blue bead.

4 Thread on another rocaille, a large lilac bead and a rocaille, then twist the wire around the opposite side of the wire frame, just above the top of the final large blue bead. Add a rocaille, a large lilac bead and another rocaille, then pass the wire back up through the heart bead.

5 Add a rocaille, a large lilac bead and a rocaille, then fasten off three beads along from the start. Re-fasten it one bead along, add a rocaille and a small lilac bead, then twist the wire around the top of the heart. Add another small lilac and a rocaille, then fasten off two beads before the start point.

6 Fasten another 30cm/6in length of wire close to the original loop. Thread on a small lilac bead, a large lilac bead, a rocaille, a small heart, a rocaille and a small lilac bead. Secure the other end of the wire to the opposite side of the lower wing just below the seventh bead of the original round.

7 Fix the wire to the frame one bead to the right, and add a small lilac and a rocaille. Twist the wire around the bottom of the heart and add a rocaille and a small lilac. Twist the wire twice around the frame, two beads to the left, add a rocaille, a lilac bead and a rocaille. Twist around the frame, three beads along, then fill the remaining space in the same way. Make the second wing as a mirror image.

8 Bind the wings together along the centre with floristry wire. Make a loop in the end of the remaining silver wire and thread on the green beads to make the head and body. Clip the wire to 6mm/¼ in to complete the body. Twist the rest of the wire to make the antennae and slip them through the top loop. Wire the body over the join. Wire a brooch backing to the wrong side if you wish.

This pretty hair comb, heavily encrusted with spirals of faux pearls, would make a perfect tiara-type hair adornment for a bride, to hold her veil in place. For bridesmaids, choose pearlized colours instead of ivory.

Pearl Hair Comb

●●●●

you will need

Thin card (stock)

Pencil

Craft (utility) knife

Heavyweight interfacing

Fabric marker

Embroidery scissors

18cm/7in millinery wire

Jeweller's pliers

Sewing needle

Matching sewing thread

Beading needle

Matching beading thread

1cm/½in pearl bead

6mm/¼in pearl beads

4mm/⅕in pearl beads

4 8mm/⅓in pearl beads

Four drop beads

Plastic hair comb

1 Trace the template from the back of the book on to card and cut out. Mark around the template twice on the heavyweight interfacing and cut out.

2 Bend a loop at each end of the millinery wire. Stitch the wire to one piece of the interfacing 2cm/¾in from the straight edge.

3 Mark the centre of each scallop on the right side. Stitch the largest bead to the middle one. Come out at the front and thread eight 6mm/¼in and enough 4mm/⅕in beads to spiral out to fill the circle. Fasten off. Couch down the pearls using sewing thread. Fill the other scallops, using 8mm/⅓in beads in the centres and filling in the remaining spaces with small pearls.

4 Slip stitch the second piece of interfacing to the back of the beaded tiara to conceal the stitches. Stitch the four drop beads between the scallops so they point upwards. Stitch the comb securely to the bottom edge of the beaded piece, on the wrong side.

These richly decorative earrings are made of rolled tubes of card covered with velvet ribbon, wrapped with metallic thread and gold wire, then studded with beads.

Wrapped Earrings

●●●●

you will need

Thin card (stock)

Ruler and pencil

Scissors

12 x 5cm/4½ x 2in wide velvet ribbon

Sewing needle

Sewing thread to match ribbon

Red metallic embroidery thread (floss)

Textured gold wire

Wire cutters

Beading needle

Matching beading thread

Small green glass beads

4 hatpins

8 4mm/³⁄₈in flower brass beads

8 6mm/¼in red glass beads

12 4mm/⅛in red glass beads

Round-nosed (snub-nosed) pliers

4 8mm/⅓in hexagonal brass beads

2 silver earring wires

1 Cut two rectangles of card, each 4 x 7cm/1½ x 2¾in. Starting from the short side, roll into narrow tubes 15mm/⅝in in diameter.

2 Cut the velvet ribbon into two pieces, each 6cm/2½in long. Roll a piece of ribbon around each card tube, right side out.

3 Fold under a narrow hem along the overlapping raw edge of the ribbon and slip stitch it down to neaten. Do the same with the other tube. Thread a needle with a double length of red metallic embroidery thread and knot the ends. Fasten to the edge of a tube, wrap evenly down in a spiral and fasten off.

4 Cut 40 pieces of gold wire, each 15mm/⅝in long. Thread a needle with beading thread and fasten on. Thread on alternate gold wires and green beads. Wrap the thread around the tube and fasten off.

5 Push a hatpin through each tube, 6mm/¼in from the top. Snip the ends, leaving an equal length on each side. Thread a flower bead, large red bead and three small red beads on each side. Twist the pin ends into a spiral with the pliers.

6 Take a hatpin for each tube, thread on a brass bead, large red bead, hexagonal bead, wrapped tube, then the same beads in reverse. Trim each hatpin end, bending it into a loop. Attach the earring wires.

This stylish and contemporary choker is woven in shades of peacock green and silver beads. Once finished, it is mounted on a strip of soft suede and can be tied loosely around the neck.

Loom-woven Choker

●●●●

you will need
Bead loom
Black nymo thread
Beading needle
2mm/¹⁄₁₂in rocailles in three shades of green
2mm/¹⁄₁₂in silver rocailles
2 6mm/¹⁄₄in beads in a contrasting colour
Soft dark blue suede
Tape measure
Dressmaking scissors
PVA (white) glue
Sewing needle
Matching sewing thread

1 Following the instructions on page 29, thread up a 50cm/20in warp of 11 threads. Knot a 1m/40in length of nymo to the first thread on the left and, using the chart at the back of the book as a guide, thread on the first row of beads. Take the needle from left to right under the warp.

2 Gently lift the beads upwards with the tip of a finger and push them so that one sits in each gap between the warp threads. Slide the needle back through the beads, keeping it above the threads without piercing them. Continue to follow the chart.

3 To make a fringe strand, add on extra beads. Go back through the last but one bead to form a stopper, then pass the needle through the remaining beads and complete the row as usual. Do the same for each strand, adding large beads as indicated.

4 When finished, remove the weaving from the loom. Cut off the knots and knot the remaining threads together securely in pairs.

5 Cut a strip of suede the same width and 50cm/20in longer than the choker. Glue the weaving to the centre, tucking under the threads. When dry, slip stitch the edges neatly to the suede.

An elegant decoration for any lapel, this sumptuous floral spray is made from wired rocaille beads using a technique that dates back centuries. Vary the colours to make a corsage to match a favourite jacket.

French Beading Corsage

you will need
Dark gold metallic rocailles
Bronze metallic rocailles
Fine craft wire in green and bronze
Artificial stamens
Green metallic rocailles
4 18cm/7in florist's wires
Florist's tape (stem wrap)
Brooch fastening
Sewing needle and thread

1 Thread the bronze beads on to the bronze wire. Bend back the last 15cm/6in and twist the bottom 7cm/2¾in for the stalk. Slip down nine beads to make the central core. Take the working wire behind and around the loose wire from left to right and pull it up. Slide down 13 beads to the left. Wrap the wire once around the top of the stem.

2 Count off another 13 beads and take them up to the right. Wrap the wire once around the loose wire, just above the top bead. Make another round in the same way with 17 beads on each side, and one more round with 23 beads on each side.

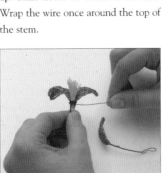

3 The final two rounds have 27 and 31 beads on each side respectively. Make five more petals in the same way. Make three small petals, of three rounds each.

4 Fold 20 artificial stamens in half and wire together. Gently curve the three small petals, then position them around the stamens. Bind them tightly in place with fine wire.

5 Curve the large petals in the same way and bind them, one at a time, around the smaller petals, placing the first three in the spaces between them.

6 Make five small petals with a centre core of five beads and two rounds of eight and thirteen beads. Bind them around a core of stamens. Make a second bronze flower in the same way.

7 Thread the green beads on to green wire. Make nine leaves from 2cm/³⁄4in to 4cm/1½in. The central core can be from four to eleven beads. Add four beads to a round to increase the size.

8 Hold a small flower at the end of the florist's wires and bind all the wires with florist's tape, adding flowers and leaves as you go and covering sharp ends. Sew on a brooch backing.

Beaded Accessories

From belts and buttons to picture frames and candleholders, beads in all their forms can be stitched, wired, woven, or glued to a vast range of surfaces. Beads add glamour, colour and texture to any item, and glass beads in particular catch the light suggesting a polished and luxurious finish has been applied. Household furnishing and clothing designers have exploited these qualities to best use on a range of small and precious items.

This simple drawstring bag, just the right size for a pair of shoes or special accessories, is personalized with a pair of initials worked in bead couching. Make a larger version to hold laundry or linen.

Monogrammed Bag

you will need

60 x 25cm/24 x 10in cotton, silk or linen, for the bag

60 x 25cm/24 x 10in cotton lawn or lightweight silk, for the lining

Tape measure

Dressmaking scissors

Pencil and tracing paper

Beading needle

Matching sewing thread

Glass embroidery beads in a variety of colours

Small glass bugle beads

Dressmaker's pins

Sewing-machine

100cm/40in silk or leather cord

Safety pin

2 large beads with large centre holes

1 Cut two rectangles each from the main fabric and lining fabric, measuring 30 x 25cm/12 x 10in. Draw your chosen initials on to tracing paper. Rub over the wrong side with pencil, and place it right side up over the right side of one of the main pieces of fabric. Trace over the lines to transfer the design.

2 Thread the beading needle with sewing thread and bring it out at the top of the first letter. Thread on enough beads to cover the first line and take it down at the end.

3 Couch the beads in place by making small horizontal stitches between them, following the shape of the line exactly. Fasten off securely at the end.

4 Continue until you have completed the whole monogram. Decorate the rest of the bag with randomly placed individual embroidery beads and small bugles in a variety of colours.

5 To make up the bag, pin the two main pieces right sides together, and machine stitch along three sides, leaving the top open. Repeat with the lining fabric. Turn the main fabric right-side out, and press.

6 Slip the lining inside the bag. Fold all the raw edges inside, pin, and slip stitch the folded edge of the lining to the folded edge of the bag. Sew two lines of stitching through both thicknesses of fabric, 3cm/1¼in and 1cm/½in from the top edge, to form the drawstring channel.

7 Snip through the stitches of the side seams between the two rows, to make gaps to insert the cords. Cut the cord in half. Use a safety pin to thread one half through from one side, and the other from the opposite side. Thread a decorative bead on to the two cords at each side, and knot to secure.

There's nothing difficult about the method used to decorate these sparkly picture frames: simply treat small beads like glitter and sprinkle them generously across a glued surface.

Bead-encrusted Frames

you will need
Flat wooden picture frames
Medium-grade abrasive paper
Emulsion (latex) or acrylic paints
Medium paintbrushes
Saucer or palette
PVA (white) glue
Small glass rocailles in a variety
of colours
Large sheet of paper
Glitter
Bugle beads in a variety of colours

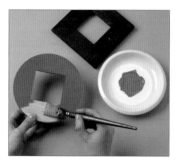

1 Prepare the frames by rubbing them down with medium-grade abrasive paper to remove any existing paint or varnish. Paint each one in a different flat, bright colour and set aside until completely dry. Add a second coat of paint, if necessary, for even coverage.

2 Paint a heart shape in each corner of a square frame, using PVA (white) glue. Sprinkle rocailles generously over the glue, using a different colour for each heart, and press them down lightly. After the beads have settled for a minute or two, lightly tap the frame to remove any that may remain loose.

3 Paint the rest of the frame with PVA glue. With the frame on a large sheet of paper, sprinkle on the glitter. Tap off the excess glitter and return it to the container.

4 Spread glue around the centre of the round frame and sprinkle with bugle beads. Continue working out to the edge, using darker or lighter beads of the same colour for a shaded effect.

5 To decorate the edge of a small block frame simply glue the sides, one by one, and then press down on to a selection of assorted beads lying on a piece of paper.

Twisted silver wire, sparingly threaded with beads, has a delicate yet sculptural quality. An assortment of toning glass beads attracts the light and looks wonderful entwining a pair of glass candlesticks.

Beaded Wire Candlesticks

you will need

Tape meaure

Wire cutters

Medium-gauge silver wire

Round-nosed (snub-nosed) pliers

Medium decorative glass beads in yellow, green, silver and clear

Pen or pencil

Small glass rocailles and square beads in complementary shades

Pair of glass candlesticks

1 Cut four 1m/40in lengths of medium-gauge silver wire for each candlestick. Use the pliers to make a small loop at the end of the first length and thread on a decorative bead. Wind the end of the wire around a pen or pencil six times to form a spiral.

2 Thread on about eight small rocailles and divide them among the loops. Thread on another medium-sized bead and repeat, forming spirals and threading beads until you reach the end of the wire.

3 Thread on the final decorative bead. Using the pliers, twist the final 8mm/⅓in of wire into a loop to keep the beads in place.

4 Make up the other three spirals in the same way, distributing the coloured beads evenly among the loops.

5 Wrap two spiral lengths around the stem of each candlestick to form an interesting shape. Secure the spirals in place by binding them gently to the stem with more wire.

No Victorian tea tray was complete without a dainty beaded cover to protect the contents of the milk jug (pitcher). Here is an updated version of this traditional idea, which is now making a come-back.

Bead-trimmed Voile Jug Covers

you will need

Dressmaking scissors

Tape measure

Checked and plain orange voile

Sewing needle and tacking (basting) thread

Sewing-machine

Matching sewing thread

Iron

Dressmaker's pins

Large orange plastic beads

Medium pink frosted glass beads

Small frosted glass beads in red and pink

Small orange opaque glass rocailles

Small square orange frosted glass beads

Checked cover

1 Cut out a 20cm/8in diameter circle of checked fabric. Turn under and tack (baste) a narrow double hem around the curved edge. Machine or hand stitch the hem, close to the inner fold, with matching thread.

2 Fold the hemmed circle into quarters, then eighths, then six-teenths. Press the folds lightly with an iron to divide the circle into 16 equal sections. Mark each of the creases with a pin.

3 Secure a length of matching thread to the hem at a pin marker, then thread on one large orange plastic bead, one medium pink frosted, one red frosted and one orange rocaille. Pass the thread back through the first three beads and make a double stitch at the hem to secure.

4 Feed the thread along the hem halfway to the next pin marker and thread on one medium pink frosted bead, one red frosted and one orange rocaille. Pass the thread back through the first two beads and make a double stitch at the hem. Repeat the pattern all around the hem to complete.

Plain cover

1 Prepare the plain voile as before and fasten on. Add a square bead, a small pink, a square, a small pink, a square, a large pink and a rocaille. Go back through the large pink and last square beads. Repeat for the other side.

2 Secure at the hem with a double stitch. Add one square, one red, one square, one small pink and a rocaille. Go back through the pink and repeat.

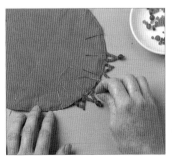

3 Double stitch at the hem to secure. Continue round the hem to complete.

Inspired by ethnic beadwork, this bag is made of traditional ikat fabric from Indonesia, lined with a plain fabric that acts as a binding and casing for the ties. An ideal first project for a newcomer to beadwork.

Little Fringed Bag

you will need

30 x 15cm/12 x 6in ikat fabric

Dressmaking scissors

Tape measure

Set square or ruler

Fabric marker

Pencil

Sheet of paper

Dressmaker's pins

35cm/14in square plain-coloured fabric, in contrasting colour

Iron

Sewing-machine

Matching thread

Sewing needle and thread to match lining

Beading needle

Black beading thread

Small black glass beads

Small multicoloured glass beads

2 50cm/20in black shoelaces

12 large beads with large holes

1 Cut the ikat fabric into two 15cm/6in squares. On the right side of each piece, mark a line diagonally from corner to corner in both directions, then mark parallel lines 2cm/¾in apart. Draw a bag shape similar to the bag in the finished picture on paper.

2 Pin the template to both pieces of ikat fabric and cut out. Cut two pieces of plain fabric 16 x 20cm/6¼ x 8in for the lining. With the marked lines right side up, tack (baste) one bag piece to each lining piece. Using running stitch, stitch along the lines. Trim the excess lining fabric.

3 To make the casing, cut two pieces of lining fabric 7 x 12cm/2¾ x 4½in. Press in half lengthways then press under a narrow turning all round. Pin one long edge to the top of a bag piece and machine stitch. Repeat with the second casing.

4 Place the two bag pieces right sides together. Pin, then machine stitch 1cm/½in from the raw, curved edges. Leave the top open.

5 Turn the bag right side out. Fold the casings over the raw edges and slip stitch in place. Thread a beading needle with beading thread and fasten just below the casing.

6 Thread on seven black beads and a coloured bead, then go back through the last black bead. Thread on six black beads and make a small stitch 1cm/½in along the seam. Repeat all around the bag.

7 Thread one shoelace through each casing for the drawstring. Thread three large beads on to the end of each shoelace and knot. Tie the two shoelaces together at either end.

These buttons are simple and satisfying to make. They would all add a unique finishing touch to a special garment, but could also be used on any soft furnishing project, from a cushion to a lampshade.

Beaded Buttons

you will need
Black felt-tipped pen
Compressed cotton sphere,
12mm/$\frac{1}{2}$in diameter
Beading needle
Black beading thread
Small black glass beads
Fabric marker
3cm/1$\frac{1}{4}$in diameter cover button
Scraps of silk
Dressmaking scissors
Sewing needle
Sewing threads to match silk
and taffeta
Large transparent glass beads
with silver-lined holes
4mm/$\frac{3}{16}$in green crystal beads
15mm/$\frac{5}{8}$in diameter cover buttons
Scraps of taffeta
6mm/$\frac{1}{4}$in green glass bead
Small copper glass beads
Small transparent glass beads

1 Colour the sphere black. Fasten the thread on at the top, stitch down a black bead, then go through the sphere. Thread on another bead and stitch it down. Take the needle around the sphere, through the top and bottom beads, then around again at right angles to divide into quarters.

2 Thread on 18 beads and pass the needle through the bottom bead on the sphere. Thread on 18 more beads, pass the needle through the top bead then around the sphere at right angles.

3 Thread on 16 beads and work from top to bottom as before, this time dividing the sphere into eight sections. Repeat with 14 beads, dividing the sphere into 16 sections, until the whole sphere is covered.

4 To make a hanging loop, fasten on at the bottom and thread on eight beads. Insert the needle back into the sphere at the same point.

▶

5 For the flower button: draw around the large button on to a scrap of silk. Draw another circle 1cm/½in larger and cut out. Mark five equal points around the inner circle.

6 Thread a needle and fasten on in the centre of the circle. Thread on 20 large transparent glass beads, then insert the needle back at the same point to make a loop.

7 Bring the needle out at one mark. Couch down the loop with a stitch between the ninth and tenth beads. Make four more petal shapes in the same way. Stitch a green crystal bead to the centre.

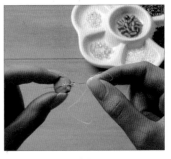

8 Run a gathering stitch 3mm/⅛in from the raw edge. Place the cover button in the centre and pull up the thread. Secure with a few small stitches and attach the underside of the button.

9 For the jewelled button: cover a small button with taffeta, as instructed. Fasten on in the centre and thread on a green crystal, a few transparent beads, then go back through the crystal. Make another stitch, then repeat to cover the button.

10 For the tassel button: cut out a 3cm/1¼in circle of taffeta. Fasten on in the centre. Thread on a green glass and eight copper beads, go back through the green bead and fasten off. Gather the raw edges and cover the button as in steps 8 and 9.

Add a touch of contemporary boho chic to your favourite outfit with this avant-garde, low-slung hipster chain belt – you can also use the same method to make a matching necklace.

Silver Chain Belt

you will need

60cm/24in medium-gauge silver wire

Round-nosed (snub-nosed) pliers

25 15mm/⅝in diameter
flat glass beads

6 6mm/¼in diameter silver beads

Wire cutters

75cm/30in silver chain with large links

60 silver jump rings

3 silver head pins

40cm/16in silver chain with small links

Fastening chain

Silver crab-claw fastener

1 Mount each of the beads on silver wire by making a small loop at one end of the wire with round-nosed pliers and threading on the bead. Trim the end to 6mm/¼in and bend in another loop in the opposite direction.

2 Cut the large-link chain into 4cm/1½in sections. Use jump rings to link alternate wired beads and chains, until the belt is the right length.

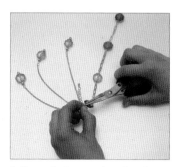

3 For each dropper, thread a silver, a glass and a silver bead on to a head pin. Clip the end and bend it into a loop. Cut the fine chain into three and fix a dropper to each one with a jump ring. Join the three chains and the fastening chain together using a jump ring and fix this to the belt. Fix the fastener to the other end with a jump ring to complete the belt.

These pulls are an ideal way to make the most of your larger beads: just one or two favourite examples can deliver real impact, and you can have the added satisfaction of using them every day.

Giant Bead Cord-pulls

you will need

Extra-long head pins

Small silver rocailles

5 coloured resin beads

2 metal cones

Wire cutters

Round-nosed (snub-nosed) pliers

Medium- and fine-gauge silver wire

2 small round metal beads

Extra-large metal bead

Coloured leather thongs

Ready-made tassel

2 large handmade foil-and-glass beads

Tape measure

Silk cord

Stranded embroidery thread (floss)

2 large, dyed bone beads

Strong non-stretch beading thread

4 long, bleached bone beads

8 small bone beads

Satin ribbon

Large, flat handmade glass bead with large hole

Sewing needle and sewing thread

1 For the metal cord-pull, take an extra-long head pin and thread with small silver rocailles and a large resin bead between two metal cones. Snip off the excess wire and bend the end into a small loop at the top. Take a length of medium-gauge silver wire, bend the end into a small loop and attach it to the top loop of the pendant.

2 Thread on two small silver rocailles, a small round metal bead, a resin bead, an extra-large metal bead, another resin bead, another small metal bead and two more silver rocailles. Snip off the excess wire and bend into a loop at the top with the round-nosed pliers.

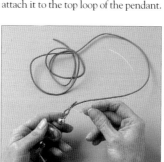

3 Thread one end of a coloured leather thong through the wire loop. Fold the last 2.5cm/1in back on itself and bind the end to the thong with fine-gauge silver wire. Ensure the ends are securely tucked under the coiled wire.

4 To make the tassel cord-pull, bend one end of a length of medium-gauge silver wire around the loop at the top of a tassel. Pass the wire through two large foil-and-glass beads, snip the wire about 15mm/⅝in above the top bead. Use pliers to bend it into a small loop. ▶

5 Pass the end of a length of matching silk cord through the loop, fold it back on itself and bind securely with embroidery thread.

6 For the decorative bone cord-pull, thread a large bone bead on to an extra-long pin between two coloured resin beads. Use pliers to bend the end of the pin into a small loop.

7 Take a short piece of medium-gauge silver wire, bend a small loop in one end and pass through a second large bone bead. Snip off the wire and bend it into a loop at the top.

8 Tie two strands of strong non-stretch bead thread to the wire loop at the top of the group of beads, leaving four long ends. Thread each through a small bone bead followed by a long bleached bone bead and finally another small bone bead.

9 Tie the threads securely to the wire loop under the top bead and thread the ends back through the bone beads to conceal them. Pass a leather thong through the topmost wire loop, fold it back on itself and bind it with wire as in step 3.

10 For a simple ribbon-pull, thread the end of a satin ribbon through a large, flat handmade bead. Fold back the short end and stitch in place, close to the top of the bead. Use pliers to bend the end of a short length of medium-gauge silver wire into a spiral, then use the rest to bind around the ribbon.

Glass rocailles, wired into simple stripes, make a lovely napkin holder, and adding a matching night-light holder makes a complete personalized table decoration that will shimmer in candlelight.

Table Decoration Set

you will need
Fine-gauge galvanized wire
Ruler or tape measure
Wire cutters
Round-nosed (snub-nosed) pliers
Plastic bottle and beaker,
to use as formers
Glass rocailles in pink,
red and orange
Fine-gauge silver wire
Adhesive pads

1 For the napkin ring, take about 1.75m/2yd of galvanized wire and bend a small loop in one end using round-nosed pliers. Wind the wire about ten times around the bottle.

2 Thread enough pink glass rocailles on to the wire to fit around the bottle once, then change to red and thread another round of beads.

3 Go on threading red and pink beads in this sequence until the wire is full, then use the pliers to bend another small loop in the end to prevent the beads falling off.

4 Bend the beaded wire around the bottle to restore its shape. Secure a length of fine wire to the first row, then bind it around the others. Do this at three other points around the ring.

5 When the ring is complete, wind the ends of the silver wire back around the previous rows to neaten, and snip off the excess.

6 To make the night-light holder, bend one end of a long piece of galvanized wire into a small loop as before. Thread the first part of the wire with orange glass rocailles.

7 Bend the beaded wire into a small spiral to form the base of the night-light holder. Attach two lengths of silver wire to the centre of the spiral and bind each row to the previous one to secure the shape. Thread on more beads until the base fits that of the beaker.

8 Use adhesive pads to attach the beaded spiral base temporarily to the base of the beaker. They will hold it in place while you construct the sides, and can then be removed.

9 Join on more wire, if necessary, by twisting the ends together with pliers. Then thread on enough orange rocailles to wind around the beaker about four or five times.

10 Wind the beaded wire around the beaker, binding each row to the last using the silver wire. Pull the wire quite tight to hold the shape.

11 Change to the red beads and repeat until the holder reaches the height you want. To finish, bind the silver wire a few times tightly around the beaded wire and back around the previous rows. Snip off the ends.

In this exquisite modern interpretation of a traditional glass chandelier, droplets of coloured glass hang and quiver from a simple structure of spiralled wire. Suspend it with a loop of clear monofilament.

Spiral Chandelier

you will need
Wire cutters
2.5m/2¾yd of 2mm/¹/₁₂in wire
Round-nosed (snub-nosed) pliers
0.2mm/¹/₁₂₀in wire
Selection of spherical and
faceted glass and plastic beads
Small glass beads
4mm/¹/₆in bugle beads

1 Use wire cutters to snip two 120cm/4ft lengths of thick wire and bend each one into a spiral. Use round-nosed pliers to make a small loop at each of the four ends.

2 Hold one end of each wire together, and carefully arrange the coils so that the two spirals run alongside each other.

3 To make the droplets, thread a piece of thin wire through a large glass spherical bead and a small bead – the small bead will act as an anchor. Pass the wire back through the beads and twist the ends together.

4 Thread on some bugle beads, then twist the wires to make a stem. Make about 30 droplets, using different beads in different arrangements.

5 Make a hanging hook for each droplet by winding a short piece of thin wire on to each stem. Use the round-nosed pliers to bend the wire back into a hook.

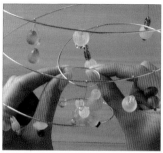

6 Suspend the droplets at intervals on the frame, alternating shapes and colours for a varied arrangement.

7 To hold the spiral shape in place, some of the droplets should be twisted over two rounds of the spiral.

8 As a finishing touch, add glass beads on to the bottom ends of the spiral wire frame.

Rocailles in restrained shades of grey, white and gold are used to make this sophisticated container, and the colours come to life in the flickering light. For safety, always use a candle in a metal holder.

Bead Candle-holder

you will need
Wire cutters
Tape measure
0.6mm/¹⁄₄₀in gold wire
Glass tumbler
Adhesive tape
Large rubber band
0.2mm/¹⁄₁₂₀in gold wire
Round-nosed (snub-nosed) pliers
4mm/¹⁄₆in grey glass beads
4mm/¹⁄₆in white glass beads
4mm/¹⁄₆in gold glass beads

1 Cut two pieces of thick gold wire twice the height and diameter of the glass plus 10cm/4in. Twist the wires together at their halfway points, then tape the knot to the centre of the glass base. Slip a rubber band over the glass to hold the wire in place. Fold the wire ends over the lip of the glass.

2 Cut two pieces of fine gold wire approximately 1m/40in long. Find their halfway points, then twist both pieces around the knot on the base of the glass. Wrap each wire around your hand first to stop it becoming tangled.

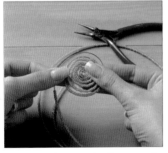

3 Thread the grey beads on to the thick wire. To begin the winding wire, bend one end of the thick wire into a 2cm/³⁄₄in flat spiral with pliers. Secure at the centre of the base by weaving the thin wire over and under the frame of thick wire and the spiralled wire.

4 Thread more grey beads on to the winding wire and continue to wind it into a spiral, weaving the thinner wire under and over the frame. Continue up the sides of the glass to within 1cm/¹⁄₂in of the top. Remove the rubber band.

5 To make a lip, ease the top of the frame outwards and thread on some white beads. Continue to weave the thinner wire under and over the winding wire and the frame. Thread on small gold beads. Open out ends of frame, remove glass, trim ends and fold over. Secure the ends to frame.

This pair of slippers is embroidered with a golden stream of bugle beads. The templates at the back of the book are for the right foot: scale them up to size and reverse the pieces for the left foot.

Child's Slippers

you will need

Tracing paper and pencil

Dressmaking scissors

50cm/20in square pale blue
wool fabric

Sewing-machine, with darning foot

Matching sewing threads

30cm/12in square dark grey velvet

Metal ruler

Dressmaker's pins

Sewing needle

Beading needle

Beading thread

Gold bugle beads

20cm/8in square grey wool fabric

20cm/8in square wadding (batting)

1 Enlarge the templates and cut out from paper to the size required. For each slipper, cut four back pieces from blue wool. Machine stitch the back seams together, then assemble each pair, wrong sides together. Work a zigzag stitch along the top and bottom edges. Using a sewing-machine with a darning foot, stitch wavy lines over the pieces to quilt.

2 To make bias binding, fold the velvet square in half diagonally, unfold and mark the line. Mark parallel lines across the cloth 3cm/1¼in apart. Cut along the lines. Match the raw edge of a length of bias binding to the outside top edge of the back piece, right sides together, and pin.

3 Machine stitch the binding 6mm/¼in from the edge of the slipper, fold the binding over to the wrong side and tuck under the raw edges. Slip stitch in place.

4 Cut one piece of fabric to the size of the template for each toe piece. Machine stitch the dart. Cut out the piece for the beaded appliqué, pin it to the toe as shown. Work a zigzag stitch around the appliqué.

5 Bind the top edge of the toe piece. Fold 30cm/12in of binding in half widthways and pin the fold to the centre front edge, right sides facing. Pin around the front and stitch 6mm/¼in from the edge.

6 At the top edge of the appliquéd piece, make a few fastening-on stitches, then thread enough bugle beads on to a beading needle to follow the line of the piece. Insert the needle at the other side.

7 Thread a second needle and make a tiny stitch over the laid thread between the first two beads. Push the third bead up close and make another stitch between that and the fourth bead. Make another 12 rows of couching in this way, following the same contours.

8 For each sole, cut two pieces of grey wool fabric and one of wadding to the size of the template. Assemble the wadding between the wool pieces. Set the sewing-machine to darning mode, attach the darning foot, then stitch a wavy line to quilt the layers. Work a wide zigzag stitch round the edge.

9 Pin and stitch the back piece around the sole, matching the centres. Pin and stitch the toe piece over the front and stitch the sides to the back where they meet. Pin and machine stitch the binding round the back base, and neaten the join with slip stitch. Fold it over the edge and slip stitch in place.

An engraving in a vintage department store catalogue provided the inspiration for this heart-shaped bridal bag, which is just big enough to hold a lace handkerchief, lipstick and other essentials.

Heart-shaped Bag

●●●

you will need

20 x 40cm/8 x 16in heavy interfacing

45 x 90cm/18 x 36in cream silk

Beading needle

60 small seed pearls

60 small long pearl beads

16 1cm/½in pearl drop beads

mounting (mat) board to size

PVA (white) glue

Cream embroidery thread

30 x 45cm/12 x 18in cream lining silk

15 x 45cm/6 x 18in striped silk

45 x 5cm/18 x 2in cream lace

1m x 3mm/1yd x ⅛in cream ribbon

Tapestry needle

2 large pearl drop beads

1 Using the template, cut two heart shapes from the interfacing. Cut two more hearts from the cream silk, allowing 18mm/¾in extra all around. Tack (baste) an interfacing heart to each silk heart. Embroider one heart with pearls, as shown, with a beading needle and sewing thread.

2 From the mounting board, cut two rectangles, 12 x 5cm/4½ x 2in, for the side. From the silk, cut two 18 x 10cm/7 x 4in rectangles, to cover. Place the board centrally on the silk and spread a thin layer of PVA (white) glue around the outer edges of the fabric. Fold over the corners, and glue.

3 Cut two hearts from the mounting board. Lay the beaded heart face-down and place a board heart on top, matching it to the interfacing. Spread glue thinly around the edge and gently stretch over the surplus silk, easing and clipping as necessary. Repeat for the second heart.

4 Use embroidery thread to slip stitch the sides together at one short end. Slip stitch the two hearts to the sides. With right sides together, hand stitch the lining and striped silk along one long edge and then the side seam. Run a gathering thread round the lower edge and draw it up.

5 Fold the lining to the inside along the seam and hand stitch the lace to the seam. Sew a row of straight stitch 6mm/¼in below the fold for a gathering channel. Pin lining in place, and slip stitch striped fabric around top of the bag. Thread ribbon through the channel; add a large pearl at each end.

Small plastic boxes with well-fitting lids can be used to keep all kinds of small treasures safe. Recycle one with style, jazzing it up with glass paints in strong colours and a sprinkling of tiny, glittering seed beads.

Glittering Trinket Box

you will need

Clear plastic box

Black relief outliner

Ruler

Flat-backed gold bead

All-purpose glue

Small glass beads

Glass paints in dark brown, crimson and yellow

Medium and fine paintbrushes

Kitchen paper

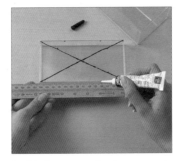

1 Mark out a simple geometric pattern on the lid of your box, using black relief outliner. Use a ruler to make sure that you keep all of your lines straight.

2 Rest the outliner on the ruler to guide it when you are outlining the edge of the lid.

3 While the outliner is still wet, press a flat-backed gold bead into the centre. As it dries, the outliner will hold the bead securely in place.

4 Cover the four panels on the cross on the lid with a thin layer of all-purpose glue.

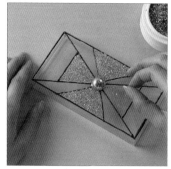

5 While the glue is wet, sprinkle small glass beads on to the surface and let them stick.

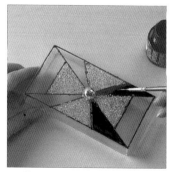

6 Fill in the areas between the beaded panels on the lid using the dark brown glass paint.

7 Paint the remaining areas on top of the lid in crimson.

8 Paint the sides of the lid in crimson, and leave to dry.

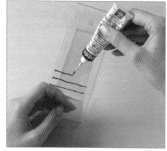

9 Using black outliner, draw vertical lines down the sides of the box at 1cm/½in intervals.

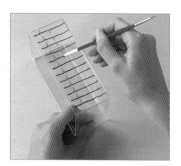

10 Immediately, drag the pointed end of a paintbrush through the lines to break them up. Drag the brush in alternate directions at 1cm/½in intervals down the sides, wiping the excess paint off the brush at the end of each stroke. Leave for at least an hour to dry.

11 Use a fine paintbrush to paint alternate stripes in crimson along the sides of the box.

12 Paint the remaining stripes around the sides in bright yellow and leave to dry completely.

This dramatic scarf is decorated with appliqué and beadwork leaves; some are velvet and others are stitched with tiny sequins. To complete the effect, beaded flowers are dotted among the foliage.

Devoré Scarf

you will need

Dressmaking scissors

28cm/11in x 130cm/52in devoré velvet, with leaf pattern

Iron

20cm/8in square fusible bonding web

Embroidery scissors

20 x 110cm/8 x 45in organza

Sewing-machine, with darning foot

Matching sewing threads

Embroidery hoop

Fabric marker

Sewing needle

Matching embroidery thread

Small silver sequins

Small silver glass beads

6mm/¼in blue oval beads

10 x 110cm/4 x 45in silk, in contrasting colour

1 Cut a square of devoré velvet 20 x 20cm/8 x 8in. Using a hot iron, fuse the bonding web to the wrong side. Cut out individual leaf shapes from the fabric using embroidery scissors.

2 Peel away the backing paper from the leaf shapes. Scatter them on one end of the organza, right sides up, and fuse in place with a hot iron.

3 Attach a darning foot to the sewing-machine and set to darning mode. Place the organza in an embroidery hoop and zigzag stitch around the edge of each leaf in matching thread.

4 Using a fabric marker, draw extra leaves over the scarf. Place the end with the devoré leaves back into the embroidery hoop.

5 Fill in the outlines of the drawn leaves with overlapping sequins: thread on a sequin then make a stitch in matching embroidery thread at the side of it. Bring the needle up on the other side, thread on another sequin, then insert the needle in the centre of the first sequin. Bring it out on the other side of the second sequin and continue.

6 Fill in some drawn shapes with small silver beads applied by hand. To make the flowers, stitch a small silver bead in the centre of a sequin. Bring the needle out on one side of the sequin, then thread on a silver bead, a blue bead and another silver. Insert the needle in the fabric and bring out on the other side of the sequin. Stitch five more petals around the sequin.

7 Cut a piece of devoré fabric 28 x 110cm/11 x 45in. Wrong sides together, machine stitch to the organza on all four sides. Cut strips of contrasting silk fabric 3cm/1¼in wide, stitch together and press to make a continuous binding. Right sides together, stitch all around the scarf. Fold the binding over the edge of the scarf, tuck under the raw edges and slip stitch in place.

Sequins make wonderful decorations, twinkling and sparkling as they catch the light. Use concave sequins to give the finished baubles a smooth surface and pin them in place with short lil pins.

Christmas Beadwork Decorations

●●●

you will need
2 compressed cotton spheres,
6cm/2½in diameter
Felt-tipped pen
6mm/¼in diameter round
concave sequins in a variety
of colours, including metallic
Lil pins
Beading needle
Beading thread
Small bronze glass beads
Fluted metal beads
Dressmaker's pins
Silver pointed oval sequins
Ribbon

1 To make a block-coloured bauble, using a felt-tipped pen, divide the surface of one of the cotton spheres into four segments, as shown. Mark around the middle of the sphere to divide it into eight sections.

2 Outline the eight sections of the cotton sphere with round concave sequins, using different colours. Use lil pins to attach the sequins and overlap them slightly. Fill in each of the sections, again overlapping the sequins slightly.

3 To make the hanging loop, thread a fine needle with beading thread and secure to the top of the ball with a few stitches. Add 8cm/3in of small bronze beads and sew down the other end. Thread a metal bead on a lil pin and press into the sphere to secure the loop.

4 To make the star bauble, mark several horizontal stripes on the other sphere. Press in a sequin at the top and bottom. Working outwards from these points, press in silver pointed oval sequins to form a star shape.

5 Fill in the rest of sphere with round sequins, as in step 2. As an alternative hanging loop, attach a 10cm/4in piece of ribbon to the top, using a dressmaker's pin and metal bead as in step 3.

Use large glass beads in strong colours to make tie-backs that will become the focal points of your window. Before you begin, gather up the curtain (drape) in a tape measure to calculate the length.

Chunky Bead Tie-backs

you will need

For each tie-back:

2 split rings

2 decorative dividers with attachments for three strings

Glue gun and glue sticks

2 flat-backed blue glass nuggets

Scissors

Pencil

Paper for template

Tape measure

Strong non-stretch beading thread

Clear nail polish

Cylindrical orange handmade glass and ceramic beads

Round blue glass beads

Large blue glass beads

1 Attach one of the split rings to the loop at the top of each triangular divider. These will be slipped over the wall hooks. Using a glue gun, attach a flat-backed blue glass nugget to the centre of each divider.

2 Cut a curved, symmetrical paper template to the required shape of the finished tie-back. Make sure it is wide enough to hold all the folds of the curtain (drape) and deep enough to accommodate all three rows of beads.

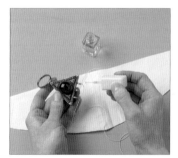

3 Cut a length of strong thread, 30cm/ 12in longer than the width of the template. Knot one end securely to the top loop of the first divider. Dab the knot with clear nail polish to keep it in place.

4 Thread on the large and small beads in a symmetrical pattern, using the main picture as a guide to the sequence. Pass both the main length of thread and the spare end through the first few beads to secure them.

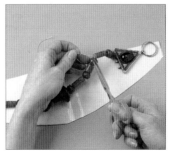

5 Thread on enough beads for the first row to fit across the top of the template and knot the loose end of thread firmly to the second divider. Trim the end and secure the knot with a blob of nail polish as before.

6 Pass the spare tail of beading thread back through the last few beads on the strand and snip off the remainder.

7 Thread up the second and third rows following the same sequence, adding extra beads to make each row a little longer than the previous one. Repeat for the other tie-back.

French-style beaded light fittings are beautiful but expensive. However, you can easily create your own by adding gold paint and swags of cheap plastic crystal beads to a second-hand find.

Beaded Wall Sconce

● ● ●

you will need

Wall sconce

Stiff card (stock)

Pair of compasses and pencil

Scissors

Metallic gold paint

Medium paintbrush

Thick sewing needle

Wire cutters

Fine brass wire

Medium-sized transparent plastic crystal drop beads

Round-nosed (snub-nosed) pliers

Transparent plastic crystal beads

Large and small coloured beads

1 Cut two circles of stiff card and paint them gold. These will be inserted in the joints where the arms unscrew, so should be a little wider than the arms at this point. Cut out the centres to fit around the flex and snip across. Pierce three equidistant holes around the edge with a thick needle.

2 Three bead drops are needed for each disc. The links are made with individual lengths of wire to give flexibility. Using the wire cutters, cut a piece of brass wire about 3cm/1¼in long. Thread on the base crystal drop bead and use the pliers to twist the wire once. Leave the ends open.

3 Take a second length of wire of about the same length and make a small closed loop at one end using the pliers. Slip this loop over one of the open ends of the previous wire and twist the open ends together to secure the link. Trim the excess wire.

4 Thread on a medium-sized crystal bead. Cut the wire to 8mm/⅓in and make a closed loop. Cut a length of wire, thread it through and make another closed loop. Thread on a small coloured bead. Repeat this process to add another medium-sized crystal bead. Add the final length of wire.

5 Repeat steps 3–5 for the remaining drops. Attach the drops to the gold-painted discs, looping the wires through the punched holes.

6 Make the swags using looped wires: use small and medium beads with a large coloured bead in the centre.

7 Paint the sconce with one or two coats of gold paint and leave to dry.

8 Twist the ends of the wire around the sconce arms to attach the swags. Fit the discs in the joints of the arms.

Easy and satisfying to make, these spheres look rich and exotic massed together. You could add ribbon loops to make opulent Christmas decorations, but they are too pretty to be put away for the rest of the year.

Glittering Bead Spheres

you will need

Polystyrene (Styrofoam) balls, 5cm/2in, 7cm/2¾in and 10cm/4in diameter

Skewer

Acrylic paints in blue and green

Artist's paintbrushes

Lil pins

Silver-lined glass rocailles

Round frosted glass beads in assorted sizes in shades of blue and green

Pen or pencil

Large faceted sequins in blue and green

Small glass rocailles in blue and green

Round metallic embroidery beads in blue and green

1 Stick the small polystyrene ball on a skewer to hold it steady while painting. Paint it with a coat of blue acrylic paint and allow to dry. Apply another coat if necessary.

2 With a lil pin, pick up a small silver-lined rocaille and a larger blue frosted bead and insert them in the ball. Repeat, pinning the beads close together all over the ball.

3 Paint the 7cm/2¾in ball with green acrylic and allow to dry. Then use a pen or pencil to mark out a grid pattern as shown: divide it into halves, then quarters, both vertically and horizontally.

4 Pin a large green sequin, a large frosted bead and a green rocaille at each intersection. Fill in the design with small rocailles and tiny embroidery bead.

5 To make the panelled design, paint the large ball blue, allow to dry and mark out into six equal sections.

6 Pin groups of large sequins, large frosted beads and small rocailles in a row along each line.

7 Fill in each panel with small glass rocailles, positioned as closely together as possible.

Elaborate pincushions were popular among Victorian women, and are simple yet effective to make. Other shapes can be used, and for a gift the beads can mark out the recipient's initials.

Strawberry Pincushion

●●●

you will need
Thin card (stock)
Pencil
Craft (utility) knife
Fabric marker
Small piece of red velvet
Dressmaking scissors
Tape measure
Needle and matching sewing thread
Sawdust or bran, for stuffing
Small glass rocailles in green and red
White pearlized beads
Green sequins
Dressmaker's pins
Scrap of green ribbon

1 Trace the strawberry shape template from the back of the book, increase in size by around 140 per cent, cut it out, and trace around it on to the wrong side of the piece of velvet, using the fabric marker.

2 Cut out the two strawberry shapes. Cut a strip of velvet for the gusset measuring 21 x 2.5cm/8½ x 1in.

3 Join the two ends of the gusset strip, right sides together, stitching the seam in back stitch and leaving a seam allowance of a scant 3mm/⅛in.

4 With right sides together, hand stitch the two strawberry shapes to the gusset, leaving a small gap on one side.

5 Carefully turn right-side out and stuff with sawdust or bran. Add the filling a pinch at a time until the shape is firm and full.

6 Tuck in the raw edges of the opening. Slip stitch neatly to close, using a double length of matching sewing thread.

7 Decorate the strawberry shape with beads and sequins. Start at the top by threading a green bead and sequin on to a pin, then fixing it into the pincushion. Work the beads and sequins in a leaf shape.

8 Continue decorating the pincushion with red rocailles interspersed with white pearlized beads to represent seeds. Finish the pincushion by pinning or stitching a loop of green ribbon to the top.

Hang these pretty tassels from keys in the bedroom or bathroom. Worked in colours that coordinate with the rest of the room's decor, they make charming decorative details.

Silken Key Tassels

●●●

you will need

2 skeins stranded embroidery thread (floss) for each tassel, plus extra for loops and ties

Stiff card (stock)

Scissors

Tape measure

Sewing needle and matching thread

2 large ceramic beads

Beading needle

Small glass rocailles in red, orange and turquoise

Large glass rocailles in red and turquoise

Medium red glass crystals

Small red opaque rocailles

1 To make a plaited tassel, wind two skeins of stranded embroidery thread around a piece of stiff card. Cut a 20cm/8in length of thread and tie it into a hanging loop, then tie the ends tightly around the top loop of the wound thread. Carefully slip the tied bundle of thread from the card.

2 Holding the knot in one hand, cut through the other end of the loop to form the tassel. Separate six threads into three pairs and make a tight plait. Use a needle and matching thread to secure the end. Make another three plaits in the same way around the tassel.

3 Trim the ends so they are level. Thread the hanging loop through the two ceramic beads, then tie the loop in a small knot to secure.

4 To make a beaded tassel, repeat steps 1–3, then tie a length of thread around the bundle about 2cm/¾in down from the top. Stitch a length of thread to the top of the tassel and thread on eight small red rocailles. Tie off with a double knot to make a ring around the hanging loop.

5 Passing the thread through alternate rocailles in the previous round, make three loops of two orange, two turquoise, two red and one large red rocailles, reversing the sequence to complete the loop. Make three more similar loops, passing the thread through the large red rocailles.

6 Link the large red beads from step 5 with a round of six red rocailles between each, then add a round of six orange rocailles. Link the large beads again with six turquoise rocailles. Suspend a pendant loop from each large red bead: thread three red, three turquoise, thee orange and one red rocaille, then one medium red glass crystal and one small red opaque. Go back through the last two beads and reverse for the other side.

7 Again passing the thread through the large red rocailles to link them, make three loops of three red, three turquoise and three orange rocailles, one red rocaille, then one large turquoise rocaille and one small red opaque. Go back through the last two beads and reverse for the other side. Finish off with a knot.

This sumptuous and eleborate bead-fringed pincushion, with its four embellished velvet hearts, typifies the nineteenth-century passion for ornament and home decoration.

Edwardian-style Pincushion

●●●

you will need

2 12cm/ 5in squares taffeta

Matching sewing thread

Sewing needle

Sawdust or bran, for stuffing

Fine sewing needle

Rocailles in gold, pink and green

4 pink crystal beads

Scraps of velvet

Brass dressmaker's pins

An assortment of glass beads in different colours and sizes

Sequins

5 rose-shaped buttons

1 Join the taffeta squares with a 1cm/ ½in seam, leaving a 5cm/2in gap at one side. Trim the corners, turn inside out and stuff firmly with sawdust or bran. Slip stitch the gap to close. Thread a fine needle with a double thread and fix to one corner.

2 Thread on 35 rocailles and secure the loop with a few stitches 1cm/½in along. Make a second loop, passing the needle through the first loop before securing. Continue all around the cushion, adding a pink crystal to each corner loop.

3 Conceal the seam with green rocailles. Cut a velvet heart for each corner. Hold in place with pins threaded with a small and a large bead: use a different colour for each heart.

4 Cut a diamond from velvet and position in the centre. Fix in place around the outside edge with pins threaded with a rocaille and a sequin.

5 Sew a rose-shaped button or a ribbon rose (see technique on page 278) to each corner and to the centre of the velvet diamond.

All types of needlework can be further embellished with beadwork: here tiny glass beads have been used to add highlights to a charming folk-art needlepoint of a boat at sea.

Beaded Boat Tapestry

you will need

10-count tapestry canvas

Tapestry frame

Drawing pins (thumb tacks) or staple gun

Ruler

Pencil

Tapestry needle

Tapestry wool (yarn) in white, red, very pale blue, pale blue, royal blue, jade green, green, yellow, grey, brown and black

Glass embroidery beads in five colours to coordinate with the wool

Fine needle and matching sewing thread

Scissors

Towel

Iron

Backing card (stock)

Stapler

Picture frame

1 Fix the canvas to the frame with drawing pins or the staple gun. Mark the centre of the canvas with a ruler and pencil: use this as a starting point to work the design from the chart at the back of the book.

2 Thread the needle with one strand of tapestry yarn and fasten it on at the centre of the frame. Begin to work the design using tent stitch, following the chart, in which one square represents one stitch.

3 Remove the canvas from the frame when the design is complete. Add the beads with a fine needle, using them as highlights on the waves and details.

4 Continue sewing on beads in complementary colours to provide points of contrast in the sky, clouds and sea.

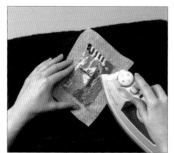

5 Measure a 3cm/1¼in border all around the design, and cut away any excess canvas. Gently stretch the canvas to regain its shape.

6 Using a towel to protect the stitches, press the tapestry from the back, using an iron on a low heat.

7 Cut a piece of backing card 1cm/½in larger all around than the tapestry. Staple the tapestry to the backing, trim away any excess canvas, and fit into the frame.

A bead loom will enable you to weave fabulous patterns, reminiscent of the traditional decorative art of Native Americans. Make the beadwork as long as you need, winding it around the spool as it grows.

Woven Bead Trim

● ● ●

you will need
Bead loom
Strong, non-stretch beading thread
Tape measure
Scissors
Fine beading needle
Small opaque rocailles
in four colours
Adhesive tape (optional)

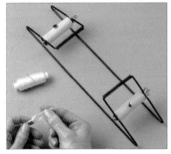

1 To make the warp, cut 19 strands of beading thread, each the desired length of the finished panel, plus 40cm/16in. Tie the ends together in a knot.

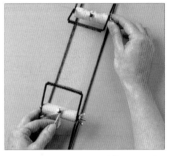

2 Prepare the warp following the instructions on page 29.

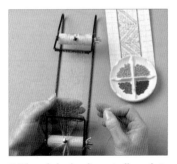

3 Thread the beading needle and tie the end of the thread in a double knot to the right-hand warp (lengthways) thread on the loom.

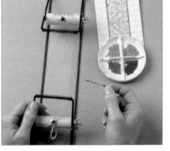

4 Following the chart at the back of the book, pick up coloured rocailles on the needle to correspond with the first row of the pattern. Place the beads under the warp threads and, using your finger, press a bead between each of the warp threads.

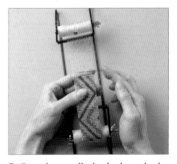

5 Pass the needle back through the beads, being sure to pass over the warp threads. Continue following the chart row by row until you have the desired length of trim. To finish, weave the beading thread under and over the warp threads for a short distance to secure the beads. Tape or stitch this woven part behind the trim before attaching it.

These brightly coloured tassels are inspired by ethnic beadwork. Stitched to each end of a bolster or to a cushion, they would certainly add a note of drama to an interior design scheme.

Beaded Tassels

you will need

Tape measure

Scissors

Fabric tape

Beading needle

Beading thread

Small turquoise and red glass beads

Large turquoise glass beads

Sewing needle and matching thread

Turquoise embroidery thread (floss)

Medium red crystal bead

Small white and light
green glass beads

2 large orange glass beads

Small dark green glass beads

1 For the turquoise and red tassel, cut 25cm/10in of fabric tape. Thread the needle with beading thread and fasten on to one end of the tape. To make the first strand, thread on 18 small turquoise, eight small red, one large and one small turquoise beads. Take the needle back through the large bead and the strand. Make two stitches to one side, then continue making strands along the tape.

2 Roll up the tape tightly to make the head of the tassel. Sew the loose end of the tape down with several stitches to keep it in place. Fasten on the turquoise embroidery thread and wind it firmly around the head to form a rounded shape. Finish off securely.

3 Fasten on to the top of the fringe. Add on 15 small beads and pass the needle down through the head. Go through the first bead, add 13, go through the final bead and down the head. Repeat to cover. Make a loop of 20 beads.

4 For the head of the looped green and white tassel, cut a 25cm/10in length of tape. Fasten on at the bottom left corner with beading thread, then add 13 white, 7 green, 24 white, 7 green and 13 white small beads.

5 Insert the needle back into the tape at the same point to make a loop. Make a stitch to secure, then make a stitch to one side. Repeat along the length of the tape.

6 Bind the head as in step 2, then cover it with turquoise, green and white beads as for step 3. Add a large red bead and a small turquoise bead at the top and a ring of turquoise beads around the base of the head.

7 For each of the eight strands of the green and orange tassel, cut a long length of thread. Thread on 20 light green, 40 dark green and 24 light green small beads. Pass the needle through the last-but-one bead, and make fastening-off stitches along the entire strand. Do the same at the other end.

8 Fold the strands in half and tie a length of thread around the centre. Thread on a needle and add an orange bead. Add a green glass bead, 17 small light green beads, another crystal and a small light green bead. Go through the crystal, add 17 more small light green beads, go back through the first two beads, then fasten off securely.

This delicate and nostalgic picture frame, made from satin ribbon encrusted with beads, will suit a special family photograph and is bound to become a family heirloom.

Sequin and Bead Frame

you will need
Pencil
Metal ruler
Mounting (mat) board
Self-healing cutting mat
Craft (utility) knife
White calico
Scissors
Sewing needle and thread
Matching embroidery threads (floss)
6cm/2½in wide satin-backed
velvet ribbon
15mm/⅝in wide green ribbon
Translucent sequins
Small gold glass beads
Clear crystals

1 Draw the frame outline on to mounting board: it measures 18 x 13cm/7 x 5in with 4cm/1½in wide borders. Using the frame as a template, cut two white calico frames 6mm/¼in larger all around. Turn under the raw edges and oversew the pieces together to cover the back and front of the frame.

2 Measure the outer edge of the frame and cut a length of wide satin-backed velvet ribbon slightly longer. Fold the ribbon so that it is 4cm/1½in wide and tack the fold. Using the frame as a guide, fit the ribbon to the frame shape, mitring the corners. Pin. Remove the ribbon. Stitch the mitres.

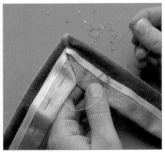

3 Sew the green ribbon over the seam with matching embroidery thread. Thread five small gold glass beads on to a needle and stitch across the green ribbon. Continue stitching until all the ribbon is covered, spacing the beads closely together. Stitch the ribbon frame to the calico-covered frame.

4 Stitch a random selection of translucent sequins and glass beads over the velvet border.

5 Sew clear crystals and small glass beads on to the grey satin part of the ribbon, spacing them closely together. Stitch a strip of the wider ribbon to the back to hold the photograph. Leave the top edge unstitched so that the photograph can be changed.

You can turn plain glass bottles into jewelled treasures with these exquisite beaded collars. Fill them with anything from bath salts to scented oils to make wonderful gifts.

Lacy Bottle Collars

Large Bottle

1 Thread a row of alternate small dark green and lilac rocailles on to a long length of thread and tie it securely around the bottle neck. Pass the thread through the beads once again, then thread on a green bugle and a lilac rocaille.

2 Go back through the bugle and the next green rocaille, and continue around the neck. Pass the thread through each lilac rocaille, adding a small dark green rocaille between each. Pull the thread up tightly to form the neck collar and tie securely.

Small Bottle

1 Follow steps 1 to 3, using lime and dark green rocailles and alternate lilac and green bugles to make the collar. Bring the thread out through a green rocaille.

2 For each point, thread on a green bugle, a lilac rocaille, a green bugle, a lilac crystal and a green embroidery bead. Pass the thread back through the crystal and repeat the sequence on the other side. Go through the second green rocaille, and continue all around the collar.

3 Passing the thread through alternate lilac rocailles, add pendant loops consisting of three lime rocailles, a small dark green rocaille, then three more lime rocailles.

4 Passing the thread between each dark green rocaille of the last round, make a round of loops, consisting of a lilac bugle, a green embroidery bead, a small green crystal, a green embroidery bead and a lilac bugle.

Here a Victorian craft – stitchery embellished with beads – has been brought up to date with a striking modern design. The glossy beadwork contrasts beautifully with the background of soft woollen yarns.

Needlepoint Photograph Album

you will need

Tapestry wool (yarn), in shades of green

Tapestry needle

48 x 34cm/19 x 13½in tapestry canvas, 10 holes to 2.5cm/1in

Embroidery scissors

Beading needle

Matching fine beading thread

Small glass rocailles in copper, light blue, gold, silver and black

Craft (utility) knife and ruler

Card (stock)

Bookbinding fabric

PVA (white) glue

Adhesive tape

Black or white paper

Hole punch

2 brass screw binders

1 Work the background in tent stitch, following the chart at the back of the book. Bring up the needle and go down one space diagonally below to the left. Come up through the space immediately to the right.

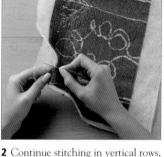

2 Continue stitching in vertical rows, leaving the beadwork motifs unstitched. One square of the chart represents one stitch: merge the shades of green as shown. Leave a border all around.

3 Add the beadwork using the different coloured beads. Thread a beading needle with fine thread and stitch them on singly, making a tent stitch in the opposite direction to the wool stitches, so they lie flat. Make an extra stitch for security every four stitches.

4 Cut two pieces of card, the same depth as the embroidery and 10cm/4in wider. Score a line 10cm/4in from one side of each piece to enable the covers to fold. Cut a piece of bookbinding fabric 2cm/¾in larger all round. Glue to the card, clip the corners, fold and stick the edges. Line with a second piece of fabric.

5 Lay the embroidery on the other card, lining up the right edge. Tape the right, top and bottom borders to the back and the left one to the front. Cut a piece of fabric 12cm/4½in x the card's depth plus 4cm/1½in. Match one edge to the edge of the embroidery and glue down. Glue back the edges, then line.

6 Cut 40 pieces of paper 1cm/½in less all the way around than the card. Mark the position of the holes on the back and front covers and the paper, then use the hole punch to make them. Place the paper between the two covers, thread the screw binders through the layers and secure.

These beautiful flowers and leaves are easily made by threading glass beads on to wire and twisting them into shape. Once you've mastered the technique, they can be used for decorating all kinds of projects.

Flowery Frame

you will need

Wire cutters

0.4mm/$\frac{1}{80}$in beading wire

Round-nosed (snub-nosed) pliers

Small glass beads in white, pink and yellow

Floss thread

Wooden frame

Drill and small drill bit

Protective goggles

0.2mm/$\frac{1}{120}$in beading wire

1 To make the leaves, cut 23cm/9in of thick wire. Twist a small knot in one end to stop the beads falling off. Mix up a few pink beads with the yellow. Bend the wire in half, thread on 18 beads, push up to the bend, then twist the wire together to form a beaded loop.

2 Wind the working part of the wire around and down the stem part by 6mm/$\frac{1}{4}$in. Make another loop and thread on 18 more beads. Wrap the working wire around the stem once more. Make another loop at the same level. Make two more pairs of loops along the stem. Twist the wire around the stem.

3 To cover the twisted stem, fasten some floss thread to one end, then wrap it around the wire in a tight spiral. Secure at the other end with a few stitches or a dab of glue.

4 Cut 40cm/16in of wire for a small flower and 50cm/20in for the large. Bend each into a circle 10cm/4in from one end. Twist to form a frame. Mix a few pink beads in with the white. Thread on 24 beads for the small flower, 30 for the large.

5 Twist the working wire around the circle to make a loop.

▶

6 To fill in the centre of the petal, thread on 16 more beads for the small flower, 24 for the large. Bend the working wire upwards and twist it around the top of the loop.

7 Add on more beads for the next petal and twist the working wire around the spiral frame. To make the remaining petals, make four more loops positioned around the spiral frame.

8 To make the flower centre, thread on 12 yellow beads and twist the wire into a half spiral. Push the working wire through the centre and twist it around the stem to finish off.

9 Make enough leaves and flowers to go round the frame and decide where they are to go. Mark the positions with pencil, then drill a small hole at each point, using a fine bit.

10 Push the stems of the beaded flowers and leaves through the holes. Keep them in place by twisting the wire into a knot on the wrong side of the frame.

11 Trim the ends of the wire using wire cutters. Secure the knots by twisting lengths of the thinner wire around them, making sure that no sharp ends are left projecting.

Shimmering droplets of water appear to cascade down this stunning three-panelled screen: the effect is created by transparent plastic crystals that have been suspended on fine silver thread.

Waterfall Screen

you will need

Saw

11m/11yd of 5 x 5cm/2 x 2in wooden batten (furring strip)

medium-grade abrasive paper and sanding block

12 right-angled brackets and screws

Pencil

Drill and drill bits

Screwdriver

Paintbrush

White emulsion (latex) paint

12 wood spheres, 7.5cm/3in diameter

Silver paint

Hammer

Long nails

1cm/½in diameter plastic tubing

6 hinges

12 screws

Dowelling

Transparent plastic crystal beads in various sizes

2 reels silver machine embroidery thread (floss)

Small silver glass beads

Scissors

1 For each of the panels, cut two pieces of wood 140cm/55in long for the sides and two pieces 40cm/16in long for the top and bottom. Sand the wood thoroughly to remove any rough edges.

2 Place the two short pieces across either end of the long pieces. Position the brackets on the inside of each corner and mark the position of the screws. Using a drill bit to match, make holes at these points. Screw the brackets in place.

3 Paint the panel with two coats of white emulsion and leave to dry. Paint the spheres with two coats of silver paint and leave to dry.

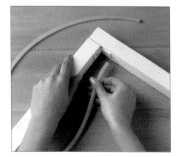

4 Hammer in a long nail 3cm/1¼in from the top and bottom on the inside of each side edge. For each panel, cut two pieces of plastic tubing 45cm/18in long and push over the nail heads.

5 Mark the position of the two hinges on the side edges of the panels, 30cm/ 12in from top and bottom. Check that the screen will fold and unfold properly, then screw the hinges in place.

6 Mark the position of the spheres at the four corners. Cut four pieces of dowelling 5cm/2in long. Drill holes in the frame and the spheres with a drill bit the same size as the dowelling. Push the dowelling into the spheres, then into the frame.

7 Thread the transparent beads in random sequence directly on to a reel of silver thread. Leave 10–30cm/ 4–12in gaps between groups of beads, knotting the thread after each group.

8 Thread on a plastic bead then pass the thread through the bead again. Thread on small silver glass beads in groups of three or more. Fasten off the end of the thread and cut.

9 Unravel a little thread from the other reel. Tie one end to the lower piece of tubing on the first panel. Pass the reel over the tubing at the top, then under the lower tubing. Continue back and forth across the width of the panel.

10 Wrap the beaded thread around the tubing in the same way. Repeat with the other two panels.

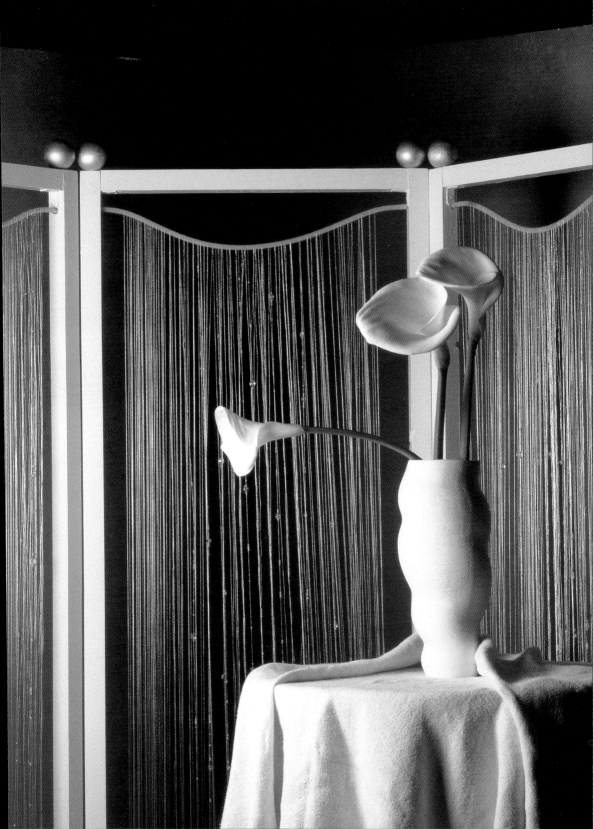

Decorative Home Furnishings

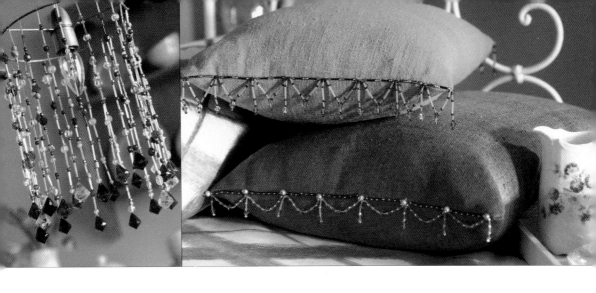

Some of the most desirable home accessories are now adorned with, or constructed from, a glittering array of beads. Bead curtains, crystal-decked wall sconces, candle holders and fringed lampshades all make the most of their light-enhancing qualities, while traditional favourite beadwork techniques, including wiring and embroidery, are still used to embellish fashionable cushion covers and picture frames.

Perfect for a small window, multicoloured beads will dress your window without blocking the light. Nylon line supports the beads, and large crystal drops at the end of each strand define the shape.

Glittering Window Decoration

you will need

Pencil

Ruler

Length of 4 x 4cm/1½ x 1½in wooden batten (furring strip) to fit outside window frame

Drill and drill bit

Scissors

Nylon fishing line

Selection of plastic beads, including drops, pendants and long or bugle beads, in various colours and sizes

4cm/1½in wide ribbon

Staple gun

2 screw-in hooks

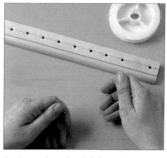
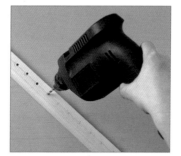

1 Using a pencil and ruler, mark points 2.5cm/1in apart all along the wooden batten, 2.5cm/1in from one edge. Allow enough space between the first and second holes at each end for the window frame. Drill a hole at each point.

2 Cut a length of fishing line twice the length of the window plus 50cm/20in. Thread both ends through the second hole, then through the loop formed by the doubled thread.

3 Pull the fishing line taut. Thread on the beads in a random manner, using bugle or long beads to space out the round beads.

4 When you reach the desired length, thread on a large pendant bead, pass the fishing line back through the last few beads and make a knot. Thread the fishing line back up the length of the strand, knotting the ends twice more, and trim the ends.

5 Repeat the process for the other strands, making them shorter towards the centre of the window. Cut a length of ribbon to the length of the batten plus 2cm/¾in. Staple it in position at either end. Attach a screw-in hook at either end of the batten from which to hang the curtain.

A bead curtain hung across the kitchen door is a tried and tested way to deter insects on a hot, sunny day. Make this jaunty, striped version from coloured drinking straws, and wooden and plastic beads.

Simple Door Curtain

1 Cut a length of wire to fit the door length plus 25cm/10in, and tie one end to a large glass bead, which will act as a weight at the bottom.

2 Thread on a large plastic bead between two medium wooden beads to cover the knot.

3 Snip the drinking straws into 7.5cm/3in lengths. Thread on three straws, alternating plain and striped, and threading a small wooden bead in between each.

4 Thread on a group of medium and large beads and repeat the sequence, using assorted colours, to fill the wire. Make more strands to complete the curtain: you will need one strand for each 2.5cm/1in of the width.

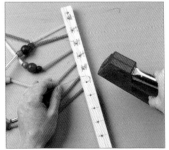

5 Mark and drill holes at 2.5cm/1in intervals all along the batten, plus a screw hole at each end.

6 Thread the end of each wire through one of the holes in the batten. Hold the batten in place to check for length.

7 Use a staple gun to secure the ends of the beaded thread in place.

Brightly painted wooden beads are ideal for fringing a plain cotton throw, as they are light in weight and easily threaded. Combine them with the occasional metallic bead to catch the light.

Beaded Throw

you will need
Florist's wire
Wire cutters
Ready-made throw with fringe
1 medium, 1 small and
1 large wooden bead and
2 brass beads for each strand to
be beaded

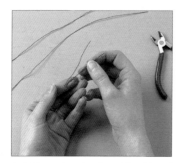

1 Make a threader from 20cm/8in of wire bent into a 'U'. To use, wrap the loop around a single strand. Slide the required beads over both ends of the wire and on to the threads.

2 Every alternate strand of the fringe is beaded. Prepare the strand by untying the existing knot at the top end and threading on a brass bead using the wire threader.

3 Twist the strand of fringe together to secure any stray thread, and make a new knot, just below the brass bead.

4 Add one small, one large and one medium bead. Finish off with a knot as before. Repeat for every other strand to the end.

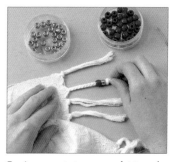

5 As a variation, try plaiting the strands of the fringe together and adding a coloured bead and a brass bead before knotting the end.

A bead curtain (drape) lets in and prettily reflects all available light. This one is made from transparent nylon line threaded with glass and silver beads, which will glitter prettily in the sunlight.

Bead Window Hanging

you will need

Length of 2.5 x 2.5cm/1 x 1in wooden batten (furring strip) to fit inside window frame

Pencil

Ruler

Tape measure

Nylon fishing line

Scissors

Large, flat glass beads with central hole, in two colours

Strong glue

Silver bugle beads

Silver rocailles

Silver square beads

Assorted large glass beads

Staple gun

2.5cm/1in wide ribbon

Beading needle and matching thread

1 Using a pencil and ruler, mark equi-distant points about 4cm/1½in apart along the length of the batten.

2 Measure the window from top to bottom and cut lengths of nylon fishing line to this measurement plus 20cm/8in to allow for knotting. You will need one length of fishing line for each mark on the batten.

3 Prepare the strands of the curtain one at a time. Thread on a large, flat glass bead and tie a knot. Trim the excess line and then apply a blob of glue to the knot for extra security.

4 Add on a 5cm/2in length of silver bugles, rocailles and square beads, then a large glass bead. Make a knot 4–8cm/1½–3¼in along the line (vary this distance as you go). Thread on 4–8cm/1½–3¼in of beads arranged symmetrically on either side of a large centre bead. Continue to the end.

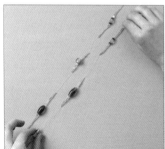

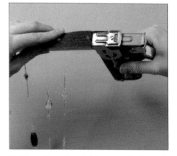

5 The next length will be slightly shorter than the first to create a staggered line at the bottom of the curtain. Lay the second length of nylon alongside the completed first length and, when threading this length, position the beads so that they roughly correspond with the beadless gaps on the first length.

6 As you complete each length, tie a double knot at the top. Staple the lengths at the marked positions on the batten; the knot will act as an anchor above the staple. It's easier to do this in a hanging position to make sure the bottom of the curtain is level.

7 Cut a length of ribbon to the length of the batten, plus 6cm/2½in. Stitch a single row of beads along the centre, then glue to the front of the batten to conceal the staples. Secure the ends with staples.

Beads add detail to this stylized flower decoration for a loose chair cover. With a design of strong shapes and contrasts, created in sturdy fabrics, the beads add a delicacy that creates a delightful surprise.

Bead-encrusted Appliqué Flower

you will need

Scissors

Fusible bonding web

Cotton fabrics in three colours

Iron

Thin card (stock)

Pencil

Sewing-machine, with zip foot

Matching sewing threads

Beading needle

Beading thread

Small glass rocailles

Bugle beads

Assorted round glass beads

Dressmaker's pins

Sewing needle and tacking (basting) thread

1 Cut a piece of fusible bonding web, the same size as each of the fabric pieces you have chosen for the flower appliqué. Following the manufacturer's instructions, iron them to the wrong side of the fabric. Copy the templates at the back of the book for the petals and the flower centre on to card, and cut out.

2 Draw around the petal template on the backing paper and cut out 12 shapes. Cut out the circular centre for the flower from a contrasting fabric.

3 Arrange the petals on a square of the background fabric, peel off the backing paper and iron them in place. Iron on the flower centre.

4 Stitch around the shapes using a decorative stitch, such as zigzag stitch or satin stitch, and matching threads.

5 Decorate the flower centre and petals with an assortment of evenly spaced glass rocaille and bugle beads.

6 Fold under a 1cm/½in hem along each raw edge of the background square and press in place.

7 Following the folded seam line, sew on an assortment of small and medium round glass beads in various assorted colours, stitching them about 1cm/½in apart.

8 Pin the panel on the chair cover, and tack (baste) in position. Thread the sewing-machine with matching thread and fit a zip foot so that the beads will not get damaged. Stitch the panel in place close to the edge.

The beads on this dramatic bolster are attached with fine wire, which creates three-dimensional, curling tendrils. The beading wire acts as a needle and thread to "stitch" through the fabric.

Velvet Bolster Cushion

●●●

you will need

Bolster cushion pad
Tape measure
Pair of compasses
Pencil and paper
Dressmaking scissors
50 x 100cm/20 x 40in blue-black embossed velvet
Fine beading wire
Small red glass beads
Sewing needle
Matching sewing thread
Sewing-machine
Dressmaker's pins

1 Measure the diameter of the end of the bolster cushion pad and divide in half to find the radius. Draw a circle to this size on paper, using a pair of compasses, then redraw, adding a 1.5cm/⅝in seam allowance. Cut two circles of embossed velvet.

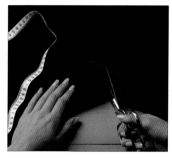

2 Measure the length and circumference of the bolster pad. Cut a piece of embossed velvet to this size plus a 3cm/1¼in seam allowance all around.

3 Tie one end of a piece of beading wire in a knot and pass the other end through the centre of a velvet circle to the right side. Thread on red beads for 10cm/4in. Insert the end of the wire back into the velvet 4cm/1½in from the knot to make a loop.

4 Thread the wire through the fabric again 5cm/2in from the first loop. Make a second loop as before. Repeat until there are about 20 loops, using extra wire as needed. Fasten the wire off. Repeat for the second circle.

5 Run a gathering stitch around each circle, using a double length of matching sewing thread. With right sides facing, fold the embossed velvet in half across the centre.

6 Machine stitch the short ends, 1.5cm/⅝in from the edge, leaving a gap for the pad. Machine stitch both circles in place, adjusting the gathering stitch to fit each end. Turn the cover right-side out through the gap.

7 Insert the cushion pad and ease it into place. Pin and slip stitch the opening to close.

Glass beads are at their most beautiful and magical when lit from behind, or in this case from within: even a plain paper lampshade can be transformed with the addition of a long bead fringe.

Fringed Lampshade

●●●●

you will need

Yellow oil-based marker pen

Tubular white paper lampshade

Tape measure

Sharp sewing needle

Scissors

Yellow and white beading thread

Beading needle

Pencil

Graph paper

Small yellow glass beads

Small purple glass beads

4cm/1⅔in purple bugle beads

Purple teardrop beads

Small transparent glass beads

1 Draw freehand stripes of varying widths down the length of the lampshade using the oil-based marker pen. Leave until dry.

2 Using a sharp needle, pierce a row of holes 6mm/¼in apart just above the bottom rim.

3 Cut a piece of yellow beading thread twice the desired length of the fringe plus 25cm/10in and double through the beading needle. Knot the ends together and pass the needle through a hole on a yellow stripe, then loop through and pull taut.

4 Mark the bead sequence on graph paper. Thread on small beads: 12cm/4½in of yellow, one purple, one yellow, one purple and one yellow. Add a bugle, then alternate five small yellow and four purple. (On alternate strands, add an extra two of each colour.) Add three yellow.

5 Add one purple teardrop and three yellow beads. Insert the needle just below the purple teardrop and make a fastening-off stitch, checking that no thread is showing. Pass the needle back up the strand.

6 Make a fastening-off stitch below the bugle then pass it up through the bugle and make another fastening-off stitch. Pull gently on the strand to remove kinks. Continue around the shade. For the white stripes, use white thread and substitute transparent beads for yellow ones.

Use an assortment of large glass beads, interspersed with smaller gold ones, for a jewel-encrusted, sparkling shade. Space the large beads randomly along the wires so that each one is framed by small beads.

Chunky Beaded Lampshade

you will need

Drum-shaped lampshade frame with
reversible gimbal, top diameter
20cm/8in, bottom diameter
25cm/10in, height 25cm/10in
Gold spray paint and face mask
Scrap paper
Fine brass wire
Jeweller's pliers and wire cutters
0.6mm/¹/₄₀in gold-plated jewellery wire
Small flat round gold crystal beads
Selection of chunky glass beads
Ceramic lamp base
Brown acrylic paint
Dish
Kitchen sponge
Clean cotton rag
Picture framer's wax gilt

1 Spray the frame on some scrap paper with gold paint. Wear a face mask and work in a well-ventilated area.

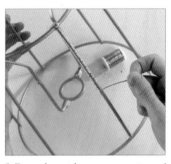

2 For each upright strut, cut a piece of fine brass wire approximately 3m/10ft long. When the frame is dry, fold the wire in half and in half again, loop it over the top ring and wind the strands down each strut. Finish at the base of the strut with a small knot.

3 Cut a piece of the thicker jewellery wire approximately 70cm/28in long and spiral one end about five times around the top ring next to a strut. Thread enough beads on to the wire to fit between the top and bottom rings, including a few large ones.

4 Spiral the long end around the bottom ring about five times and pull up tightly. Thread on the same number of beads, then spiral the long end around the top ring. Snip the end with the cutters. Continue back and forth in this way all around the shade.

5 Cut a piece of the fine wire approximately 3m/10ft long, fold in half and in half again. Loop the wire around an upright strut and spiral the strands closely around the bottom ring, finishing with a small knot. Wrap the top ring in the same way.

6 To decorate the base, squeeze some brown acrylic paint into a dish, dab a sponge in the paint and wipe it over the base in an uneven criss-cross manner, avoiding the brass fitting. Leave to dry completely.

7 Using a clean cotton rag, wipe gilt wax over the paint, rubbing harder in some areas to give an uneven finish. Leave to dry completely before attaching the shade.

This lampshade gives you the perfect opportunity to sort out your bead collection and use all your prettiest shapes in rainbow colours. A large crystal drop at the bottom of each strand gives weight to the fringe.

Bead Pendant Light

●●●●

you will need

Enamel spray paint

Face mask

Scrap paper

Flush pendant lamp ring

Fine jewellery wire (this design used about 20m/22yd)

Scissors

Large crystal drop beads

Medium round and shaped beads

Bugle beads

1 Spray-paint the lamp ring on a piece of scrap paper in a well-ventilated area and leave it to dry.

2 Cut a piece of jewellery wire a little more than twice the length you want the finished fringe to be and thread on a large crystal drop bead.

3 Take the bead to the centre of the length of wire and hold the two ends together. Thread on an assortment of beads in different sizes and colours, spacing them with bugle beads.

4 Complete the strand with a long bugle bead, making sure you have left enough wire to tie on to the lamp ring. Attach the strand of beads on to the metal ring by tying the two ends of the wire together.

5 Continue making beaded strands to tie evenly all around the ring. Thread the two wire ends back through the beads on each strand to conceal them.

The plainest cushion cover can be dramatically transformed with a fringe of beads: these three designs show how beads of different sizes and colours produce different effects.

Bead-fringed Cushions

you will need

Tape measure

Square cushion pad

Dressmaking scissors

Yellow velvet

Iron

Sewing-machine and matching thread

Dressmaker's pins

Beading needle

Matching beading thread

6mm/¼in white glass beads

7mm/³⁄₈in opaque yellow beads

Small copper glass beads

7mm/³⁄₈in opaque white beads

7mm/³⁄₈in opaque blue beads

Rectangular cushion pad

Striped fabric

Fabric marker

Graph paper

Pencil

Small glass beads in pink and yellow

7mm/³⁄₈in yellow disc-shaped beads

Rectangular cushion pad

Pink velvet

Small glass beads yellow and pink

6mm/¼in white glass beads

6mm/¼in turquoise glass beads

Yellow cushion

1 Cut a piece of yellow velvet the size of the pad and two back panels the same depth and two-thirds the length. Hem one short side of each panel. With right sides facing and hems overlapping, join with a 1cm/½in seam. Clip the corners and turn through.

3 Make a tiny stitch, then thread on a blue or white opaque bead and a copper bead. Pass the needle back through the blue or white bead, then insert the needle 2cm/¾in farther on. Repeat the sequence of steps 2 and 3 along each side of the cover.

2 Thread a beading needle with double beading thread and fasten to one corner. Thread on two white glass beads, a yellow and a copper bead. Go back through the yellow bead and thread on two white glass beads. Insert the needle 2cm/¾in to the right.

Striped cushion

1 Cut a piece of fabric the size of the cushion pad plus 2cm/¾in on the width and 20cm/8in on the length. Cut two back panels the same depth and two-thirds the length.

2 Hem one short side of each. Then, right sides facing and hems overlapping, sew 1cm/½in from each long edge. Turn through. Stitch a line 10cm/4in from each raw edge and fringe the fabric to this line.

▶

Pink cushion

3 Mark the length of fringe, 10cm/4in, on graph paper. Cut thread four times this measurement and double through the needle. Insert the needle at the inner edge of the first stripe of the fabric and secure with a knot, pass the needle through the loop and pull taut.

4 Mix a few pink with the yellow beads. Thread on 9.5cm/3¾in of beads, using the graph paper as a guide. Thread on a disc and a small yellow bead. Pass the needle back through the disc, make a finishing stitch, pass the needle up the strand and make another finishing stitch. Pull gently on the strand to remove any kinks. Trim the thread. Repeat with the other stripes.

1 Make up the pink velvet cover as in step 1 (yellow cushion). Mark points 15mm/⅝in apart along two opposite sides. Fasten a double length of thread on to one corner.

2 Mix a few yellow with the pink beads, and thread on 2cm/¾in. Add a white bead, 2cm/¾in of pink or yellow and one turquoise and one copper bead. Go back through the turquoise bead, thread on 2cm/¾in pink or yellow, a large white, then more pink or yellow. Insert the needle at the third point.

3 Make a back stitch to bring the needle out at the second marked point. Thread on 2cm/¾in of pink or yellow beads, then pass the needle through the large white bead already in place, on the strand to the right.

4 Thread on another 2cm/¾in of pink or yellow beads, one turquoise and one copper bead. Repeat this three-step sequence along each side of the cushion, to make the lattice edge.

These more intricate bead edgings, made from rocaille, bugle, pearl and crystal beads, have a delicate appearance, but they are stitched along the seams with strong thread and are unlikely to break.

Beaded Cushion Trims

you will need

50cm/20in each purple and green linen

Dressmaking scissors

Tape measure

Dressmaker's pins

Sewing-machine

Matching sewing thread

2 cushion pads, measuring

35cm/14in square and

30cm/12in square

Beading needle

Strong non-stretch beading thread

Iridescent beads in pink and green

Rocailles in gold, silver and red

Frosted bugle beads in pink,

blue and green

Green metallic bugle beads

Small crystal beads in pink,

blue and yellow

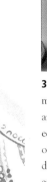

1 First make up the covers. Cut a 38cm/15in purple square for the front of the large cushion, and two back panels measuring 38 x 28cm/15 x 11in. For the small cushion, cut a 33cm/13in square and two 33 x 23cm/13 x 9in panels.

2 Hem one long edge of each back panel. Place them on top of the front, with right sides facing and hems overlapping at the centre. Machine stitch around all four sides of both cushion covers with a 12mm/½in seam. Turn right-side out and insert the pads.

3 The trim for the purple cushion is made up of alternate swags and drops and is stitched along two opposite edges of the cushion. Measure one edge of the cushion and divide it at equidistant points approximately 5cm/2in apart. Mark each point vertically with a pin.

4 The first row of beads is worked along the seam line. Fasten on at the bottom left corner and thread on an iridescent pink bead followed by a gold rocaille. Take the needle back through the pink bead, into the seam and back out along the stitching, beside the pink bead.

►

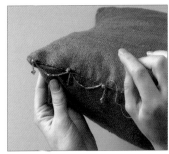

5 Thread on 2.5cm/1in of alternate pink bugles and gold rocailles. Make a small stitch through the seam to secure, then repeat until the first marker pin. Secure the thread. Attach a green iridescent bead with a gold rocaille as for the pink bead. Repeat to the second corner.

6 Starting again at the corner, make the drop from a silver rocaille, a blue bugle, a silver rocaille, a blue bugle, a silver rocaille, a pink crystal and another silver rocaille. Take the needle back through the crystal and the rest of the strand. Secure with a small stitch in the seam and come out one bead to the right.

7 For the swag, thread a silver rocaille and a frosted bugle. Repeat twice, then add a silver rocaille, a gold rocaille and a pink crystal. Thread the beads on the other side of the crystal as a mirror image. Secure at the seam, just under the iridescent bead. Continue making drops and swags to the end of the row.

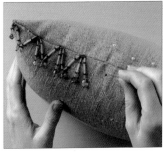

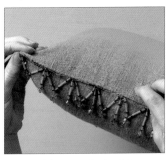

8 Pin at 3cm/1¼in intervals along the green cushion. For the drop, thread two red rocailles, a blue bugle, a red rocaille, a green bugle, a red rocaille, a blue bugle, a red rocaille, a blue crystal and a red rocaille. Go back through the crystal and the strand. Secure, then come out one bead along. Starting with a single red rocaille, thread the same sequence but using a yellow crystal and a rocaille. Go back through the crystal.

9 Thread the second side of the triangle as a mirror image of the first. Secure to the seam just to the left of the next pin and secure. Continue making alternate drops and triangles to the end. Starting again at the corner, conceal the seam as before with a line made up of a gold rocaille, a green metallic bugle, three gold rocailles, a green bugle and a gold rocaille.

Clusters of beads make an original addition to mosaics, and are perfect for creating intricate shapes. Mix sizes and colours for the fish, but stick to just one type of bead for the starfish for a contrasting effect.

Fish Mosaic Splashback

you will need

Pencil

Paper

Piece of plywood to fit splashback area

Carbon paper

Coloured glass mosaic tiles

Wood glue

Interior filler

Mixing container

Spoon

Acrylic paints in a variety of colours

Selection of beads including metallic bugle beads, frosted and metallic square beads, large round beads and mixed beads

Mosaic clippers

Tile grout

1 Following the picture opposite as a guide, sketch the design to fit the required size of the splashback on a large sheet of paper. Keep the shapes simple and bold. Use a sheet of carbon paper to transfer the design on to the plywood by drawing firmly over all the lines using a sharp pencil.

2 Begin by adding the mosaic squares on to the border, which uses complete square tiles. Lay them out around the top and side edges in two rows, alternating the colours to give a chequered effect. Then apply a thin layer of wood glue to the border, a small section at a time, positioning the tiles textured side down as you go.

3 Following the manufacturer's instructions, mix up a small amount of interior filler, then add some acrylic paint to colour it to match the beads.

4 Spread green filler thickly over the seaweed fronds, then carefully press in metallic green bugle beads. Fill in the fish fins using green filler and metallic green square beads.

5 Make sure all the beads are on their sides so that the holes don't show. Spread orange filler thickly over the starfish and press in square frosted beads. Use some darker beads for shading.

6 Glue on a large bead for the fish eye using wood glue. Thickly spread white filler on to a 5cm/2in square section of the fish body and press in mixed beads. Repeat, working in small sections, until the fish is complete. Glue on large beads for bubbles.

7 For the background and rocks, use mosaic clippers to cut the mosaic tiles into 1cm/½in squares. Clip the edges where necessary to fit closely around the curves.

8 Stick the clipped tiles down with wood glue in the marked areas. When the design is complete, Mix the tile grout and spread over. Spread very lightly and carefully over the beaded areas. Wipe off the grout with a damp cloth and leave to dry.

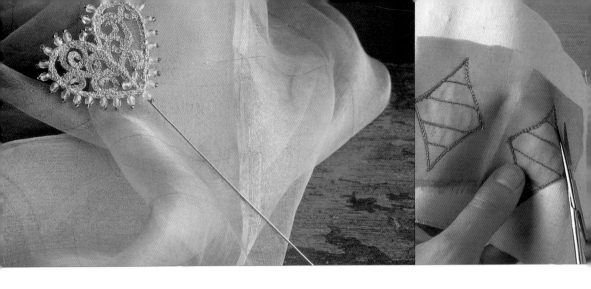

Machine
Embroidery

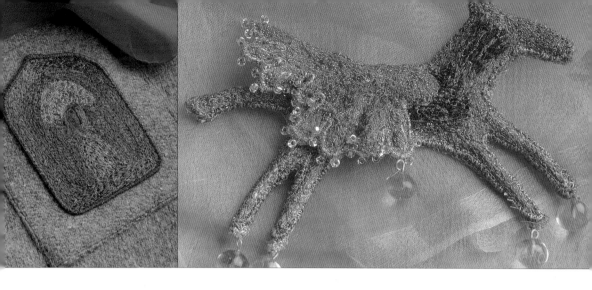

The versatility of machine embroidery enables needleworkers to experiment with a wide range of decorative stitches and techniques to produce truly original pieces. The great appeal of this craft is its speed – designs can be realized in a few hours and ideas captured with immediacy and spontaneity. Metallic threads are an ideal medium for this delicate form of jewellery: they can even be used on soluble material that is then dissolved to leave ethereal, glittering webs of stitches.

As would be expected with a craft dependent on modern technology, machine embroidery is a fairly recent development in the history of textile design and needlework.

History

Embroidered textiles have been in evidence for centuries, in all cultures, and have always been highly prized for their skill and workmanship. Embroidery as the art of embellishing existing fabric with threads and other materials has been practised since the times of the ancient Egyptians. In most cultures of the world, men and women have used embroidery to decorate clothing.

Until last century, embroidery was a laborious process requiring many hours of skilled labour. Embroidered items were expensive and affordable only to the upper classes and the church. Embroidered items denoted rank and status and as such were desired and highly prized. Since the advent of the domestic sewing machine, the time and patience required for embroidery has been halved, enabling designers to achieve wonderful results with less of the painstaking labour.

Originally, hand embroidery was an activity for the upper classes. Upper- and middle-class ladies were kept idle as a mark of their wealth. The only pastimes considered suitable for a lady of rank were those that confirmed her femininity, emphasizing qualities desirable in women: charitable acts showed her compassion, while embroidery demonstrated her delicacy, dexterity and patience. Pattern books of popular motifs such as flowers, hearts and animals were produced especially for this market. Homes were full of the produce of women's leisure hours: tablecloths, cushions and stitched samplers were displayed to demonstrate the maker's patient, industrious nature.

Machine embroidery is the antithesis of these restrictive concepts. It is a craft for people who may have less patience for results than that imposed by time-consuming hand embroidery, and for those whose

Left: Worked on a water-soluble base, this machine embroidered garment has been carefully made, using a grid of stitches and a restricted colour palette. The lacy effect is achieved relatively quickly.

Above: Small items of jewellery can be made quickly with machine embroidery. With their small surface area such projects are a good method of trying different combinations of colours and fabrics.

priority is creativity over occupation. It also appeals to those who like working with technology. The great appeal of machine embroidery is its speed. Designs can be realized in a matter of hours, while fleeting ideas can be captured. Working with such immediacy is a distinct advantage in the creative process, as new ideas for texture and shape may be born from mistakes and the direction of a piece can be changed at will.

Machine embroidery has much to do with the process of drawing and painting. With practice, the embroiderer learns to use the needle with dexterity and fluidity, much as an artist uses a pencil. Stitches can be used to create different textures and densities. Areas of colour are applied by stitchwork or appliquéd fabrics. The texture of the threads and fabrics chosen adds the most tactile dimension to the work.

As long ago as the 1790s, manufacturers were toying with the possibilities of producing a sewing machine. During the 19th century, industry developed embroidery machines such as the Cornelly machine for decorative chain stitch, but these were for factory use only. Domestic machines did not appear on the market until much later in the century. And when they did they were fixed-needle machines which produced a straight line. To get a zigzag the embroiderer had to move the fabric rapidly from side to side, a manoeuvre that took great dexterity and skill.

In the 1880s, technicians at the Singer sewing machine company were employed to produce "art" pictures with satin and zigzag stitches on domestic treadle machines. They depicted the popular Victorian images of animals, portraits, landscapes and seascapes or copied well-known paintings. With the advent of electric sewing machines, Singer realized the potential for, and the interest in, domestically-produced machine-made embroidery. In 1911 the company published a book, which was called *Singer Instructions for Art Embroidery*. It

contained lessons for lace making, appliqué and free embroidery.

Later guides were written by a technician and teacher at Singer, Dorothy Benson, who published *Machine Embroidery: The Artistic Possibilities of the Singer Sewing Machine*, for Singer, and the more popular *Your Machine Embroidery*, for Sylvan Press in 1952. She was a skilled technician and probably the first to see the creative possibilities for embroiderers. As a teacher she influenced and inspired a great many women, one of whom was Rebecca Crompton, an artist and head of women's craft, dress and embroidery at Croydon School of Art, near London. She used hand embroidery with machine embroidery, and experiment-

Above: This patchwork cushion could be worked by hand or machine. The appliqué motifs are quickly stitched in place and their details enhanced with machine embroidery.

ed with colour and techniques to create texture. Her unconventional approach has left a lasting legacy in the field of machine embroidery.

Today, designers and needleworkers can allow their imagination free-rein, with almost limitless scope for invention, and for exploring the use of colours, textures and structures, as well as new materials, which seem to appear on the market on an almost weekly basis. This freedom to create unique pieces of work is the essence of machine embroidery.

One of the joys of machine embroidery is its sheer versatility; it can be used as expressively as paint, or it can be used to build up a design in three dimensions.

Gallery

Machine embroidery has many applications that are limited only by the imagination and skill of the craftworker. From simple embellishments on everyday clothing and home furnishing to textile art that challenges the boundaries of the craft, there is something to appeal to everyone whatever their level of skill. Small-scale items are quick to make, but need accuracy. Large-scale projects may need a more painterly and artistic approach. There are so many different threads, experimental products and fabrics available to the maker nowadays that the sky really is the limit when it comes to designing and making a project. The work shown on these pages demonstrates the versatile nature of machine embroidery and represents a cross section of contemporary design.

Below: APPLIQUÉ CUSHIONS
The vibrant effect of these cushions was achieved by using a combination of appliqué and decorative zigzag and free stitches to build up layers of colour.
LORNA MOFFAT

Above: EMBROIDERED FAN
This piece was created by alternating layers of machine stitching and appliqué on felt to achieve a complex design reminiscent of the countryside.
LINDA CHILTON

Right: EMBROIDERED BUTTONS
These witty designs appear to be sketched on to the buttons, and the designer has played with the textures and effects possible with stitching. A single line is used in some places, while others have been filled in by stitching over the same area several times.
MICHELLE HOLMES

Below: PISCES PICTURE
Layers of translucent and textured fabrics have been layered and then machine stitched with a mixture of metallic and coloured threads. Hand stitching completes the image.
KAREN HALL

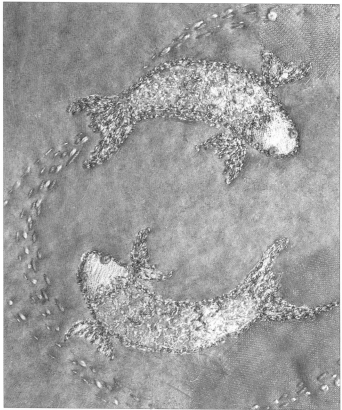

Below: LINEN SCARF
Cotton fabrics were machine-appliquéd to a loose-weave linen scarf to create this delightful design. Additional decorations were screen-printed on to the fabric.
RACHEL HOWARD

Most of the materials used for machine embroidery can be purchased from craft shops or department stores. Virtually any fabric can be machine embroidered; silk and cotton are easy to handle.

Materials

Embellishments 1

Buttons and beads come in a range of shapes and sizes and a variety of materials, such as plastic, glass, wood, metal and bone.

Fabric cord 2

Cord is usually couched on to fabric or covered in stitchwork.

Fabrics 3

Fabrics are available in many textures and colours: metallic organza, silk, chiffon, satin and velvet. Cotton ticking, calico and cotton will all provide a firm base for many designs.

Self-adhesive felt can be applied to the back of the embroidery.

Threads 4

Hand embroidery threads are available in skeins and can be couched or stitched on the work to enhance machine embroidery.

Invisible thread is a strong transparent thread used to stitch beads on to embroidery. It must be secured firmly.

Machine embroidery threads are available in every imaginable colour and in different strengths. They are more lustrous than sewing threads.

Metallic machine embroidery threads are available in many colours as well as shades of gold, bronze and silver. When stitching at high speeds occasionally the thread will snap. Some metallic threads are twisted with matt colours for a less glittery effect. These threads shed so you may need to change your needle more frequently.

Sewing threads are used for constructing pieces or when lustrous stitchwork is not desired.

Texture threads are available in metallic shades and colours. They can be difficult to use and work best when used in conjunction with a coloured thread in the same needle.

Wool threads are matt, textured threads which work well on woollen fabrics. They can be used in the bobbin or on top of the sewing machine.

Stabilizers 5

Stabilizers should be used to prevent puckering and distortion of the fabric. **Water-soluble polythene** will stabilize open-work and sheer fabrics. It pulls away after immersion in cold water, although it can simply be worn away or dabbed with water to remove. It can be used as a template over textured fabrics or to create free-standing embroidery.

Hot water-soluble stabilizer can also be used but the embroidery may lose some colour and become stiff.

Also available is **vanishing muslin**, which disintegrates when heated, although scorching may occur and fibres may be difficult to remove.

For heavier fabrics use **lightweight paper** or **non-woven interfacing**, which can be torn or pulled away after stitching.

The most vital piece of equipment for machine embroidery is, of course, a sewing machine. Any machine is adequate as long as it has a straight and zigzag stitch facility.

Equipment

Compasses

A pair of compasses are used to make scallop templates and draw circles.

Embroidery hoops

A wooden hand embroidery hoop can be used for machine embroidery if the inner ring is wrapped with bias tape. Machine embroidery hoops with spring closures are available.

Fabric dyes

Dyes for hot and cold water are available and can be mixed to give interesting and unusual shades. Use fabrics with a high percentage of natural fibres for the best results. It is worthwhile to dye a number of fabrics in a variety of colours before creating an appliqué piece. Remember to fix dyes according to the manufacturer's instructions. Fabric paints are water-based, non-toxic paints that are fixed by ironing.

Glue

Fabric glue can be used in place of fusible interlining to bond fabrics. PVA glue can be used to varnish paper and embroidery.

Iron

Embroidery should be pressed on the wrong side to prevent scorching or flattening the fibres. Set the temperature so as not to damage the least heat-tolerant fabric or thread.

Needles

Hand-sewing needles Use a selection of needles with larger eyes for hand-stitching with thicker thread. Use a fine beading needle to stitch tiny beads.

Bobbins It is useful to have a number of bobbins to save time unwinding before refilling with another thread.

Machine needles Choose a needle that is the right size for the thread. Extra fine and metallic threads require 70/10 or 80/12. Most other threads require 80/12 or 90/14. Heavy textured and double threads require 100/16 or 110/18.

Outliner

Gutta is applied using a special dispenser to draw a line of even thickness on to fabric. Gutta is available in a variety of colours, metallics and transparent.

Pens

Fabric pens are used to draw on fabric.

Ruler

Metal rules are used for drawing straight lines and reducing or enlarging designs.

Scissors

Use dressmaker's shears for cutting fabric. Use embroidery scissors for cutting away threads and trimming.

Set square

Set squares are used for finding a right-angle on a design or fabric.

Sewing machine

The machine should have a free arm and a detachable bed for ease of movement. Take care of the machine: clean and oil it regularly to prevent stitch problems.

Machine feet For most embroidery a darning foot should be used, although a presser foot will give a cleaner satin stitch. You can work without a foot, although the thread will tend to snap more frequently.

Tape

Masking tape is used to hold fabric taut over templates.

Tape measure

Tape measures are flexible measuring tools ideal for measuring fabric.

Templates

Stencil paper is available in a waxy yellow finish. Cut out stencils with paper scissors or a craft knife.

Transferring designs

Dressmaker's carbon is used to transfer designs to fabric. You could also use a soft pencil and a light box.

If your sewing machine is capable of zigzag stitch you can use it to create many different effects: all the designs in this chapter are achieved by varying basic stitches. Start by practising simple shapes and outlines.

Basic Techniques

On a domestic sewing machine the size of the stitch is predetermined by a control mechanism, which can be altered, as well as by the thickness of fabric that the needle is stitching through. The direction of stitch is controlled by the presser foot and the feed dog, which is the raised part that lies on the bed immediately below the foot. If the feed dog is removed, stitches of any size can be made. Many machines have a darning function that lowers the feed dog; on others, the feed dog should be covered and the stitch length set to 0. Use a darning foot on the sewing machine.

The fabric needs to be stretched taut in an embroidery hoop, since the speed at which the stitching moves, even if only slowly, can make the fabric pucker. Place the fabric right side up in the outer ring and press the inner ring over it so that the fabric lies flat on the machine bed.

Practise stitching with the machine set at a slow speed if possible. Set the stitch width to 0 and lower the presser bar to engage the top tension. Work a few stitches to secure the threads, then trim the ends. With the feed dog lowered, stitches are made at differing lengths depending on how quickly or slowly the fabric is moved below the needle. You can either manoeuvre the hoop or place your fingers at each side of the foot to guide the fabric. Keep the fabric moving steadily and practise working spirals filling stitches, drawing and writing.

For regular stitching the tension should be even top and bottom, but interesting effects can be achieved by altering it. If you loosen the bobbin tension, for example, the top thread will lie on the surface as if couched. Different textures and weights of fabric will also have an effect on the stitching.

Above: Any sewing machine is suitable for machine embroidery, as long as it does straight and zigzag stitch.

Stitch problems

Oil the machine regularly and remove lint and threads from the bobbin case. If stitches are not properly formed or the threads break, check first that the machine is correctly threaded, the needle is correctly fitted and is not blunt or bent, and that it is the appropriate size for the thread.

If the needle breaks

Check that the top tension is not too tight. If the fabric is moved too forcibly it can bend the needle, causing it to hit the needle plate or bobbin case.

If the top thread breaks

Check that the top tension is not too tight, the top thread is not knotted and the presser bar is lowered.

If the bobbin thread breaks

Check that the bobbin tension is not too tight, the bobbin thread is evenly wound, and there are no threads caught in the bobbin case.

If the fabric puckers

Check that the tension is not too tight, the stitches are not too long, and the thread is not too thick for the fabric. If the needle hits the bobbin case, the timing may be out and the machine will need a service.

Transferring designs

There are plenty of ways of transferring a design on to fabric, so whatever fabric you are using, there will be a suitable method. Start by creating a template, scaling up the design if necessary using graph paper or the enlarge facility on a photocopier.

Enlarging an image

1 Trace the template on to tissue paper and lay it over a piece of graph paper. Using an appropriate scale, enlarge the template on to a second piece of graph paper, copying the shape from each smaller square to each larger one.

Transfer using a fabric marker

Draw around the template with a water-soluble fabric marker or dressmaker's marking pencil.

Transfer using carbon paper

Place the carbon paper face down on the right side of the fabric and position the traced design on top. Draw over the lines with a ballpoint pen.

2 Place the sketch on to thin card and cut around the outline using paper scissors.

Transfer using a light box

Tape the design to a light box or window and then tape the fabric over it. Trace over the design with a fabric marker.

Transfer using tailor's chalk

If you are using a dark fabric, mark out the design with tailor's chalk. It will leave a fairly powdery texture that is easy to brush off.

Stabilizers Light fabrics may be distorted during embroidery if they are not stabilized with a firmer backing.

Transfer using water-soluble fabric

If a design cannot be drawn on to a textured fabric with a fabric marker, trace the design on to a piece of water-soluble polythene and pin it to the right side of the fabric. Dissolve after stitching.

Non-woven stabilizer

A non-woven interfacing or light-weight paper should be pinned to the wrong side of the fabric for heavy embroidery or on lightweight fabric, to add body and prevent the fabric from distorting.

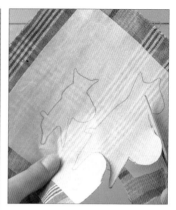

Fusible interlining

1 Fusible interlining is useful for stabilizing appliqué pieces, as it binds on to the fabric with an iron. You can then cut around the shape to be appliquéd, with the interlining in place to act as a stiffener.

Transfer using tissue paper

Trace the design on to a piece of tissue paper and pin it to the wrong side of the fabric. Remove after stitching.

Water-soluble stabilizer

Use water-soluble film to support lightweight fabric, lace or openwork during stitching.

2 Fusible interlining has a backing paper that can be peeled off. The pieces can then be pressed in place on the ground fabric.

Appliqué Used in patchwork and embroidery, appliqué is the application of one fabric to another. Usually the applied fabric is cut to a shape and its outline is machine or hand stitched in place.

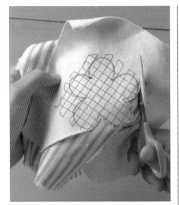

Machine appliqué: satin stitch

1 Pin the appliqué piece to the ground fabric and stitch around the outline. Trim away the excess fabric close to the stitched line.

Machine appliqué: straight stitch

1 Cut out the shape, leaving 1cm (½in) allowance all around. Press the allowance to the wrong side, snipping away corners and curves.

Shadow appliqué

1 Work the appliqué pieces using one of the methods described previously, then pin and tack a piece of sheer fabric over the design.

2 Work a zigzag stitch around the outline, covering raw edges. This can be followed by a second line of satin stitch.

2 Pin the piece to the fabric and work a straight stitch all around.

2 Use matching sewing thread to stitch over the sheer fabric, close to the stitches on the appliquéd pieces.

Stitches These stitches will all be useful when making jewellery and related items. Practise them on spare scraps of fabric, and experiment freely with different threads and tensions to create original effects.

Whip stitch

Loosening the bobbin tension and tightening the top tension produces a beaded effect as the bobbin thread is brought to the surface. It is most effective when the bobbin is threaded with a contrasting colour.

Cable stitch or mock couching

The thread appears to be couched in place. This is a method for embroidering heavy threads which cannot pass through the eye of a needle. The heavier thread is wound on to a bobbin and the bobbin tension is loosened so that the thread can pass through easily. Tighten the top tension. Work the piece from the wrong side.

Satin stitch

This can be worked in free embroidery or as regular stitching. Set the stitch width as desired; this can be varied along the line by altering the dial. Move the hoop slowly so that the stitches lie next to each other.

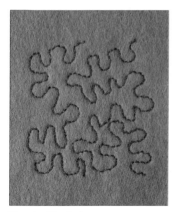

Vermicelli stitch

This is a filling stitch particularly effective for quilting, or for cable stitching with gold thread.

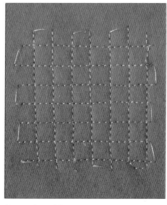

Cross-hatching

This is used as a filling. Set the sewing machine for regular stitching and attach the presser foot.

Looped stitch

Work whip stitch, tightening the top tension and loosening the bobbin. Remove the top thread with a needle and bond a piece of fusible interlining to the wrong side to hold the looped stitches in place.

Zigzag filler

Set the stitch width as desired and move the fabric from side to side. To add shading, work several rows of stitching making the edges jagged so that subsequent layers will blend into the previous ones.

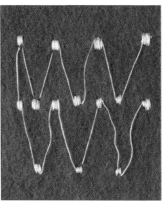

French knots

Set the stitch width to the size of the knot desired. Work a solid satin stitch over one spot several times. Do not cut the threads between the dots. The dots can be cut with a stitch ripper to create tufts to secure the threads. Bond a piece of fusible interlining to the wrong side to hold the thread.

Double threads

Thread two different threads through the eye of a large needle and use a looser top tension to accommodate the extra thickness. Double threads will give a subtle two-toned effect and tone down bright metallic threads.

Couching

The fabric should be backed with a stabilizer. Lay a piece of thick thread or piping along the line of the design. Set the stitch width to the width of the piping and stitch down with a satin or zigzag stitch.

Couched yarn with straight stitch

Arrange a yarn around the outline and work a straight stitch along the centre of the yarn.

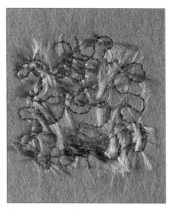

Trapped threads

Cut small pieces of thread and lay them on the fabric. Work a vermicelli stitch over the threads.

Layers of contrasting fabrics and glittering machine embroidery make this a spectacular piece. The rough texture of the felts is wonderfully highlighted by shimmering organza and metallic machine embroidery.

Sparkling Starfish Brooch

you will need

Pencil, thin card (stock) or paper and scissors (for templates)

Dressmaker's pins

Purple felt

Tailor's chalk

Fabric scissors

Rust felt

Shot organza

Sewing machine with darning foot

Needle size 70/10–80/12

Metallic machine embroidery thread

Needle and matching sewing thread

Brooch back

1 Draw two freehand starfish shapes on to thin card or paper, one larger than the other. Cut the templates out roughly. Pin the large starfish template to the purple felt and draw around it with tailor's chalk.

2 Cut out irregular pointed shapes from the purple and the rust felt. Pin them down along the points of the starfish outline. Cut out the smaller starfish shape from organza and pin it on top of the felt starfish.

3 Thread the machine with metallic thread and stitch over the edges of the organza. Build up layers of texture and colour with different threads.

4 Cut out the felt starfish shape and a small circle of felt. Stitch this on to the centre back of the starfish. Stitch on the brooch back.

The heart is a timeless jewellery motif, evoking love and friendship. This filigree machine-embroidered hatpin, which can also be worn as a lapel pin, was inspired by baroque gilding found in a Czech church.

Heart Hatpin

you will need
Water-soluble film
Fabric pen
Embroidery hoop
Sewing machine with darning foot
Needle size 70/10–80/12
Metallic machine embroidery thread
Thin jewellery wire
Wire cutters
Hatpin
Beading needle
Invisible thread
Plastic beads in two sizes

1 Copy the template from the back of the book, enlarging as required, and trace it on to water-soluble film with a fabric pen. Place the piece in an embroidery hoop and lower the sewing machine feed. Using metallic thread, stitch around the lines of the heart motif. Fill in the filigree outline, stitching in small circles.

2 Stitch back and forth several times over the circular stitchwork. Remove the work from the machine and turn the embroidery the other way up in the hoop.

3 Set a narrow zigzag width. Curve a length of jewellery wire around the stitched outline of the heart, starting and finishing at the point at the bottom of the heart. Couch the wire in place and trim the ends.

4 Remove the piece from the hoop. Lay the hat pin in the centre of the heart. Set a medium zigzag width and couch the pin in place.

5 Immerse the piece in cold water and pull away the film. Using a beading needle and invisible thread, stitch the beads around the edge of the heart. Sew through a large bead, then a small one and back through the large bead. Make a stitch in the edge of the embroidery to secure the beads.

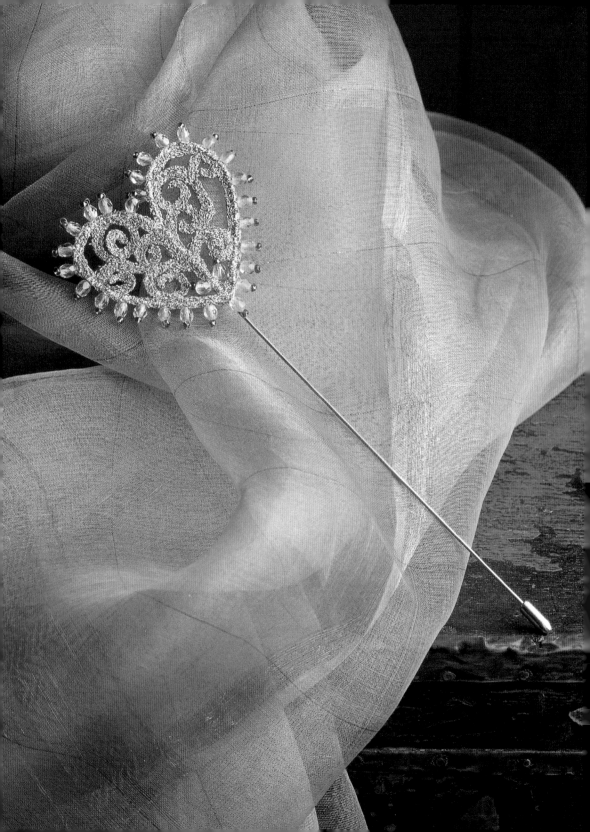

This exotic character with his flamboyant headdress is embroidered using filling stitchwork in richly contrasting threads on a background of interfacing, and is designed for stitching on to a blazer pocket.

Blazer Badge

you will need

Pencil, thin card (stock) and scissors (for template)

20cm/8in square non-woven

Heavyweight interfacing

Fabric pen

Fabric paints

Paintbrush

Iron

Sewing machine with darning foot

Needle size 80/12–90/14

Coloured and metallic machine embroidery threads

Needle and sewing thread

Embroidery scissors

1 Follow the photograph opposite to draw the design, enlarging as required. Cut out a template from thin card. Lay this on a piece of interfacing and draw around the shapes with a fabric pen.

2 Using fabric paints, paint the background design in areas of solid colour, so that the white interfacing does not show through the stitching. Press with a medium-hot iron to fix the colours.

3 Lower the feed on the sewing machine. Fill in the design areas in the desired colours by working a straight stitch back and forth.

4 Work the face in a spiral from the centre point to the outline. To give a raised effect to the face, push the stitching out from the wrong side to form a dome shape.

5 Thread a needle with a dark thread and sew the eyes and nose details. Use gold thread to add the stars and the headdress details. Cut out the badge shape close to the outline. Set a medium stitch width and work a satin stitch all round the edge.

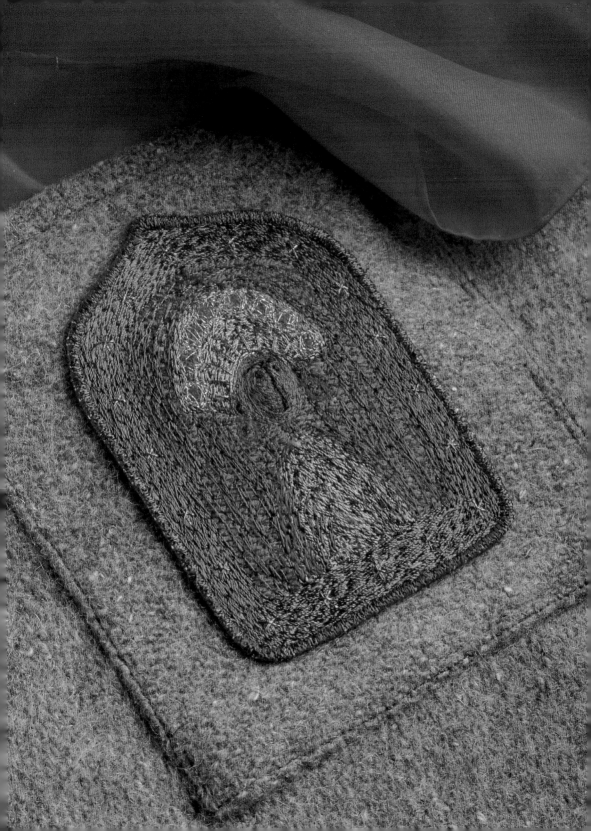

A decorative hatpin is a stylish way to jazz up a plain hat. This outsize brass pin is topped with an elaborate shining sun in machine-embroidered velvet, backed with rays of hammered metal.

Embroidered Sun Hatpin

●●●

you will need

Yellow velvet

Scissors

Piece of any type of fine fabric

Embroidery hoop

Sewing machine with darning foot

Needle size 80/12–90/14

Coloured and metallic machine embroidery threads

Brass sheet

Tin snips

Metal file

Small ball hammer

Brass wire

Wire cutters

Round-nosed (snub-nosed) pliers

Epoxy resin glue

Glass beads

Hatpin

1 Cut out a yellow velvet sun. Place a piece of fine fabric in an embroidery hoop (to act as a stabilizer) and machine-stitch the sun to it. Thread the machine with contrasting threads in the top and bobbin and whip-stitch around the edge. Then make a deeper decorative band of stitching around the edge. Stitch a spiral on each ray in contrasting threads and finish with the face in the centre. Trim the velvet sun away from the fine fabric.

2 Cut out a larger sun shape from the brass sheet using tin snips, and file the edges until smooth. Hammer the brass to give it some interesting texture. To make an enclosure for the hatpin, form a spiral at each end of a piece of wire and hammer flat. Centre the wire over the brass sun and glue in place. Cut out a small circle of brass and glue over the wire.

3 Now glue the velvet sun on to the centre of the brass sun. Thread some glass beads on to the hatpin and glue them in place at the end. To assemble the finished piece, bend the wire spirals slightly backwards so that you can easily slide the hatpin through the top and bottom spirals.

A winged horse makes a stunning brooch, with subtle glints of light in the embroidery hinting at precious metal. The three-dimensional form is created after stitching and the back is varnished to hold the shape.

Horse Brooch

you will need

Tracing paper, pencil, paper or card (stock) and scissors (for templates)

20cm/8in square calico

Scissors for cutting fabric

Water-soluble film

Dressmaker's pins

Embroidery hoop

Sewing machine with darning foot

Needle size 90/14

Metallic and coloured machine embroidery threads

Small piece of velvet

Fine cord

Acrylic varnish and paintbrush

Beading needle

Invisible thread

Beads

Brooch back

1 Copy the templates from the back of the book, enlarging as required. Cut the horse and wing shapes out of calico and pin them on to a piece of water-soluble film. Now place the piece in an embroidery hoop.

2 Lower the feed on your machine and stitch around the edges of the shapes. Cut some velvet to the shape of the horse's body and pin it in place. Fill the bobbin with contrasting thread and use two threads in the needle: one metallic and one coloured. Stitch over the velvet randomly to hold it in place.

3 Fill in the wing area in a contrasting metallic thread. Stitch over the raw edges of each shape in small circles to neaten them.

4 Curve a length of fine cord around the outline of each shape. Set a medium zigzag width and couch the cord in place.

▶

5 Set the stitch width to 0. Work a narrow band inside the couched cord in a contrasting colour.

6 Take the embroidered pieces out of the hoop and immerse in cold water. Pull away the water-soluble film and leave to dry.

7 Stitch one end of the wing on to the horse's back using thread of a matching colour.

8 Shape the horse and the wing by curving them over your hand. To hold the shapes, paint two coats of acrylic varnish on to the wrong side of the pieces. Allow to dry.

9 Thread your beading needle with invisible thread and stitch small beads around the edges of the wing. Stitch a larger bead on to each hoof. Finally, stitch a brooch back on to the wrong side of the piece.

The intensely coloured ground fabric of this bracelet contrasts wonderfully with metallic embroidery in a strong, simple geometric pattern, embellished with embroidered domes topped with beads.

Harlequin Bracelet

you will need

Pencil, ruler, paper or card (stock) and scissors (for template)

Scissors for cutting fabric

30cm/12in square silk

Fabric pen

Iron

Dressmaker's pins

Non-woven interfacing

Embroidery hoop

Sewing machine with darning foot

Needle size 80/90–12/14

Metallic and coloured machine embroidery threads

Embroidery scissors

Metallic fabric paint

Paintbrush

White paper

Small coin

Water-soluble film

Beading needle

Invisible thread

Beads

Brass jewellery wire

Wire cutters

File

Round-nosed (snub-nosed) pliers

Clasp fastening

Needle and matching sewing thread

1 First, cut out a paper or card template to the size required and then use this card template to cut out two pieces of silk, making sure that you leave a 2.5cm/1in seam allowance all around the edge. Now draw the pattern on to one of the pieces of silk with a fabric pen. Turn under the seam allowance on both pieces and press.

3 Working carefully, cut away the interfacing close to the machine stitching. Now paint diagonal lines between the stitched areas with your metallic fabric paint. Press the piece between two completely clean sheets of white paper, in order to fix the metallic paint.

2 Pin the patterned fabric to a piece of non-woven interfacing and place in an embroidery hoop. Lower the feed on the sewing machine. Fill the bobbin with contrasting thread and use a metallic thread in the needle. Using whip stitch, fill in each diamond and triangle shape, working in a spiral from the centre to the outside edge.

4 Use a coin to draw four circles on water-soluble film. With metallic thread on top and coloured thread in the bobbin, work back and forth from a circle's centre to its outline, then work a spiral from centre to outline. Immerse the piece in cold water, pull off the film and press each circle into a dome.

5 Thread a beading needle with invisible thread and sew a bead to the pinnacle of each dome. Stitch each dome at four points around its base over the point where two diamond shapes meet.

6 Cut seven pieces of jewellery wire 10cm/4in long. File the ends smooth and twist a spiral at each end using round-nosed pliers. Set a medium zigzag width and, using metallic thread, couch the wires on to the bracelet, one through each diamond and one at each end of the bracelet.

7 Pin the second piece of silk to the embroidered piece, wrong sides together. Set the stitch width to 0 and work a line of stitching all around the edge. Hand-stitch a clasp fastening to the ends of the bracelet.

These embroidered diamond-shaped earrings are padded to make them three-dimensional while remaining extremely light. A rich combination of colours and textures gives a precious, jewel-like quality.

"Diamond" Earrings

you will need

Pencil, paper or thin card (stock) and scissors (for template)

Fabric pen

Small pieces of calico

Small pieces of organza and silk

Dressmaker's pins

Sewing machine with darning foot

Needle size 80/12

Embroidery hoop

Coloured and metallic machine embroidery threads

Small, sharp scissors for cutting fabric

Wadding (batting)

PVA (white) glue

2 small paintbrushes

Metallic acrylic paint

Needle

2 eye pins, 2 metallic beads and 2 glass beads

Round-nosed (snub-nosed) pliers

Earring wires

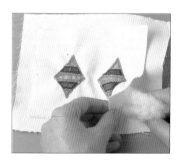

1 Cut out a diamond-shaped stiff paper or card template to the required size, and then use it to draw two diamond shapes on to the calico. Now draw four horizontal lines across each diamond, using a fabric pen. Pin a piece of organza over each marked shape. Lower the feed on the sewing machine and place the fabric in an embroidery hoop. With matching thread, stitch the horizontal lines and several lines around the design.

◄ **4** Pin a second piece of calico to the wrong side of the embroidery. Place it in the hoop and stitch around three sides of each diamond. Stuff both diamonds with wadding, right into the corners. Close up the fourth side with stitching. Cut out the shapes close to the stitched outline. With a brush, apply PVA glue to the edges of the shapes to varnish and stiffen them. Leave to dry.

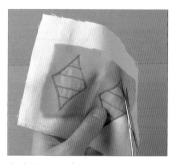

▲ **2** Now, working very carefully, use your scissors to trim away the excess organza, cutting close to your stitched outline.

◄ **3** Cut two pieces of silk in a contrasting colour. Pin them over the diamonds. Place the piece in a hoop. Stitch some lines around the horizontal stripes with matching thread. Trim off excess fabric close to these lines. Work lines of stitching around the stripes to cover raw edges, plus more lines around the design with metallic thread.

5 Now paint the back and the edges of the diamond shapes, using metallic acrylic paint. When the paint has dried, make a hole at the top of each diamond with a needle. Thread each eye pin through a small metallic bead, a glass bead and then the embroidered diamond. Using round-nosed pliers, twist the wire at the back to secure in place and attach the earring wires to the eye pins.

This unusual fan-shaped comb is decorated with deeply worked embroidery. There are no solid areas of colour, but a subtle, densely mottled surface created by whip stitching one colour over another.

Glittering Hair Comb

1 Copy the templates from the back of the book, enlarging as required, and draw around them on to the calico. Now cut out the fabric pieces and pin them to water-soluble film. Place the whole piece in an embroidery hoop. Lower the feed on the sewing machine. Using contrasting threads in the bobbin and the needle, work whip stitch in circles to fill in the outline. Stitch areas of different colours bleeding into each other to give a mottled effect. Stitch in circles to neaten the raw edges.

2 Turn the piece over in the hoop. Fill the bobbin with metallic thread and use contrasting thread in the needle. Work a whip stitch along the zigzag edge of the larger piece.

◄ **3** Immerse the pieces in cold water and pull away the film. Cut a 2.5cm/1in square of card and eight 1m/1yd lengths of jewellery wire. Wrap a length of wire around the card. Cut the wire at one end and twist the strands together at the other end to make a tassel. Repeat with the other lengths. Set a medium zigzag width and, using metallic thread, couch the tassels in place between the points on the larger piece of embroidery.

4 Lay the smaller piece on top of the larger, matching up the lower edges. Set the stitch width to 0 and join the two pieces using matching thread, stitching in circles. Hand-stitch the top bar of the hair comb to the lower edge of the embroidered piece. Draw around the larger template on to a piece of self-adhesive felt and cut out the shape. Peel off the paper backing and stick the felt on to the back of the embroidery.

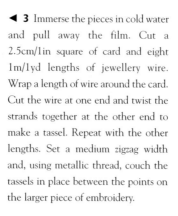

This stunning necklace features cords that appear to be wrapped but are in fact embroidered. Unusually shaped beads picking up a colour in the stitchwork are suspended between the cords on jewellery wire.

Beaded Necklace

●●●●●

you will need

Sewing machine with darning foot

Needle size 90/14

Fine metallic and coloured machine embroidery threads

40cm/16in and 72cm/29in lengths thick cord

60cm/24in thin cord

Pencil, stiff paper or thin card (stock) and scissors (for template)

Pen

Felt

Scissors for cutting fabric

Dressmaker's pins

Water-soluble film

Embroidery hoop

Pin board

Needle and matching sewing thread

Round-nosed (snub-nosed) pliers

Brass jewellery wire

Wire cutters

Beads

Necklace clasp

1 Lower the feed on the sewing machine. Fill the bobbin with a metallic thread and use a coloured thread in the needle. Set a medium to wide zigzag width and feed each of the cords through the machine several times, changing the colours each time to give a mottled effect. Create bobbles at intervals along the cords by stitching back and forth over a point with metallic thread.

2 Draw a heart shape approximately 1cm/½in tall on thin card. Use this template to draw four hearts on a piece of felt and cut them out. Pin the felt hearts on to a piece of water-soluble film and place in an embroidery hoop. Set the stitch width to 0 and fill in the shapes with whip stitch, spiralling outwards from the centre to the edge. Immerse the piece in water and pull away the film.

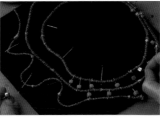

3 On a pin board, pin out the shortest length of cord to make the inner ring and the medium length 2cm/¾in from the first to make the outer ring. Pin the longest length of cord around the outer ring, making curves along its length. Hand-stitch the points where the curves meet the outer ring. Using pliers, bind the ends of the cords

together with brass jewellery wire. Cut 22 pieces of wire, each 5cm/2in long, and thread a bead on to each one. Using pliers, twist one end of each wire around the inner cord and the other end around the outer cord. Attach some of the beaded wires between the curved cord and the outer ring. Trim the ends of the wires.

4 Cut four 6cm/2½in lengths of wire. Use a needle to pierce a hole at the top and bottom of each embroidered heart. Thread each wire through a bead, then through the heart and through another bead. Twist the ends of each wire into spirals and attach both ends to the cords. Hand-stitch the clasp to the ends of the cords.

Metallic threads, iridescent paper and shimmering beads combine to make these glittering pieces of jewellery. The embroidery is done on a base that dissolves to leave only the sparkling tracery of stitches.

Iridescent Earrings and Pendant

●●●●●

you will need
Water-soluble film
Embroidery hoop
Dressmaker's pins
Tracing paper, pencil, stiff paper or
thin card (stock) and scissors
(for templates)
Fabric pen
Iridescent paper
Sewing machine with darning foot
Needle size 90/14
Metallic machine embroidery threads
General-purpose scissors
Iron
Kitchen paper
Self-hardening clay
Stiff wire
Blue-green watercolour inks
Paintbrush
Metallic paints
Card
Felt
Plastic sheet
Acrylic spray varnish
Beading needle
Selection of small beads
2 split rings
Pliers
2 jump rings
Earring wires or posts

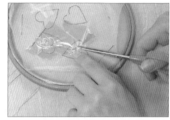

1 Stretch a layer of water-soluble film in an embroidery hoop and then pin another layer to the back. Copy the templates provided at the back of the book, enlarging them if necessary, and draw round them on the film. Now pin pieces of iridescent paper to the back of the film over the centres of the motifs. Thread the bobbin and needle with metallic thread. Set the machine stitch width to 0 and lower the feed. Work stitching in circles around the centres of the motifs and then carefully cut away any excess iridescent paper from the back.

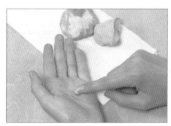

4 Make small balls of self-hardening clay for the beads, and push them on to a stiff wire. Leave to dry, stuck into a piece of clay.

2 Machine-stitch right around the outlines of the motifs, and then fill in the area around the centres with whip stitch, spiralling outwards to the edge.

3 Immerse the embroidery in water to dissolve the film. Iron dry between kitchen paper.

5 Paint the clay beads with blue-green watercolour inks. Leave to dry, then add highlights with dots of metallic paint.

6 Cover a large piece of card with felt and then with plastic sheet, to make a soft backing sheet. Pin the motifs to the backing and coat the clay beads and the embroidered motifs with acrylic spray varnish.

7 Using a beading needle, attach metallic thread to the top of a motif. Thread on two small beads, then a clay bead and two more small beads. Take the thread through a split ring and then back down again through the beads and into the motif. Fasten off. Sew a ring of small beads around the centre of the motif.

8 To make an earring, open a jump ring with pliers and thread through the split ring. Join it to the ring on the earring wire or post. If you are making a pendant, then thread a machine-embroidered chain through the slip ring.

Felt, Rags and
Leather

Felt, rags and leather are textiles that offer endless scope for creating all kinds of unique and decorative pieces to wear, or with which to fashion home furnishings. Leather scraps can be bought from gloving manufacturers, while rags are readily available from favourite items of worn clothing or fabric remnants. Felt is made from carded wool, best bought as wool tops, or from pure woollen clothing that can be recycled.

Felt, rag-rug crafts and leather are age-old techniques, familiar to every culture. Leather goods were once the preserve of skilled craftspeople, while rag-rug making was a thrift craft available to everyone.

History

Feltmaking

Felt is a strange and unique fabric. It has no warp or weft, like woven fabrics, no right or wrong side, no beginning and no end. It is made with the minimum of equipment, yet a strange alchemy occurs between wool, moisture, heat and friction to create a fabric which is warm and hard-wearing. It can be fine enough to drape in heavy folds, or of such density and thickness that it can take on a sculptural quality. It can be left its natural hues or dyed with all the brilliance of the colours of the rainbow.

Below: Rag-rug making has developed from a thrift craft based on necessity to become an art form.

The use of felt pre-dates all other textiles and its manufacture with minimal materials and equipment must have been known to every culture, who may each have discovered it by accident! Sheep's wool placed in a hard shoe to ease a blister, or used to line a boot, would soon become felt with the friction, heat and sweat of the wearer. Today felt is widely known as carpet underlay, fuzzy felt and the material for hats, piano key pads and the tips of pens. More recently handmade felt has become recognized as an art and craft medium. Its history, however, belongs with the nomads of Central Asia who have used felt in many forms and who have made felt for more than 2500 years.

Above: Felt is a hardwearing fabric. It is warm material, good for making winter clothing.

Felt was so fundamental in the lives of the nomads that in 400BC the Chinese called their territory the land of felt. Ghengis Khan referred to the nomads he ruled as "the generations that lived in felt".

The story of felt past and present is as tangled as the fibres of the fabric. Felt is still made today in the same way that it would have been made 2,000 years ago, and the most effective way of making it is still the simplest. Who has not put a favourite sweater in the washing machine by mistake, to find it shrunk beyond all recognition and as stiff as a board?

Felt is a truly timeless fabric.

Rag-rug making

The history of rag rugs is sketchy. Historically most rugs that were made of worn clothing were designed to be used and were discarded once they were worn out and the last bit of use was eked out of them. Adapting textiles to make practical floor coverings to provide insulation and warmth is an idea that has evolved in different ways with the materials that were available to different peoples.

Rag-rug making reached the height of its popularity during the late 19th century. It was a thrift craft; to make a rug cost nothing but time. Long before recycling became an environmental concern, it was a way of life.

Old clothes were handed down until they were no longer serviceable. They then became the source material of rug making. Clothing was cut into long strips for "hooking", or short clippings for "prodding". Old sacking, made from woven jute cloth, imported from India as packaging for grain and other foodstuffs, was recycled for the background fabric. Hooks and prodders were adapted from any suitable household item too, such as a wooden clothes peg or large masonry nail, sharpened into a pointed hook.

Rag rugs could be made in several different ways depending on the traditions of the maker. Cloth could be hooked through to the front of the sack cloth creating a looped pile effect. The pile could then be slashed to create a thickly textured rug. Similarly the strips could be prodded through to the back of the rug, and once densely packed, the quantity of rags would hold the piece together.

The modern revival in ragwork is strongly associated with environmental conerns and the ways in which the maker can reuse waste materials. The techniques are simple enough. For beginners and professionals alike, the attraction of working with rags begins with the initial search for fabrics.

Leatherwork

Leather is an extraordinarily beautiful material and one which offers great potential because of its versatility. It has been produced all over the world since ancient times. The Egyptians made sophisticated leather goods, such as bags, cushion covers, flooring, harnesses, tyres, shoes, sandals, dog collars, chair seats and tents. It was valued on a level with gold and silver.

The benefits of leather as a hard-wearing material have long been recognized; it has been used for armoury since records began. Leather-

Above: Leather was once essential to every trade. Nowadays it is associated with the luxury goods market.

covered wooden shields were used worldwide and the armies of ancient Greece wore boots, shirts, leg guards and helmets all made from leather. Its use has continued throughout history. Leather permeated every aspect of medieval life: men wore leather doublets (jackets), travel was dependent on leather for harnesses and saddles, for trunks and cases, money was kept in leather pouches, drink was poured from leather jugs. Every trade needed leather to function and tanners began to specialize. But in later centuries with the development of man-made materials came a sharp decline in the need for handcrafted leather. Leather is still the standard material for footwear and is a popular material for clothing and baggage.

Many textiles have historical associations with different types of industry or ways of living. Today's textile artists are successfully challenging perceptions of the way age-old materials are used.

Gallery

Felt, rags and leather are all materials that have been used throughout history. All have a strong resonance of materials that are strong and serviceable, used to provide warmth and comfort, as well as for other practical purposes. The main purpose of each was always functional before beautiful, but such basic materials have an innate quality that is appealing and reassuring. With current trends in recycling fabrics, rags and felt have come into their own as decorative crafts used to make attractive and desirable objects, while leatherware has retained its appeal to the luxury goods market.

Below: PINKISH AND BLUEISH
This pair of wallhangings explores the colour spectrums of pink and blue. Each uses lengths of fabric wrapped with coloured rayon threads. The strips are woven in an order which enhances the colour movement.
ANGELA HARRISON

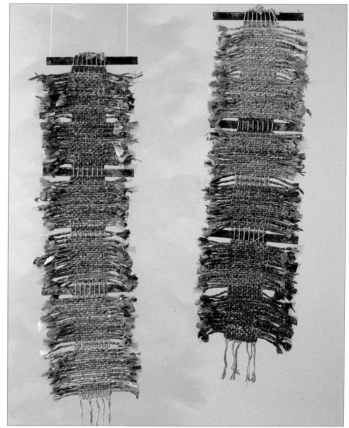

Below: LITTLE CHAMOIS DOG
This traditional-looking child's toy is made from chamois leather, which gives it a deceptive aged appearance.
MARY MAGUIRE

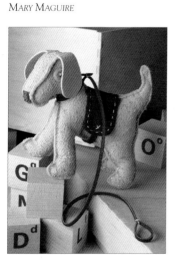

Above: FELT WALLHANGING
Painterly effects can be achieved with felt by blending two colours of fleece together.
DAWN DUPREE

Below: FELT BALLS
The marvellous range of colours available in felt can be used to great effect, as illustrated by this collection of felt balls.
VICTORIA BROWN

Above: BABY'S BOOTEES
These adorable bootees are made from lambskin, a natural product that is warm and snug. Each bootee consists of just two pieces of fabric, the upper and the sole, which are simply stitched together.
MARY MAGUIRE

Made by turning wool fibres into solid fabric, felt is an ideal jewellery material as it is lightweight and can be created in any number of lovely colours. Wool can also be mixed with fibres such as silk and mohair.

Feltwork Materials

Carded sliver

This wool is commercially sorted into fibres of the same length, bleached and carded into a long rope ready for spinning or felting. You can buy it pre-dyed in a range of vibrant colours or you can dye it yourself.

Commercial felt

Felt is available from craft suppliers in a wide range of colours.

Dye

Acid dyes – so-called because an acid such as vinegar must be added to the dye bath – are ideal for wool. They need very hot water to work well, but give good colourfast results.

Felteen

This is a clear fabric stiffener commercially used in the making of felt hats. PVA (white) glue diluted with water can also be used to stiffen felt, but will leave a surface sheen.

Glass beads

Beads in a wide range of sizes and shapes can be stitched directly on to felt items as decoration.

Jewellery findings

Standard findings are easily attached to felt pieces, using either thread or epoxy glue. Use nylon-coated jewellery wire to thread felt beads.

Thread

Ordinary sewing thread can be used in a sewing machine to create embossed lines or relief effects on thin felt. As

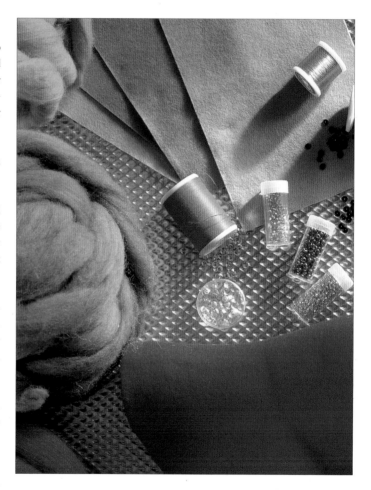

well as being used for embroidered decoration, metallic thread can be trapped under a thin web of fibres and felted into the fabric.

Uncarded fleece

Fleece needs to be cleaned, dyed and carded, but it gives greater scope for experimentation than prepared sliver. Felt is best made from wool with a staple or fibre length of 2.5–5cm/ 1–2in: longer fibres will tangle. The ideal wool for feltmaking is Merino.

Much of the equipment needed for feltwork can be improvised; felt made from carded sliver requires no specialist items. The most important thing is a cloth or mat in which to roll the felt.

Feltwork Equipment

Bamboo mat

Rolling the fleece on a bamboo or sea-grass beach mat increases friction and speeds the felting process.

Craft (utility) knife

A very sharp blade is essential for cutting cleanly through felt balls.

Drum carder

This will card a large amount of wool quickly, but is an expensive piece of equipment, only really necessary if you do a lot of feltmaking.

Hand carders

Wool can be carded by hand quite quickly. If you have no carders, use pre-carded sliver, which can be teased open with your hands.

Needles

For sewing felt choose "straw" or "milliner's" needles, which are extra long with small eyes that do not create a bulge in the shank. A needle with a large eye and a sharp point is useful for threading felt balls and beads.

Scissors

To cut through felt smoothly scissors need to be really sharp. Dressmaker's shears are needed for cutting out flat pieces of felt, and small sharp-pointed scissors for embroidery and beadwork.

Soap flakes

All soap will make felt, but some kinds have properties less advantageous to the feltmaker. For example, washing powder is too harsh and hand soap

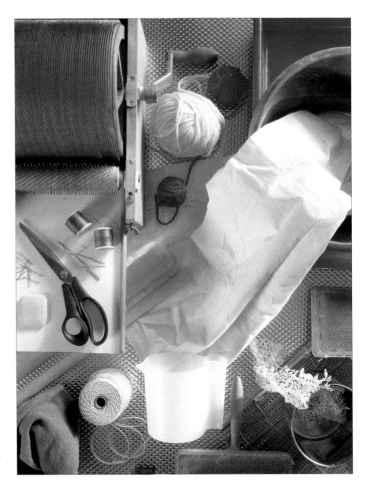

washes out too quickly. Pure soap flakes suitable for hand-washing are most suitable as they are very mild and easy to rinse out.

String

Any string that will not disintegrate in hot water or stain the wool when wet can be used to hold carded wool in hanks during the washing and dyeing processes. Cotton string is best as knots will not slip and it can be re-used many times.

The transformation of a mass of loose wool fibres into a solid piece of felt is a mysterious and intriguing process, as it requires only the action of heat, moisture and friction, aided by soap.

Feltwork Techniques

Making flat felt

1 It is not essential to use a tray to make flat felt, but it will contain any excess water, and will protect the felt if it has to be moved or left at any stage. If you are using a tray, line it with a piece of clean cloth before you start to lay out the first pattern of felt.

2 Different patterns can be laid on both faces of felt. For the pattern that is laid down first, you must remember to lay down the detail before the background. Lay the pattern on to the lining fabric, teasing out pieces of wool into the pattern required. This enables you to "sketch" with the wool.

3 When the pattern has been laid out, the background colour is put over the top. The wool must be teased out from carded slivers so that the fibres run in the same direction. This is most important if the felting process is to be successful. If the first layer of wool is laid out so the fibres run from top to bottom of the tray, the second layer must be placed at right angles to this, so the fibres run from side to side.

4 Use at least three layers of carded wool to make the felt, each layer at right angles to the last, to ensure a strong and even fabric. Keep the layers thin, and add more layers for a thicker fabric. Patch up any thin or uneven layers with wool.

5 A second pattern may be laid on the final layer of fleece. Dissolve one or two handfuls of soap flakes in hot water, using slightly more soap than you would use to wash a sweater.

6 The fleece must be soaked with the hot soapy water but sprinkle it on gently with your hand.

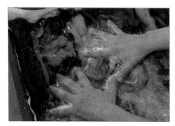

7 Press the water into the wool with the palms of your hands, and flatten the layers.

8 Start the felting process gently, by rubbing the surface in a circular movement. If the wool sticks to your hand, add more soap. Rub the wool until the fibres begin to lock together.

9 Turn the edges of the lining faric over the fleece. This will keep the edges straight and firm. Place a rolling pin at one end of the tray, and roll up the fabric with the fleece.

10 Fold a long piece of string in half, make a slip knot and pull it tighter over one end of the roll. Criss-cross the loose ends down the roll and tie firmly.

11 Roll the bundle backwards and forwards on the tray or a ridged surface. Move your hands along the length of the roll to keep an even pressure. When the string becomes loose, unwind the roll and lift the felt away. Turn the felt 90 degrees, smooth it out and then roll up the cloth again. Tie and roll the bundle back and forth as before. Repeat until the felt has been rolled in every direction.

12 The felt will have shrunk and become a firm piece of cloth. Rinse it under hot and cold running water to remove the soap. This helps the final stage of felting. Allow to dry.

Making felt balls A small ball will take about 20–30 minutes. When the wool is fully felted the ball will have shrunk considerably and will bounce if thrown hard on to a table.

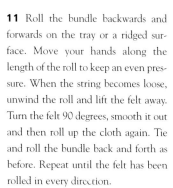

1 Twist a length of carded wool into a tight ball. If the finished ball is to be cut in half, for example, when making buttons or earrings, use several colours to achieve a marbled effect.

2 Cover the ball in another layer of carded wool, wrapping it around evenly. Keep the ball in your hand to stop it falling apart. Dip the ball in hot, soapy water, squeezing it to wet it through to the middle.

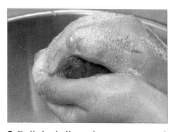

3 Roll the ball gently in your cupped hands. As the fibres begin to felt, increase the pressure steadily and dip the ball back in the water from time to time. When the wool has fully felted, rinse out the soap and leave to dry.

The felting properties of wool are such that if any other openweave fabric is placed on top, it will become part of the felt. The wool fibres lock around the non-wool fibres during felting, locking them in place.

Lace Collar

you will need
50g/2oz fleece
Tray
1m/1yd lace
Soap flakes
Iron
Scissors
Buttons
Needle and matching sewing thread

1 Place three very thin layers of fleece in the bottom of the tray as described on page 206.

2 Place the lace on top of the fleece. Dampen the fleece and lace with hot, soapy water and start to make the felt gently with your hands following the instructions on pages 206–7, making sure the lace stays in place. Don't lift a corner to see how the felting is progressing as this would break off the fibres and spoil the collar.

3 When the felting is complete, rinse the felt, then press while still wet with a hot iron, pulling out the edges and stretching out the lace. Allow the felt to dry.

4 When the felt is dry, carefully cut out the shape of the collar. Stitch buttons along one cut edge and make button loops along the other to fasten the collar.

This bright necklace is fun to wear and easy to make. The large beads are very light and will not weigh you down. Experiment with different shapes of beads, and try mixing colours to create a marbled effect.

Felt Bead Necklace

you will need

50g/2oz fleece, in carded slivers, in various colours

Soap flakes

Bowl

2 crimp beads

Nylon-coated jewellery wire

Necklace clasp

Small pliers

Large needle

1 Divide the fleece into bundles to make 19–21 beads, each containing two or three colours. Wind and twist each bundle into a tight ball, keeping it in your hand to stop it falling apart.

2 Dip each of the balls that you have just made in hot, soapy water. Now squeeze and roll each ball in your hands to felt the fibres until you can feel that the ball is hard all the way through. Rinse each bead under a hot tap then a cold one, and allow to dry. (A spin dryer will help speed up the drying process.)

3 Lay the beads out in the order in which you want to thread them. Thread a crimp bead on to the nylon-coated wire and then one half of the clasp. Turn the wire back through the crimp bead and crush the bead, using a small pair of pliers, to secure the wire.

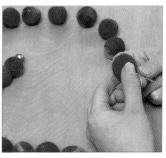

4 Thread the wire on to a large needle then push this through all the beads to thread them on to the wire. Attach the other half of the necklace clasp as described in step 3.

Though this bracelet has a chunky look it is light and soft to wear. You can vary the end result by adding embroidery, sewing on beads or artificial flowers, or incorporating other yarns under the surface of the felt.

Felt Bracelet

you will need
40g/1½oz fleece in carded slivers, three colours
String
Heavy weight
Soap flakes
Bowl
Scissors
Needle and matching sewing thread

1 Divide each length of fleece in half. Make the wool up into two plaits, each of the three colours, leaving two additional strands unplaited. Tie the two plaits and the two strands together at one end with string and attach the string to a heavy weight. Twist the plaits and strands tightly together and tie the other end of the twist securely with string.

2 Wet the wool thoroughly with hot, soapy water, keeping the plaits and strands in a twist. Rub the length of the fibres with plenty of soap, using one hand to keep the twist pulled taut against the weight all the time. The fibres will soon felt together, after which the twist will not unwind.

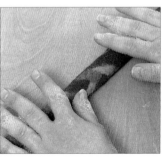

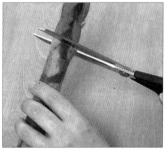

3 When the wool has felted on the outside, untie the string from the weight and roll the wool "sausage" firmly on the worktop to felt the fibres in the middle.

4 While the sausage is still flexible, cut off the ends tied with string. Wrap the felt around your wrist to check the fit and make sure that it will go over your hand when the ends are joined up. Trim down as required.

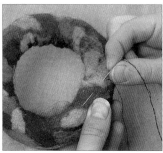

5 Stitch the two ends together using a long needle and strong thread. Take the thread from end to end inside the felt as well as stitching around the edges, to make the join very strong.

6 Felt the bracelet again in hot water and soap to shrink the inside curve and hide the stitches at the join. Rinse and allow to dry.

Felt brooches were popular in the 1930s and 1940s, when their bold colours gave a lift to a dull winter coat or plain hat. This design uses a thinner commercial felt than would have been available then.

Felt Flower Brooch

●●●

you will need

Tracing paper, pencil, card (stock) and scissors (for templates)

10 x 5cm/4 x 2in commercial felt pieces, one each of pink, mauve and orange

14.5 x 3cm/5¾ x 1¼in felt pieces, one each of yellow and three shades of green

Scissors for cutting felt

Needle and matching sewing thread

45cm/18in string

Sewing machine

Brooch back

1 Trace the templates from the back of the book. Transfer to the felt and cut out two flower shapes each in pink, mauve and orange, and four leaves in various shades of green.

2 Put the petals together in contrasting pairs. Now cut a fringed edge along three strips of yellow felt for the flower centres. Roll them up and place them in the centre of the paired petals.

3 Stitch the flower centres in place. Pinch the backs of the petals, and stitch through all the layers to give the flowers more shape.

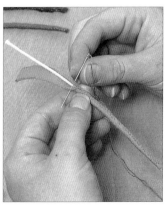

4 Cut the string into three 15cm/6in lengths, then slip-stitch a thin strip of green felt around each length to create the stalks.

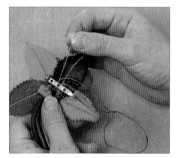

5 Using a sewing machine, satin-stitch along the centre of each leaf to make a rib. Sew the four leaves together in a fan shape. Fold the stalks in half and sew them to the leaves. Then sew the flowers to the leaves over the folds of the stalks.

6 Now turn the brooch over and stitch the brooch back on very firmly, right in the centre.

The fact that felt can be moulded to any shape makes it the perfect choice of material for hat making. Felt can be purchased in cone-shaped pieces ready to make into hats.

Felt Hat

you will need

2 heatproof bowls, 1 head sized,
1 to fit inside

Teapot lid

Cone-shaped felt hood

Scissors

Plant mister

Kettle

Steam iron

String

Capeline felt hood

Sharp knife

Tailor's chalk

Tacking (basting) thread

Needle and matching sewing thread

Tape measure

1 Select a suitable heatproof bowl to use as the hat block and a smaller bowl which must fit, upturned, inside the larger bowl. This will raise the larger bowl up off the work surface allowing it to be spun around and worked on from all sides. The teapot lid will sit on top.

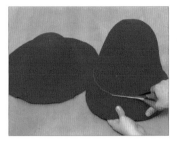

2 The cone-shaped felt hood is too deep for the crown of the hat so cut off approximately 12.5cm (5in) from the rim and set this aside to use as a hat band.

3 Use the plant mister to spray the inside of the hood with warm water. Steam the inside of the hood until it is warm, damp and soft. You should use a kettle that will sit on the hob. This will supply a steady amount of steam.

4 Push the teapot lid up into the centre of the hood. Use a hot iron to soften the felt above it, then mould it to the shape of the lid. Secure the felt in place with string. Make a slip knot and wind the string tightly round the shape of the lid.

5 Place the lid on top of the upturned bowl and pull the felt over the lower part of the lid. Use the hot iron to help stretch the felt over the curve and shrink it in under the lid. Tie string round to hold the shape.

6 Using the plant mister and steam from the kettle, damp down the felt with warm water. Pull the felt down evenly over the bowl. Use the hot iron to help define the shape of the rim.

7 Lift the bowl up and turn the felt underneath. Press it dry with the iron and cut away the excess felt gathered up inside the bowl. Allow the felt to dry on the bowl. When the felt is completely dry remove the string. If you remove it before the felt is completely dry, the hat will lose its shape.

8 Stab into the capeline hood with a sharp knife to make a starting hole. Cut out with scissors and discard the middle, leaving the brim. (The discarded felt could be used to make a cap.) Dampen the felt for the brim and press it flat with the iron. Allow it to dry flat.

9 Press the felt cut off which was set aside in step 2. Wrap it around the crown and mark a cutting line with tailor's chalk. Remove the band and cut it to the correct length and width.

10 Butt the two cut edges of the band together and tack, then sew in place. Place the brim beneath the crown and tack in place. Mark the cutting line for the brim and cut to neaten. Trim any excess felt.

This purse makes perfect recycling use for a favourite sweater that has been shrunk in the wash and become too small. Choose and cut the motifs and colours carefully from the garment.

Appliquéd Purse

● ● ●

you will need

Paper and pencil

Scissors

Felted wool knitting in several different colours

Dressmaker's pins

Tacking (basting) thread

Matching sewing thread

Sewing machine (optional)

Needles

Steam iron and pressing cloth

Lining fabric such as fine cotton or silk

Tape measure

Braid, 2.5cm/1in wide

140cm/55in cord

Button

Press stud (snap fastener)

1 Use the template at the back of the book to make a paper pattern for the purse, enlarging it to size. Cut out the base pieces from the felted knitting and pin and tack them together. Sew on each appliqué piece with matching thread, using a sewing machine with a zigzag stitch, or hand-sew the pieces with blanket stitch.

2 Build up the design, laying down four layers of fabric, pinning, tacking and sewing each one in place before starting the next layer. Trim off loose threads as you work.

3 Embroider the detail by hand or use the sewing machine. Press the piece using a steam iron and pressing cloth. Measure the piece (it may have stretched) and cut a piece of lining to fit.

4 Place the lining on the back of the felt. Pin and tack the edges of the purse and lining together. Cut the braid 2.5cm/1in longer than the perimeter of the puse. With a 5mm/¼in seam allowance, sew the braid to make a circle and pin it on the felt side, 5mm/¼in from the edge. Straight stitch the braid in position using the sewing machine, keeping just inside the edge. Trim away the excess fabric close to the edge of the braid. Fold the braid over the edge of the purse then pin, tack and sew it in place. Over-sew the edges together on each side.

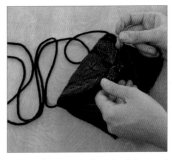

5 Tie a knot at each end of the cord and stitch in place inside each side seam of the purse. Locate the centre of the flap and sew on a button. Underneath, sew on the top half of a press stud. Sew the other half to the centre of the bottom half of the purse.

A felt ball cut in half to reveal an intricate pattern makes a delightful pair of earrings. Cutting through the ball to reveal the marbled colours is so exciting it will probably prompt you to make more than one pair.

Marbled Earrings

●●●

you will need

5g/⅛oz fleece, in carded slivers, various colours

Soap flakes

Bowl

Craft (utility) knife

Felteen hat stiffener or PVA (white) glue

Epoxy resin glue

Earring posts and butterfly backs

1 Make a ball by twisting and wrapping two or more colours of fleece together. The more twists, turns and colours you use in the middle of the ball, the more intricate the resulting pattern will be. Dip the ball in hot, soapy water and squeeze and roll it to felt the fibres all the way through. When hard, rinse under a hot tap then a cold one.

2 Leave the ball until it has dried out completely, then cut it in half using a craft knife. The pattern should stay in place; if the ball has not been felted all the way through, the middle will bulge out at this point.

3 To make the felt really hard, dip it in felteen hat stiffener. The felt must be absolutely dry as water reacts with the stiffener and will make a cloudy white film on the surface. An alternative is to dip the felt in PVA glue diluted with water, although this leaves a shiny surface.

4 Mix up a little two-part epoxy resin glue according to the manufacturer's instructions and use it to attach an earring back to the domed back of each earring.

These beaded felt buttons are ideal for a special cardigan or jacket, but they could also be used as eye-catching ornaments, or threaded on a leather thong, knotted at intervals, to make a necklace.

Acorn Buttons

●●●●

you will need

6g/¼oz fleece in carded slivers, brown and gold

Soap flakes

Bowl

Craft (utility) knife

Needle and strong button thread

1,000 small faceted glass beads

Polyester thread

1 Divide the brown and gold fleece into three and make each into three balls by dipping them in hot, soapy water and rolling in your hands. For the brown fleece, keep rolling and felting the balls until they are very hard and bounce when dropped.

2 For the gold fleece, squeeze and roll the balls as before but when they are beginning to go hard, distort them into the shape of rugby balls with your fingers. Rinse all the balls thoroughly in hot, then cold water.

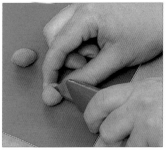

3 Leave the balls to dry out completely, then cut each one in half using a sharp craft knife. When halving the gold rugby balls, cut across the narrow width.

4 With their cut faces together, sew the gold half balls to the brown half balls using strong button thread. Make a stitch straight through the middle of each acorn and back, and pull the thread tight to form a small dimple at the top of each gold ball.

5 With the thread emerging from the base of the brown ball, make three small loops, one on top of the other, and use these as the foundation of a buttonhole shank.

6 Use polyester thread to sew beads round the rim of each acorn cup then spirally down to the shank to cover the cup. Sew the beads in groups of six: back-stitch three beads and catch down the thread before bringing the needle back out at the sixth bead.

Since the essence of ragwork is its economical use of recycled fabrics, the materials and equipment needed are minimal. The most unlikely materials, even including plastic bags, can be used to great effect.

Ragwork Materials and Equipment

is strong and pliable and the threads open and close easily when hooking. It is available in different weights – 250g/9oz is perfect for ragwork.

Hook

A tapering, sharp-ended brass hook with a turned wooden handle is pushed through the hessian to make a large hole, through which the fabric is hooked. A large crochet hook can also be used to hook small pieces.

Hoop

Hessian needs to be stretched taut on a frame for ragwork; an embroidery hoop is suitable for small projects such as jewellery.

Plastic bags and foils

Strips of plastic sheet, such as carrier bags, can be used with or instead of fabrics. Add sparkle with foil-backed crisp (chip) packets and gift wrap.

Scissors

You need two pairs: sharp dressmaking shears for cutting fabrics and pile and another pair for paper, foil and plastic, as these will blunt the blades.

Sewing materials

Findings such as brooch backs and earring clips can be stitched to ragwork pieces, and backing fabric can be slip-stitched in place. Embroidery thread (floss) is used for decorative finishes.

Wire

Thin wire is useful to stiffen ragwork shapes.

Adhesives

Latex carpet adhesive can be used to back finished pieces of ragwork. Use clear impact adhesive to attach backing fabric and strong epoxy resin glue to secure jewellery findings.

Fabrics

Cotton – Jersey fabrics, such as old T-shirts, fray very little and make excellent looped surfaces. Printed shirts and dresses are also ideal.

Nylon – Thin jersey (such as coloured tights) makes a fine-textured surface.

Felt

Black felt makes a smart backing fabric to finish pieces of jewellery such as brooches and earrings.

Hessian (burlap)

Old sacking was the traditional recycled foundation for hooked rag rugs but nowadays hessian, made from jute, can be bought by the metre or yard. It

All ragwork involves cutting fabric into strips but several techniques can be used to work them into the finished item. Use contrasting materials and surface treatments to create a wide range of textures.

Ragwork Techniques

Hooking   This is the commonest and most versatile technique, in which fabric strips are hooked through hessian (burlap). They can be left as a loop pile or sheared to create a cut pile surface. A combination of the two surfaces gives a sculpted, three-dimensional effect.

1 With the hessian in a frame, push in the hook and feed on a loop of fabric. Pull the hook back, bringing the end of the strip to the top. Push the hook back in 1–2 warp threads away and then feed a loop on to the hook as before.

2 Pull the hook back to make a fabric loop approximately 1cm/½in high. Repeat in order to create rows of loops to cover the hessian. When you reach the end of a strip, pull it through to the top. Trim to the same height as the loops.

3 To create a cut pile surface, pull the fabric through in loops as before but hook them to a height of approximately 2cm/¾in. When the area is filled, shear across the tops of the loops with a large pair of scissors.

Backing and Finishing   Once the ragwork is complete the edges of the hessian need to be neatened and the back covered. Backing jewellery pieces with a soft fabric such as felt will prevent the hessian irritating the skin.

1 Trim around the finished piece to leave a hessian border at least 2cm/¾in wide. Spread latex adhesive all over the back and leave to dry for 3–5 minutes, then fold in the edges.

2 Cut any excess hessian away at the corners to make the underside as flat as possible.

3 Cut a piece of felt slightly larger than the ragwork. Pin around the edge and slip-stitch in place, turning in the excess felt as you go.

This matching set is very easy to make in hooked ragwork. The domino spots, in loops of contrasting colour, stand out strongly against the cut pile background. Cotton jersey fabrics are ideal for this project.

Domino Hairslide and Earrings

you will need

Pencil, ruler, card (stock) and scissors (for template)

30cm/12in square hessian (burlap)

Felt-tipped pen

Embroidery hoop

Cotton jersey fabric in two contrasting colours

Hook

Scissors for cutting fabric

Latex carpet adhesive

Clear impact adhesive

10 x 4cm/4 x 1½in black felt (NB: extra will be needed for the earrings)

Needle and matching sewing thread

Hairclip fastening and earring clips

bonding adhesive

1 First, make yourself a card template that measures 10 x 4cm/4 x 1½in. Place it right in the middle of the piece of hessian and draw round it, using the felt-tipped pen. Now place the hessian piece in the embroidery hoop. Cut the jersey fabric into strips that measure 1cm/½in. Hook one of the colour blocks, making sure that you are working from the outside edge towards the centre.

2 Shear off the tops of the loops to create a cut pile surface. Repeat to make the second block of colour on the other half of the domino.

3 To make the spots for the domino, hook small loops in the contrasting colours. Do not cut these loops. Trim the excess fabric ends.

4 Remove the work from the hoop and place face down on a flat surface. Cut around the shape, leaving a border of 2cm/¾in all round. Apply a thin layer of latex adhesive over the back of the work and the border. Leave to dry for 5 minutes then turn in the border and press down firmly.

5 Apply clear impact adhesive to the back of the ragwork and cover with black felt. Slip-stitch all round the edge. Attach the hairclip fastening to the back of the hairslide (barrette) using bonding adhesive and leave to dry for 1 hour. Make the earrings in the same way, using a 2.5cm/1in square template or a circle of the same size.

This set of hairslide (barrette) and hairbobbles is made from plastic carrier bags and remnants of nylon fabric! It shows what you can do at very little expense, and you can make the whole project very quickly.

Hooked Hair Accessories

you will need

Pencil, ruler, card (stock) and scissors (for template)

25cm/10in square hessian (burlap)

Felt-tipped pen

Embroidery hoop

Nylon fabric

Scissors for cutting fabric

Coloured plastic carrier bags

Hook

Latex carpet adhesive

12 x 6cm/4¾ x 2½in black felt

Needle and matching sewing thread

Clear impact adhesive

Hairclip fastening

Bonding adhesive

Elastic hairbands

1 Make a sawtooth card template measuring 11 x 5cm/4½ x 2in for the hairslide (barrette). Place it in the centre of the hessian and draw round it with a felt-tipped pen. Put the hessian in the embroidery hoop.

2 Cut the nylon fabric and the plastic into strips 1cm/½in wide. Start by hooking the fabric to outline the marked area, working in rows.

3 Using the plastic, hook loops to fill in the central triangles. Bring the ends of the fabric and plastic strips through to the top of the work as you reach them. Trim any excess lengths.

4 Remove the hessian from the embroidery hoop. Place face down on a flat surface and cut round the shape, leaving a border of 2.5cm/1in. Apply a thin layer of latex adhesive over the back of the work and the border. Leave to dry for 5 minutes, then turn in the edges and press down firmly.

5 Lay the card template on the black felt, draw round it and cut out the backing. Apply clear impact adhesive to the back of the ragwork. Place the felt on the back of the hairslide and slip-stitch in position.

6 Carefully drop a small amount of bonding adhesive on to the top surface of the hairclip fastening, then hold it in position on the back of the hairslide. Leave to dry for 1 hour before wearing. Make the hairbobbles in the same way, using a round template of 2.5cm/1in diameter. Stitch the bobbles to the elastic hairbands.

The long, rectangular shape of this hairband lends itself to a bold repeat pattern of squares or triangles. Two different but equally simple designs have been shown here for inspiration.

Geometric Hairband

you will need

Card (stock)

Ruler

Hessian, 61 x 30cm/24 x 12in

Marker pen

Staple gun

Wooden frame

Nylon fabrics, in assorted colours

Hook

Scissors

Latex carpet adhesive and applicator

Clear impact adhesive

Black felt, 33 x 5cm/13 x 2in

Needle and matching thread

Dressmaker's pins

Ribbon, 1m/1yd

1 Make a rectangular card template measuring 32 x 4cm/12½ x 1½in. Place it in the centre of the hessian and draw around it, using a marker pen. Use a staple gun to attach the hessian to the frame.

2 Cut the nylon fabrics into strips 1cm/½in wide. Begin by hooking the outline of your chosen design, working in close loops. Shear across the tops of the loops to create a cut pile surface.

3 Fill in the shapes, using contrasting fabrics alternately. Shear across the tops of the loops periodically as the work progresses.

4 When the design is completed, remove the hessian from the frame. Cut round the hooked rectangle, allowing a border of at least 2.5cm (1in). Apply a thin layer of latex adhesive over the back, including the border. Leave to dry for 3–5 minutes.

5 Turn in the border and press down firmly. Apply small dabs of clear adhesive on the back, then cover with the black felt. Slip-stitch the felt in place, turning under any excess. Pin the ribbon along the centre back of the hairband, leaving equal lengths at each end to make the ties. Stitch the ribbon in place.

This project uses a different ragwork technique to great effect. Fabric strips are wrapped round wire and bound with coloured embroidery threads, then coiled and sculpted into unusual brooches or earrings.

Wrapped Jewellery

●●●

you will need

Three different fabrics

Scissors

70cm/27½in wire

Stranded embroidery thread (floss) in four colours, including a metallic thread

Thick cotton thread

Beads or sequins

Pen or pencil

Needle and matching sewing thread

Brooch back

Earring clips or wires

1 Cut the different fabrics into strips 1cm/½in wide and the same length as the piece of wire. Starting at one end, wrap three different fabric strips round the wire, using embroidery thread to bind them in sporadic

patches. When you are near the end of the wire, add a loop of thick cotton thread facing the end, and then continue wrapping the embroidery thread over this loop.

2 Thread the end of the embroidery thread into the loop with one hand, and with your other hand pull the two ends of the loop around until the thread end is tied off. Bind more embroidery thread in the other colours in patches along the length. Add a string of beads or sequins for extra decoration.

3 Wrap the metallic thread round one end, then wind it back on itself to tie in the end. Continue binding with the metallic thread, binding in the ends as before.

4 Wrap the finished bound length of wire around a pen or pencil to shape it into a spiral.

5 Remove the pen or pencil from inside the coiled length and sculpt it, working outwards and flattening it to make a cone shape. Stitch the fabric coils securely together and stitch on the brooch back. Make the earrings in the same way, but form the coiled lengths into lozenges instead of the cone shape. Stitch the earring findings to one end.

Even crisp (chip) packets can be hooked to make a loop pile surface just like fabric or yarn. In this heart-shaped brooch and matching ring the shiny plastic foil contrasts beautifully with the dark fabric border.

Textured Brooch and Ring

●●●

you will need

Pencil, card (stock) and scissors (for template)

30cm/12in square hessian (burlap)

Felt-tipped pen

Embroidery hoop

Scissors for cutting fabric

Dark fabric

Hook

Foil crisp (chip) packets

Latex carpet adhesive

12cm/5in square black felt

Clear impact adhesive

Needle and matching sewing thread

Brooch back and ring fitting

Bonding adhesive

1 Make a cardboard template for your textured brooch by drawing a heart shape that measures approximately 8cm/3in across. Now place the card template on to your hessian square and draw round it, using the felt-tipped pen. Place the hessian into the embroidery hoop.

2 Cut the dark fabric into strips 1cm/½in wide. Begin the hooking by following the outline of the heart shape. Make the loops close together, approximately 1cm/½in high.

3 Cut the crisp packets into strips 1cm/½in wide. Fill in the centre of the heart shape with loops of the same height as the fabric loops. Bring all the ends through to the top of the work, and trim any excess lengths.

4 Remove the hessian from the embroidery hoop and cut around the shape, leaving a border of 2.5cm/1in. Apply a thin layer of latex adhesive to the back and the border and leave to dry for 5 minutes.

5 Using scissors, make snips in the border at regular intervals. Turn in the border and press down firmly. Draw round the template on the black felt and cut out the backing. Apply clear impact adhesive to the back of the work, then cover with felt. Slip-stitch around the edge.

6 Position the fastening on the back of the brooch and stitch, using double thread. Make the ring in the same way, using a 2.5cm/1in diameter circle for the template. Attach the ring fitting with bonding adhesive.

This wonderful hat has everything – a hooked loop pile band decorated with motifs, a machine-embroidered silk top, striped piping, and a soft silk lining. Use machine embroidery skills to decorate the hat top.

Hooked Hat

●●●

you will need
Tape measure

Hessian, the size of the hatband plus at least 8cm/3in all around

Marker pen

Ruler

Rotary cutter

Cutting mat

Four fabrics: striped, coloured lining, coloured felt and coloured silk each 50 x 50cm/20 x 20in

Assorted fabrics, for hooking

Old blanket fabric

Wooden frame

Staple gun

Needle and matching threads

Scissors

Latex carpet adhesive and applicator

Dressmaker's pins

Strong thread

Paper and pencil

Pair of compasses

Drawing pin

Sewing machine

Lurex sewing thread

1 Measure the circumference of the head just above the ear and add 5cm/2in to give the length of the hatband. The width of the hatband is 8cm/3in. Draw out these measurements on the hessian with a pen.

2 Draw a freehand design within the hatband shape. Simple flower, leaf and heart motifs are used here. Mark the hatband into sections.

4 The top piece of piping has two seams. Stitch the striped fabric to the lining fabric along the long edges, with wrong sides together, leaving 1cm/½in seam allowances. Stuff piping with cord or a strip of old blanket.

5 Attach the hessian to the frame, using the staple gun. Stitch the right side of the bottom piping to the hessian, along the lower edge of the hatband. Stitch the piping with the two seams at the top of the hatband as shown.

3 For the piping, cut two strips of striped fabric on the bias, the length of the hatband plus 6cm/2½in and the width 11cm/4¼in wide. With wrong sides together, stitch along the length of one strip with a 1cm/½in seam allowance for the bottom piping.

6 Prepare the fabrics for hooking the hat band. Cut them into strips about 1cm/½in wide, varying the width according to the weight of the fabric.

7 Begin hooking the design, working close loops. Change the background colour between sections as shown. When the hatband is complete remove the hessian from the frame. Cut around the hatband, allowing an extra border of 4cm/1½in.

8 Spread latex adhesive over the back of the hooking, and leave to dry for 3–5 minutes, then turn back the hem. Leave the side edges open. Pin the side edges of the hatband together. Using strong thread, stitch the seam together closely. The stitches will be hidden by the pile surface.

9 Make a paper pattern for the top of the hat. Take the length of the hatband plus 2cm/¾in, and divide by 6.3. Add a 1cm/½in seam allowance. Draw a circle on paper to this measurement. Cut two layers of silk using the circle template.

10 Machine embroider the layers of fabric together with the felt uppermost. Cut a silk lining band the same size as the hatband. Pin and stitch in place. Decorate the hat top and stitch to the hatband.

Ragwork can be combined with other textile techniques to give a richly textured surface. In this design, flat pieces of patterned fabrics are appliquéd to padded hessian, then surrounded by hooked loops.

Textured Shoulder Bag

●●●

you will need

Hessian, at least 46 x 46cm/18 x 18in

Marker pen

Ruler

Piece of old blanket

Scissors

Needle and thread

Assorted fabrics, for hooking and appliqué

Staple gun

Wooden frame

Hook

Sewing machine

Lining fabric, 92 x 92cm/36 x 36in

Latex carpet adhesive and applicator

Cord, 1.5m/1½yd

2 tassels

Press stud (snap fastener)

1 Draw a rectangle on the hessian measuring 25 x 18cm/10 x 7in, using a marker pen. Draw your design inside this. Tack (baste) the blanket to areas of the hessian, as padding for the appliqué. Choose appliqué fabrics and stitch in place, turning under the raw edges.

2 Using the staple gun, attach the hessian to the frame. Begin hooking round the appliqué shapes, using a rich mixture of fabrics. Continue until the design is completed, then remove the hessian from the frame.

3 Cut three pieces of lining the same size as the hooked panel, plus a seam allowance all round. Place two pieces right sides together. Machine stitch round, leaving one short side open.

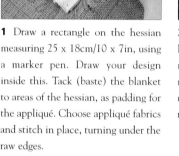

4 Cut out the hooked panel, allowing an extra 2cm/¾in border all round. Apply a thin layer of latex adhesive over the back, then turn under the border. With wrong sides together, hand stitch the third piece of lining fabric to the panel, turning in the seam allowance and leaving the top edge open.

5 Stitch the cord along both long sides of the bag, extending it in a loop at the top for carrying. Stitch the tassels to the bottom corners, concealing the cord ends. Place the inner lining inside the bag, wrong sides together. Stitch round the top edge, turning under the raw edges. Stitch the press stud to the centre top edges of the bag, with one half on each side.

Leather offers a distinctively unusual material for jewellery. Leatherwork is a skilled craft, but small-scale jewellery projects can be accomplished using little more than basic sewing materials and equipment.

Leatherwork Materials and Equipment

Adhesives

PVA (white) glue can be used to stick pieces of leather together if the surfaces are roughened to provide a key. Use epoxy resin glue to attach jewellery findings.

Leather

Hide can be bought by the full skin or in cut sections that are ideal for small projects. Skins are available natural or pre-dyed in a wide range of different finishes and colours, including metallics. Skiving leather is a natural undyed hide that has been pared down in order to make it thin enough for moulding. Leather can also be purchased in different thicknesses.

Leather stain

Stains are water- or alcohol-based. Unlike dyes or paints, which colour the surface, stains penetrate the skin. They may fade in strong sunlight.

Felt-tipped pens

For small items, natural leather can be decorated using permanent felt-tipped pens. Translucent pens allow the grain to show through the colour. Treat leather decorated in this way with beeswax before polishing it.

Needles

Leather needles – Embroidery needles may be sturdy enough for very fine skins, but leather needles are better able to pierce thicker hide.

Glover's needles – These have a three-sided point that acts as a cutting edge. They are available in a range of sizes.

Punch

A rotary leather punch is used to make holes. Choose a good-quality punch with replaceable cutting tubes.

Scissors, knives and shears

Special leather scissors are sturdy with rounded ends. Small shapes can be cut using a craft (utility) knife and cutting mat. Use pinking shears to add a decorative edging to lightweight leathers.

Sewing thread

Linen thread is used for most leatherwork, and is waxed to help it slip through the skin easily. Cotton thread may be strong enough for fine skins, and embroidery thread (floss) can be added for decoration.

It's a good idea to practise any techniques for shaping or decorating leather on scraps or offcuts of a similar colour and thickness before using them on your chosen piece of skin.

Leatherwork Techniques

Punching

A row of punched holes, perhaps combined with a pinked edge, makes an effective decoration for fine leather.

It's best to place a scrap piece of thick leather under the item you are punching to protect the cutting tubes. If you need to get to a point beyond the reach of the punch, try folding over or gathering the leather.

Moulding Leather

When dampened, vegetable-tanned, undyed leather can be moulded into shapes that it retains when dry.

Thick leather needs to be soaked to soften the fibres, but small thin pieces need only be moistened with a sponge and warm water. Press the leather into the desired shapes using your fingers.

Staining Leather

Protect the work surface and work in a well-ventilated area if you are using alcohol-based dye. The leather must first be cleaned so that it is completely free of grease, as this can resist the dye.

1 To clean the leather, make a solution of oxalic acid (5ml/1 tsp to 600ml/1 pint water) and rub over the surface using a soft cloth. Leave to dry. Dampen the leather with a sponge then apply the dye with a cloth, working over the surface in a circular motion.

2 It is easier to obtain an even colour if you apply several layers of dye, allowing each to dry before applying the next. Apply polish to seal the surface and make the colour permanent.

Designed to keep paper money and credit cards safe, this purse is a useful and attractive accessory. Tan deerskin is the basic material and it is beautifully soft and supple.

Oak-leaf Purse

you will need

21 x 33cm/8½ x 13in deerskin or suede

16 x 22cm/6¼ x 8½in tan soft leather or suede

Strong scissors

Pencil

PVA (white) glue

Thick sand and rust-coloured embroidery cotton (floss)

Darning needle

Dark brown sewing cotton (thread)

Thin leather needle

Pinking shears

Double-sided tape

Hole punch (no 1)

1.2m/4ft thin rust-coloured cord

1 Cut out the four component parts from deerskin and soft leather, enlarging the templates at the back of the book. Place the leaf template on piece A in the position shown and draw around it with a pencil.

2 Cut out the oak-leaf shape using scissors, then glue piece A on to piece B, ensuring that the suede is facing upwards and there is an even border around the edge. Leave to dry.

3 Using embroidery cotton and a darning needle, stitch through the oak-leaf shape from the back and make one long stitch from top to bottom to represent a central vein for the leaf. Couch this down with dark brown sewing cotton, using a thin leather needle.

4 Trim all around the border using pinking shears.

▶

5 Place piece D on to piece C and stick together with double-sided tape to hold them in position temporarily. Using a hole punch, make holes through both pieces all around the edge of piece D, 5mm/¼in in from the edge. In the same way, punch holes all around the edges of piece A and piece B, as shown. This ensures that the pieces are lined up for stitching.

6 Using contrasting coloured embroidery cotton, stitch piece D on to piece C to form a pocket. Punch holes around the edge of piece C to correspond to piece A. Using rust-coloured embroidery cotton, stitch piece A to piece B around the oak-leaf section.

7 Continue stitching with the rust-coloured embroidery cotton to join the pocket section to the backing. Make sure that the two pieces are joined so that the oak-leaf section folds over the pocket section.

8 Knot the ends of the cord together to form a loop with 4cm/1½in ends. Place the knot at the base point of the purse and stitch around the cord to join it to the purse as shown. Once you have reached the top of the front section, stitch back around the purse so that you form a cross stitch.

9 Unravel the ends of the knotted cord to make a decorative tassel.

Natural vegetable-tanned leather can be moulded with your fingers when dampened and is used here to decorate a headband with flowers, which are easily coloured with permanent marker pens.

Floral Headband and Brooch

you will need

Tracing paper, pencil, card (stock) and scissors (for templates)

Scraps of vegetable-tanned, undyed leather

Scissors for cutting leather

Felt-tipped pens

Sponge

PVA (white) glue

Large brooch back

Epoxy resin glue

Elastic, 2cm/³⁄₄in wide

1 Following the templates at the back of the book, cut out all the elements for the headband and brooch from undyed leather. Using felt-tipped pens, colour in the leather "leaves" on the headband and brooch background. Using thin opaque pens, delineate outlines and markings on each flower. Then colour in with thicker translucent fluorescent pens.

2 Dampen all the elements with a moistened sponge, then shape the leaves and flowers with your fingers. Leave until completely dry. Scuff the surface of the leather on the headband and the brooch backing at the points of contact with the flowers. Then glue on the flowers with PVA glue. Attach the brooch backing with epoxy resin glue. Leave to dry.

3 Cut a V-shaped slot in each end of the headband backing. Cut the end of a piece of elastic into a point and slide it through one slot from front to back; glue into position with epoxy resin glue. Once dry, repeat with the other end, after trying on the headband to check the fitting.

The oak-leaf motif is perfect for the warm autumnal colours of suede or leather. You'll need a tough piece of skin for the base layer of the hair ornament, but the buttons can be made from thin leather.

Oak-leaf Hair Clasp and Buttons

●●●

you will need

Tracing paper, pencil, card (stock) and scissors (for templates)

Pen

Small, sharp scissors for cutting leather

Small pieces of suede or leather in three colours

PVA (white) glue

Stranded embroidery thread (floss)

Sewing thread

Small leather needle

Glover's needle

Pinking shears

Hole punch

Bamboo knitting needle

Saw

Abrasive paper

Large self-cover buttons

1 Scale up the templates that have been provided for this project at the back of the book and then use them as guides to cut out two backing ovals and one front piece from different colours of either suede or leather. Now cut out your oak-leaf stencil and then draw around it on to the top piece of suede.

2 Cut out the oak-leaf shape from the suede using a pair of small scissors.

3 Glue the cut-out top piece on to the first backing piece using PVA glue. Leave to dry.

4 Stitch through the first backing piece with stranded embroidery thread to make a central leaf vein. Couch this down with sewing thread in a darker colour.

5 Using embroidery thread to match the backing leather and a glover's needle, make a running stitch border around the edge of the top piece.

6 Neatly trim the edge of your first backing piece with the pinking shears. Then use more PVA to glue on the base layer. Once completely dry, use the pinking shears to trim the edge of this piece, too.

7 Carefully punch a hole at each side of the oak leaf using a No 6 hole punch. Saw a bamboo knitting needle down to a length approximately 5cm /2in longer than the hair clasp and rub the sawn end to a point with abrasive paper. Push the knitting needle down through one hole and out through the other.

8 Finally, to make the buttons, cut out circles of leather or suede large enough to cover the self-cover buttons. Cut out one oak-leaf shape for each of the buttons from complementary colours of suede.

9 Glue each leaf to a backing circle. Lay a short length of stranded embroidery thread down the middle of the leaf and couch down with darker sewing thread.

10 Stretch the circle over the button dome, place the backing in position and snap it shut to secure.

Popular in the 1930s and revived in the 1960s, these simple interlink belts are once again in fashion. The shape of the links can be changed: experiment by cutting out patterns in folded pieces of paper.

Leather Chain Belt

you will need

Small scissors

Thin suede or leather

PVA (white) glue

Long shoelaces

Ruler

Leather thonging

1 Using the template at the back of the book, cut out enough suede or leather shapes to fit around your waist, allowing one shape for each 2.5cm/1in. Glue two shapes together and leave to dry. Cut out the centre circles in all of the other shapes.

2 Cut out the circles from the double shape and use this as the centre back of the belt. Attach the other sections of the belt by linking them through the holes and doubling them over as shown. Continue adding links, making sure that you have the same number on each side of the central shape, until the belt is the correct size.

3 Cut out four strips from the same suede or leather, each measuring 5 x 7cm/2 x 2¾in. Fold over each piece lengthways and glue the ends together. When dry, snip a fringe along the folded edge about 1.5cm/⅝in deep.

4 Tie knots in both ends of each shoelace. Apply a little glue to the uncut ends of the fringing and roll up the fringes around the ends of the shoelaces. Secure with thin strips of leather thonging and glue or tie to hold in place.

5 Loop and knot a shoelace through one end of the belt, as shown. Repeat with the second shoelace at the other end of the belt. These will act as ties.

Leather or suede tassels are highly individual and can look stunning when used to adorn formal furnishings. The tassels here are made from thick suede; the thinner the material, the skinnier the tassel.

Suede Tassels

you will need
Paper, pencil, scissors
15 x 23cm/6 x 9in suede or leather
Strong scissors
Hole punch (no 1 and no 5)
Metal ruler
Craft (utility) knife
Thick cord
Suede thonging

1 Make a paper stencil following the template at the back of the book. Place the stencil on the suede or leather and cut out the shape to form the basis of the tassel. Mark out all points to be punched with a pencil.

2 Cut out the triangular points with scissors. Punch out the large holes using a No 5 hole punch, and the smaller holes using No 1. Using a metal ruler and craft knife, cut slits in the leather, following the template markings.

3 Carefully cut fringing in the leather from the inner points of the triangular edging up to each first small hole. Taking each pointed end of fringing in turn, loop it back and pull it through each respective slit to create a decorative twist.

4 Thread thick cord through the single hole in the corner of the shallower end of the suede. Tie a knot in the end of the cord and wrap your tassel base around it, starting from the wider edge.

5 Tie a knot at the end of a length of suede thonging. Thread through the hole in the top corner. Wrap it around the tassel three or four times and secure it by threading it through the last large hole on the bottom row. Knot and trim.

Made from soft and supple leather, this purse has a reassuring and satisfying feel, particularly when it is full of money. It is not difficult to make and only requires cutting, gluing and punching holes.

Coin Purse

you will need

Paper, pencil, scissors

30 x 40cm/12 x 16in soft leather

PVA (white) glue

Hole punch

Metal ruler

2 long shoelaces

2 scraps of contrasting leather

1 Make a paper stencil for the purse pieces following the templates at the back of the book. Cut out the leather pieces using the stencil. Mark the positions of the holes using a pencil.

2 Glue the purse reinforcer on to the main purse piece, with the suede sides facing. Leave to dry. Using a No 6 hole punch, carefully punch out the marked holes around the edges of the purse.

3 Thread both ends of one shoelace from the inside outwards on the lower holes of the reinforcement. Cross over the laces and thread them in and out around each side of the leather circle until they meet at the opposite side.

4 Repeat with the second shoelace, starting from the opposite side. Pull the strings to make a purse shape.

5 Cut two triangles and two circles from contrasting coloured leather. Punch holes in each shape. Thread the ends of one lace through a circle and a triangle and knot the ends to secure. Repeat with the second lace to complete.

This is a delightful project to make and would also make a wonderful gift. Once made, furnish the purse with scissors, embroidery cottons, pins and needles.

Sewing Purse

●●●

you will need

Pair of compasses

30cm/12in square of purple soft pig suede, 50g/2oz weight

30cm/12in square of interfacing

30cm/12in square of red soft pig suede, 50g/2oz weight

Ruler, pencil, scissors

Needle, sewing cotton (thread)

Scraps of coloured thicker leather

Paper

Hole punch

Medium rivets

Riveting hammer

Block of wood

PVA (white) glue

Stitching wheel

Thick embroidery cotton (floss)

Embroidery scissors

Darning needle

Velcro tape

Felt

1 Using compasses, draw a circle measuring 25cm/10in in diameter on each of the following: purple suede for the lining, interfacing and red suede for the cover. Cut out the circles.

2 Cut out a 23cm/9in strip of purple lining suede. Stitch this across the centre of the purple circle, making cross stitches at five points.

3 Cut a strip of purple leather measuring 12 x 2cm/4½ x ¾in to make a strap. Then, following the templates at the back of the book, cut out a leaf and flower from the coloured leather scraps, and a paper pattern for the petal shape of the purse.

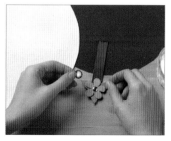

4 Place the leaf on one end of the strap and place the flower on top. Punch a hole through both, then rivet them together. Cover the rivet by gluing a red leather circle over the top. Cut a slot in the large red leather circle wide enough to insert the strap and about 2.25cm (⅞in) from the edge of the circle. Push the strap in 3cm (1¼in) deep and glue this on to the underside. Glue the interfacing to the underside of the red circle. Leave until the glue is dry.

▶

5 Carefully glue the top layer on to the purple layer, sandwiching the interfacing, making sure that the strap lines up with the purple strip. Trace around the petal shape from the pattern, so that the strap is positioned mid-heart. Cut out the shape.

6 Mark 5mm/¼in in from the edge of the petals all around the shape. Mark dots along the line at 5mm/¼in intervals.

7 Using a No 1 hole punch, punch holes all around the edge, following the marked dots. Move the strap forwards while you punch behind it.

8 Using contrasting embroidery cotton, stitch the layers together following the punched holes. Glue a piece of red Velcro tape to the inside of the strap, and its counterpart on to the outside of the front in position.

9 Cut out small felt segments and glue to the purple side of the purse with a dab of PVA glue. These are for keeping pins and needles secure.

10 Before folding the actual purse, practise on the paper pattern, checking the picture to see how it is folded. Fold in both sides first, leaving a flat bottom where the inside strip passes by. Then form creases down the sides of the hearts. Use a ruler to achieve a crisp crease. Fold the strap down to close.

This fashionable bag, made from thick red suede and stitched together with royal blue suede thonging, is easier to make than it looks. The
handles have rope cores which make a comfortable grip.

Shopping Bag

you will need
Paper, pencil, scissors
Thick suede or leather
Hole punch (no 4)
Mallet
Block of wood
Royal blue suede thonging
50cm/20in rope, 2cm/³⁄₄in thick

1 Make a paper pattern following the
templates at the back of the book.
Using the pattern, cut out two side
pieces and one gusset piece from thick
suede or leather. Cut two straps.

2 Mark holes at regular intervals
around the edge of each of the cut-out
suede or leather pieces. Punch out the
holes using a hole punch.

3 Make the handle attachment holes
in each side panel. When the part of
the leather you are trying to punch is
inaccessible to a rotary punch and you
do not have a single punch, place the
item to be punched on a wooden board
with a thick piece of scrap leather
beneath the spot to be punched and
another thick piece of leather between
the jaws of the punch. Close the punch
tightly and hit the bottom (which will
be facing upwards) with a hide mallet.

4 Working with a very long piece of
thonging and leaving an excess of
15cm/6in, lace the thonging through
the gusset and one side piece, joining
them together.

▶

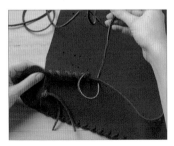

5 Once one side of the stitching is complete, start on the other side piece, tying the ends of the thonging together at the top of the gusset.

6 Cut two pieces of rope, each 25cm/10in long. Glue one piece into the centre of each handle and wrap the suede around to encase the rope. Allow to dry.

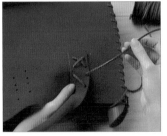

7 Attach the handles to the side pieces of the bag using 40cm/16in of thonging to make large cross stitches. Start the stitching from the inside top outer corner to make the first diagonal, then make the second diagonal from bottom to top. Secure with a knot on the inside.

8 Punch two holes above the top cross stitch on each handle. Thread through a length of thonging and bind it tightly around the handle to cover it.

◀ **9** To finish, join both excess ends on each handle with a reef knot to prevent them from unravelling.

Ribbonwork History
and Techniques

For centuries, ribbons were one of the few affordable adornments for all, and from the Middle Ages to the 1800s they were used as fastenings and decorations for garments and hairstyles, crafted into tokens of love and worn as badges of allegiance or awards. From the 1900s ribbons were used less as elements of clothing and more as an attractive and widely available craft material. Ribbons in a dazzling variety of colours can now be seen embellishing the smartest gifts, millinery, soft furnishings and fashionable outfits.

From the very earliest times, ribbon has served both practical and decorative purposes. Its history is closely aligned to the history of fashion, but its use and popularity has changed dramatically.

History

The earliest examples of ribbons – in the general sense of narrow strips of fabric – are from ancient Egypt and can be dated to about 3000BC. It is impossible to say for certain how or where weaving was first developed, but, having produced lengths of fabric, people began to use them as clothing, and embellished them in various ways.

During the Middle Ages, a variety of elaborate borders began to be used to decorate clothing. In England,

Below: A pedlar selling ribbons. A travelling salesman would bring his wares to isolated farms and villages.

gowns had become relatively complex garments. The bodice was slit down either side from arm to hip and fitted with ribbons, which were used to tie the material tightly across the upper part of the body. By the middle of the 12th century, skirts had become fuller with dozens of knife-pleats, and the tightness of the bodice was accentuated with a belt resembling a deep cummerbund, which was tied at the back with ribbons.

By the 16th century, trade with the New World had developed and a middle class emerged, eager to spend its wealth on imitating the style of the aristocracy. Henry VIII loved richly decorated garments and headdresses and, to protect himself and the Court from being copied, he introduced legislation preventing anyone but royalty and the aristocracy from wearing decorative embroidery, ribbons woven with gold and silver thread, brocades and jewellery.

The use of ribbons and other adornments was relatively modest during the Puritan period of the 17th century, but the restoration of the English monarchy in 1660 and the coming of age of France's Sun King, Louis XIV, in 1661 brought about a complete change of attitude in both countries. Louis XIV's powerful and dazzling court in France and the

Above: This Flemish woman from the 17th century wears a dress embellished with huge silk ribbon bows.

self-indulgent rule of Charles II in England were reflected in the costume of men and women. Men's petticoat-breeches, doublets and shoes were decorated all over with bunches of ribbon. Tight stockings were generally pulled over the breeches and fastened with a garter, which was also decorated with a bunch of ribbons. Women's skirts were divided or drawn up with lavishly tied ribbon to reveal extremely ornate petticoats beneath.

The Court of Versailles dominated all matters of taste and fashion among the European aristocracy in the early 18th century. At the same time, the middle classes experienced increasing

Right: The interior of Hill Bros Millinery Goods in the 19th century, with hundreds of rolls of ribbon for hat trimming.

prosperity and for the first time fashion became the domain of the majority. Ribbons played an essential role, being used to trim gowns and bonnets, tie up hair for a ball, lace dainty shoes and in the form of waistbands, sashes, frills, favours and rosettes. Children were smothered in ribbon, and curtains and cushions were embellished with broad bands of silk. Ribbons were produced in a dazzling variety of weaves and colours; plain, striped, checked, watered, shot, shaded and figured ribbons were all widely available. During the Napoleonic wars, weavers were recruited for the army, leaving the trade short of labour. The smuggling of vast quantities of French ribbon almost became an industry in itself in coastal villages, and yet the demand was still not met.

In 1813, a scalloped-edged ribbon became the rage and weavers had never known a time of such fierce demand for their product. In London, for a period of two years while the craze lasted, manufacturers could ask whatever prices they wished.

By the first half of the 19th century, the Industrial Revolution was in full swing and fashion was no longer dictated by nobility. Department stores sprang up in all major cities and off-the-peg clothes appeared for the first time. Parasols, large-brimmed hats and the new fashion accessory, the handbag, were all extravagantly decorated with rosettes and bows.

In 1823, jacquard looms were introduced in Coventry, in the English Midlands, thus extending the variety of fancy ribbons available. Ribbon factories and mills were built, all making use of steam-powered looms, although hand looms were still used, particularly in the countryside. The increased prosperity of the time meant that working women could indulge in a piece of ribbon to trim a hat, and Coventry found a new middle- and lower-class market.

The period between 1850 and 1870 was one of unprecedented prosperity for an enormous number of people. Women's clothes became increasingly complex, made from two or three different materials and trimmed with a medley of folds, frills and pleats. Ribbons and braids were an integral part of the garments, and by the 1880s, bustles became known as the "upholstered style" because they were made from draperies more suited to furnishing a room than trimming a dress. The turn of the 20th century saw a general softening of the silhouette and tucks, frills, ruchings and other ribbon trims were gradually modified. As the size and complexity of dresses diminished, hats grew larger and were trimmed with a profusion of ribbons and feathers. These extravagant hats gradually gave way to more modest creations: the cloche hat of the 1920s was quite plain but often trimmed with a fancy rosette on one side.

From the 1930s until quite recently, the significance of the ribbon as a fashion item diminished, with just the occasional reappearance as trends dictated – during the 1960s for example. There is today a revival of interest in ribbons and ribboncrafts, although the emphasis is now as much on home decoration as on fashion. Ribbon embroidery is the new stitchcraft and ribbon weaving, pleating, plaiting and ruching are all being rediscovered.

Ribbons are an extremely versatile medium and presented here is a selection of work by contemporary designers that illustrates just some of the wide range of effects that can be achieved.

Gallery

Textile artists working in techniques from weaving and stitching to leatherwork and millinery are today using lengths of ribbons on their own to create texture and pattern, or in small amounts to add colourful detail to their designs. The simplicity of the ribbon hat on the left makes the most of the natural flow of the coiled

ribbon, and the woven cushion overleaf exploits the subtle shades of soft velvet, whilst the gloves and hydrangea picture show a more traditional use of ribbon as embellishment.

Below: CHRISTENING GOWN
Double-face satin ribbon to match the cream lace has been appliquéd on to the gown using various simple techniques.
JENNY BANHAM

Below: WAVES WALL HANGING
Ribbon makes an ideal material for weaving, and offers dramatic effects. The inspiration for this design came from the shapes that are created by the weaving techniques employed. Small-scale undulations, or waves, are produced through the interaction of the bands of a thick wool warp and thin ribbon weft.
PATRICIA TINDALE

Above: RIBBON SPIRAL HAT
This elegant ribbon hat was inspired by
the natural way in which the ribbon spirals when pulled from the roll.
JO BUCKLER

Right: EMBROIDERED GLOVES
These hand-stitched gloves, which are
embroidered with ribbons, are based on
an original 17th-century pair. The decoration is typical of the period when ribbons
were used in profusion.
PAMELA WOODS

Right: RIBBON EMBROIDERY
This beautiful embroidery was inspired by
the pretty, delicately coloured hydrangea.
It is composed mainly of machine embroidery with ribbon embellishment. First the
bracts were drawn, outlined and shaded
in. Then the tiny flowers were worked by
hand using ribbon, beads and French
knots. The foliage was machined without
any further drawing on to the fabric.
DAPHNE J. ASHBY

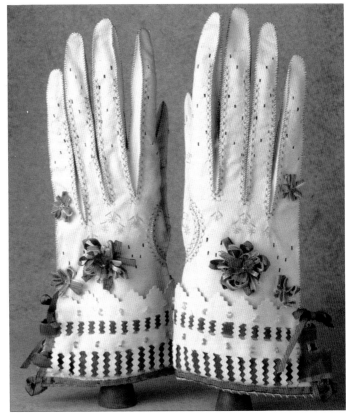

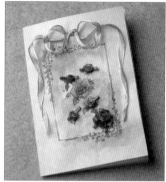

Left: INVITATION
This card was made by drawing a decorative border of delicate roses on to parchment paper. It was then colour-washed in watercolour before being decorated with ribbon rosebuds and bows.
LINDSAY CHALFORD BROWN

Above WOVEN CUSHION
The charm and beauty of this woven cushion lies in the fantastic colour scheme and texture of the velvet ribbons.
HIKARU NOGUCHI

Below: AFRICAN HANGING
This wall hanging was made by stitching together two layers of simple patchwork in a grid pattern. Selected areas of the patchwork were then cut away to reveal the layer underneath. The surface was covered with couched "ribbons" of hand-dyed silk to create geometric patterns.
JENNY CHIPPINDALE

Above: TREASURE CHEST
The lid of the chest is made up of a square of ribbon weaving worked in fine ribbons in shades of blue. It is enhanced with extra ribbons, held in place with single strands of metallic embroidery thread, worked in cross stitch and French knots. To give a three-dimensional effect, the weaving was mounted on to card. This shape suggested the lid of a treasure chest, inspiring the designer to make the rest of the chest.
M. MAUREEN VOISEY

A simple sewing kit of needles, thread and scissors is all that you need for basic ribbonwork, but a few of the projects that follow require more specialized items, which are readily available from craft suppliers.

Equipment

out of the reach of children. PVA or white craft glue is ideal for larger-scale sticking and dries clear. Double-sided tape is good for paper projects and gives a neat finish.

Sewing thread

Polyester thread comes in a wide range of colours, so you should always be able to find a reel to match the ribbon you are using.

Scissors

Use small, sharp-bladed scissors for trimming thread and cutting ribbons, and larger dressmaking shears for fabric. Keep a third pair especially for cutting paper only.

Stub (floral) wire

Florists use this thick, straight wire for supporting the flower stems. It is used to make the stalks of ribbon roses.

Tape measure

This is useful for checking the length of ribbons before cutting and also for measuring the progress of bead weaving, bracelets or necklaces.

Weaving board

A heat-resistant, fabric-covered soft board that will take pins easily is needed for weaving, although an ironing board is a good substitute.

Wire cutters

An essential tool for cutting florist's and stub wire. Some pliers, such as those illustrated here, can be used to cut wire, as well as to shape it.

Dressmaker's chalk

This makes an easily removed line to mark templates or specific intervals on to fabric or ribbon.

Dressmaker's pins

Long, straight pins have many uses in ribbonwork. Glass- or pearl-headed versions are easier to handle and are used for weaving.

Florist's tape (stem wrap)

Flexible and stretchy, this green self-sticking tape is used to conceal wire stems and bind the stems of fresh flowers together.

Above: Equipment such as a glue gun, florist's tape and stub wire is required for a few of the projects in the book. However, for many of them a good range of sewing equipment is all that is needed.

Glue

Although not essential, a glue gun will be much used once purchased. They apply glue with speed and accuracy, even in tricky areas, and are available in various sizes. A small gun is ideal for beginners. As with any adhesive product, it is important to keep glue guns

Ribbons come in myriad textures, colours and widths, and there is a ribbon for every occasion and season, from baby pastels and frothy sheers to designer prints and brocades.

Types of Ribbon

Cut-edge craft

This ribbon is made from a wide fabric and then cut into strips. It is available wired or unwired and is suitable only for craft applications. The special finish stops the ribbon from fraying but means it is not washable.

Grosgrain

These ribbons have a distinctive crosswise rib and are a stronger, denser weave than most other ribbon types. Grosgrains are made in solid colours, stripes, dots and prints; satin and grosgrain combinations are also available.

Jacquards

An intricate pattern is incorporated in the weave of the ribbon. This can be multicoloured or single-colour combinations, florals or geometric patterns, which give a beautiful tapestry-like effect.

Lace-edged satins and jacquards
These are sometimes embellished with a lace edge that is stitched or bonded on to the selvedge. It is particularly popular for bridal applications.

Merrow-edge
This describes the fine satin-stitched edge, usually incorporating a wire, that is added to elaborate cut-edge ribbons for stability and decoration. It is often in lurex thread but can also be in a contrasting colour.

Metallics
These ribbons are made from or incorporate metallic or pearlized fibres. Many different weaves and finishes result in a number of combinations.

Moiré
This effect is the result of a water-mark finish applied during manufacture. It gives a lustrous finish.

Ombré taffeta
A finely woven taffeta with colour shading across the width. Variations include plaids and interesting colour blends giving a lustrous finish and subtle tonal effects.

Plaids and checks
Popular classics, plaids and checks are usually taffeta weaves but are also available in cut-edge ribbon.

Satins
Satins are either double-face or single-face. They are available in plain colours or printed. Some incorporate edgings such as picot- or feather-edge.

Sheers
These fine, almost transparent ribbons are available as plain ribbons or with satin, lurex or jacquard stripes. A thicker yarn is used along the selvedge to give stability. This is known as a monofilament edge.

Shot-effect taffeta
The use of different, often contrasting colours for the warp and weft results in a shot effect giving a really lustrous, colour-shaded finish, similar to shot silk. This product is available both wired and unwired.

Velvets
The deep, plush pile of velvet is unmistakable and the depth of colour is exceptional. Imitation velvets are also available.

Wire-edged taffeta
A fine weave with a matt rather than shiny finish. This product looks the same on both sides and is available plain or with lurex incorporated. Weaves include plaids, checks and ombrés. Taffeta can also be printed or given a shimmering watermark finish. The wire edge is usually encased so it is not visible.

Woven-edge ribbon
These ribbons are woven in narrow strips, with a non-fraying selvedge running along both edges. They are ideal for projects that need to be laundered or that will have heavy wear. The ribbon reels should carry laundry instructions and details of crease resistance and colour fastness.

Ribbon Conversions

1.5mm/1/16in	36mm/1 3/8in
3mm/1/8in	39mm/1 1/2in
5mm/3/16in	50mm/2in
7mm/1/4in	56mm/2 1/4in
9mm/3/8in	67mm/2 5/8in
12mm/1/2in	70mm/2 3/4in
15mm/5/8in	77mm/3in
23mm/7/8in	80mm/3 1/4in
25mm/1in	

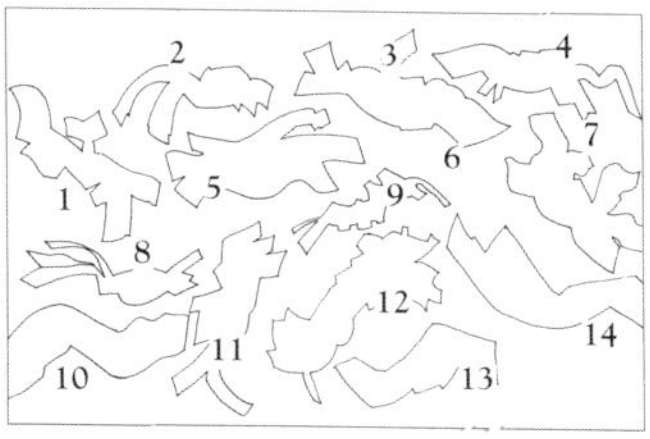

1 Ombré taffeta; 2 Grosgrain; 3 Sheer; 4 Jaquard; 5 Wire-edged taffeta; 6 Lace-edged; 7 Shot-effect taffeta; 8 Plaid and check; 9 Velvet; 10 Merrow-edge; 11 Moiré; 12 Metallic; 13 Cut-edge craft; 14 Satin.

Ribbons are a wonderfully versatile craft material with which to work. They can be woven, braided, appliquéd, used in embroidery, or simply made into beautiful rosettes, flowers and bows.

Basic Techniques

Ribbon Bows

Bows are probably the first thing that comes to mind when thinking about ribbon. There are several ways of making a bow; be it large and floaty or small and dainty, all are easy to accomplish. Satin ribbon is the most popular choice, but sheers, prints and lurex all have their own special qualities. As a general rule, if the ribbon can be tied in a tight knot, it is suitable for hand-tying. A stiffer ribbon will need to be pleated and stitched or bound at the neck. The hanging tails of the finished bow need to be in proportion to the loops. Leave them slightly longer than is required, then trim diagonally or into a chevron. This not only looks attractive, but also prevents a woven ribbon from fraying.

you will need

Ribbon

Florist's wire

Craft scissors

Glue gun

Needle and matching thread

Hand-wired Bow

1 Fold each half of the ribbon across the centre to make two loops and two tails. Hold the ribbon at the neck and bind it with wire. Conceal the wire with a narrow ribbon, secured with glue or a couple of stitches.

Double-loop Bow

1 Fold a length of ribbon into the desired number of loops. Form the neck by stitching through the ribbon or binding it tightly with wire, exactly halfway along the loops.

2 Hide the wire or stitches by wrapping a small piece of ribbon around the neck. Secure with glue or a couple of stitches at the back.

Pompom Bow

1 Fold the end of a length of cut-edge ribbon into a loop the diameter of the finished bow. Wrap the ribbon ten times around this loop and flatten into a rectangle. Cut off the corners.

2 Refold so that the cut corners meet in the middle to form the neck. Bind the neck securely with wire. Pull out each of the ribbon loops individually and twist them in different directions. Trim the ends diagonally or in a chevron, as shown here.

Ribbon Roses

Despite their sophisticated look, ribbon roses are deceptively easy to make. There are several techniques, employing various ribbon types, and each method will produce a slightly different flower; for example, satin ribbon roses will be more delicate and less full than those made from wire-edged taffeta. Experiment also by using different widths of ribbon – the wider the ribbon, the larger the finished rose will be. The fuller you wish to make the rose, the more ribbon you will need to use.

Stemmed Wire-edged Rose

This quick and easy flower is perfect for trimming special gifts or evening wear garments. They can also be used as accessories for bridal wear. The addition of a stem makes the rose suitable for use as a buttonhole or as an attachment to a hair-slide. A group of roses can be arranged in a vase.

you will need
Wire-edged ribbon
Needle and matching thread
Stub (floral) wire
Wire cutters
Florist's tape (stem wrap)
Artificial leaves

2 Twist the end of a stub wire gently around the stem and wrap the wire strand around the end of the stem. Fold back and wrap the raw end of the ribbon, securing it with a few stitches as necessary.

3 Bind the stem with florist's tape, adding on the leaves as you work. Ease the ungathered edge of the ribbon into the shape of the petals.

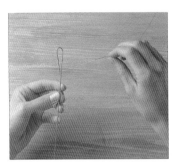

1 Tie a knot at one end of the ribbon and gather it by carefully pulling up one of the wires from the other end. Hold the knot and wrap the gathered edge around it to form the rose.

Stitched Ribbon Rose

Use this highly decorative rose for adorning fashion accessories or soft furnishings, either singly or in groups for extra romantic appeal. A stem and leaves can be added as before.

you will need
Ribbon
Needle and matching thread
Dressmaker's pins

1 Fold one end of the ribbon at a right angle so it extends 2.5cm/1in below the edge of the remaining ribbon. Stitch through both layers. Working from left to right, turn the ribbon six times to make a tube. Stitch at the base to secure the centre.

2 For each petal, fold the ribbon to the outside at a right angle, 2.5cm/1in from the centre, so the loose end hangs down vertically. Pin the fold and turn the bud into the fold until the ribbon is horizontal. Secure with a stitch and remove the pin.

3 Continue folding and stitching until 8cm/3in of ribbon remains. Fold again and stitch the raw edge to the base, pleating as necessary.

Ribbon Weaving

Weaving ribbons is an immensely satisfying craft, which can produce some dazzling effects, as can be seen in the Basket-weave Cushion and Woven Ribbon Waistcoat projects. It can be used for many different soft furnishings or on a smaller scale in panels on accessories or evening wear. The methods described here are all fused on to iron-on interfacing. Any type of ribbon can be used for weaving, but if the item is to be laundered you should work with washable, woven-edge ribbons. When working with velvet, place the ribbon face down to protect the woven pile and iron the interfacing on to the back of the finished woven piece.

Basic Steps for Weaving

you will need
Felt-tipped pen
Ruler
Tape measure
Iron-on interfacing
Weaving board
Ribbon
Glass-headed pins
Scissors
Steam iron or dry iron with damp cloth

2 Weave in the weft, or horizontal, ribbons and pin down both ends, angling the pins outwards. Cut the interfacing to the size of the weaving area, marking in a 2.5cm/1in seam allowance all around.

1 Pin the piece of interfacing to the board, glue upwards. Pin the top ends of the warp, or vertical, ribbons along the top edge.

3 Pin down the bottom of the warp ribbons, then fuse the completed weave to the interfacing using a moderate dry iron. Press the outer edges with the tip of the iron.

4 When the ribbons are secure, remove all the pins. Turn over and press again with a steam iron or with a damp cloth, then leave to cool.

RIBBON QUANTITIES FOR WOVEN SQUARES
The quantities given are for the whole square. If using two or more colours, divide the quantity by that number. All measurements include a 2.5cm/1in seam allowance.

RIBBON WIDTH	RIBBON LENGTH		
	10 x 10CM (4 x 4IN)	20 x 20CM/ 8 x 8IN	30 x 30 CM/ 12 x 12IN
5mm (³⁄₁₆in)	6m/6½yd	20m/22yd	42m/46yd
7mm (¼in)	4.2m/4½yd	14.6m/16yd	30.2m/33 yd
9mm (⅜in)	3.4m/3¾yd	11m/12yd	23.2m/25yd
15mm (⅝in)	2.2m/2½yd	6.6m/7¼yd	14m/15¼yd
23mm (⅞in)	1.4m/1½yd	4.6m/5yd	9.2m/10yd

Plain Weave

you will need
For a 30cm/12in square:
Lightweight iron-on interfacing,
    35cm/14in square
Red ribbon, 15.1m x 6mm/16½yd x ¼in
Blue ribbon, 15.1m x 6mm/16½yd x ¼in

1 Prepare the interfacing as in Basic Steps for Weaving. Cut both ribbons into 15cm/4in lengths. Pin the top ends of the red warp ribbons, edge to edge, along the top of the interfacing.

2 Weave the first blue weft ribbon over the first warp, under the second, then under and over to the end. Push it up to the top line and pin tautly at each end. Weave the next weft under the first warp and over the second, and so on to the end.

3 Alternate the weft ribbons in this way until the whole of the weaving area is covered. Check the ribbons are all neatly lined up before pressing as shown in the Basic Steps.

Patchwork Weave

you will need
For a 30cm/12in square:
Lightweight iron-on interfacing,
    35cm/14in square
Blue ribbon (A), 8.5m x 10mm/
    13¼yd x ⅜in
Yellow ribbon (B), 12m x 10mm/
    13¼yd x ⅜in
Red ribbon (C), 5.5m x 10mm/6yd x ⅜in

1 Prepare the interfacing as in Basic Steps and cut all the ribbons into 35cm/14in lengths. Pin the warp ribbons along the top edge in the following sequence: blue, yellow, red, yellow (ABCB).

2 Starting at the top-left corner, pin the ends of the weft ribbons down the side in the same order.
Weave them in the following sequence of four rows:
row 1: over AB, under C, then over BAB, under C to the end.
row 2: under A, over BCB to the end.
row 3: over A, under B, over C, under B to the end.
row 4: as row 2.

3 When complete, bond the ribbons to the interfacing as in Basic Steps.

Zigzag Weave

you will need
For a 30cm/12in square:
Lightweight iron-on interfacing,
    35cm/14in square
Yellow ribbon, 15.4 x 6mm/16¾yd x ¼in
Blue ribbon 14.6m x 6mm/16yd x ¼in

1 Prepare the interfacing as before and cut the ribbons into 35cm/14in lengths. Pin alternate yellow and blue ribbons along the top and left edges.

2 Weave the weft in the following four-row sequence:
row 1: under two, over two to the end.
row 2: under one, over two, under two, over two to the end.
row 3: over two, under two to the end.
row 4: over one, under two, over two under two to the end.

3 Bond the ribbons to the interfacing as detailed in Basic Steps.

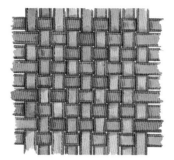

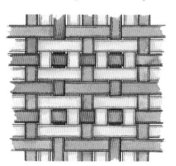

Basic Stitching Techniques

Ribbon embroidery is exactly the same as any other embroidery, the only difference being that the stitches are worked with ribbon. The texture and width of the ribbon produces raised embroidery, and the amazing range of shades available means that very life-like floral results can be achieved. The real secret of successful ribbon embroidery is to remember that you are trying to recreate the look and feel of the original subject, be it daisies, roses or tulips.

Running Stitch

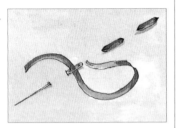

Pass the needle regularly in and out of the fabric, keeping the stitches small and evenly spaced on the back and front.

French Knots

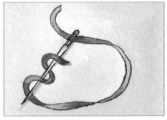

1 Bring the needle up through the fabric to the right side. Hold the ribbon taut with one hand and twist the needle around the ribbon twice.

2 Still holding the ribbon, turn the needle to go back down through the fabric close to the point where it emerged. The needle and ribbon should go through the twists.

Spider's Web Rose

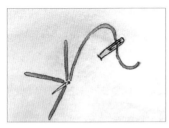

1 Stitch a circle of five spokes in a strong thread. Secure the thread at the back of the fabric and fasten off.

2 Bring the ribbon up through the centre of this circle of spokes and start weaving in and out of the spokes in a spiral. Let the ribbon twist naturally as you form the rose.

3 Pass the needle under the rose and back down through the fabric.

Lazy Daisy Stitch or Detached Chain Stitch

1 Bring the ribbon up through the fabric. Push the needle back down again at almost the same spot, leaving a loop of ribbon. Come back up through the fabric inside the loop and pull the ribbon up gently.

2 Take the needle back down again, over the loop to secure it in place. Bring the needle up at the tip of the next petal. Repeat to the end.

Chain Stitch

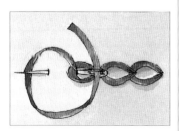

Loop the ribbon under the needle's tip. Hold the ribbon down as you draw the needle through the fabric. Push the needle back through the hole it left to form the next stitch.

Blanket Stitch

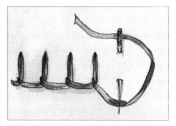

Work a line of vertical stitches and, as you draw the needle through the fabric, catch the ribbon under the needle's tip. Pull the ribbon through then insert the needle into the fabric parallel to the previous stitch.

Cross Stitch

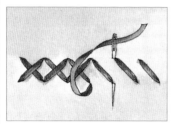

Cross stitch is worked in two parts and the top stitches should always lie in the same direction, usually from bottom left to top right. Work a row of diagonal stitches from right to left, then complete the crosses with a second row of diagonal stitches worked in the opposite direction.

Back Stitch

Back stitch produces an unbroken line of stitching suitable for outlining designs. First make a small stitch and pull the needle through the fabric. Insert the needle into the hole at the end of the previous stitch, then bring it up through the fabric a stitch length further on and repeat.

Slip Stitch

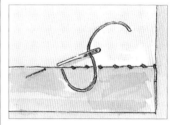

This dressmaking stitch is worked in sewing thread, and should be nearly invisible. Pick up two threads of the single fabric and slip the needle through the fold for about 6mm/¼in. Draw the needle through to make a tiny stitch and repeat to the end.

Tips for Ribbon Embroidery

To thread the needle, pass the end of the ribbon through the eye of the needle. Then push the point of the needle through the same end of the ribbon and pull. As with other types of embroidery, it is best to work with an embroidery hoop. Use your finger or a large needle to prevent the ribbon from twisting. Don't tie knots too tightly in case you need to undo them. Try to weave in the ribbon ends at the back of the embroidery.

Ribbonwork
Accessories

Ribbon is a surprisingly versatile textile medium, and the many creations on the following pages reveal just a few aspects of what can be achieved. Small-scale gift boxes, jewellery, Christmas decorations and present-wrapping ideas are shown alongside more ambitious and complex projects, which involve other skills such as basic woodworking, floristry or dressmaking. Today's stunning variety of colours, widths, patterns and styles of ribbon make ribbon projects even more adaptable, innovative and decorative.

Any aspiring young prima ballerina, flowergirl or junior bridesmaid would be delighted with the way that satin ties and a cluster of ribbon roses transform these plain ballet pumps into pretty shoes fit for a princess.

Ballet Shoes

you will need
3 toning shades of double face satin ribbon, 20 x 1cm/
8 x ½in of each
Scissors
Needle and matching threads
Pair of ballet shoes
Single-face satin ribbon to match ballet shoes, approximately
2m x 15mm/2¼ yd x ⅝in

1 For each satin rose you will need a 10cm/4in length of 1cm/½in wide ribbon. Start by rolling one raw end of the first length inwards to the left two or three times. Secure by stitching neatly through the roll at the lower edge.

2 To make the first petal, hold the roll in one hand and fold the ribbon away from you with the other. Turn the rolled end from right to left, turning tightly at the bottom and loosely at the top. Stitch the base of the petal in place.

3 Continue folding the ribbon, rolling the rose and stitching each petal until the rose is the desired size. Cut the ribbon square approximately 5mm/¼in from the rose. Fold the end neatly on to the rose and stitch to secure.

4 Make five more roses from the remaining ribbon in the same way. Stitch three roses, one of each shade, to the front of each shoe, just below the bow. Use a double length of thread for extra security.

5 Cut the 15mm/⅝in ribbon into four equal lengths. Stitch one length inside each side of the ballet shoes to form ties. Neatly hem the end of each tie to prevent fraying.

Extravagant bows and rosettes add true distinction to special gifts. Choose wrapping paper in interesting textures to complement them, and combine ribbons in several different shades for enchanting effects.

Luxurious Giftwrapping

you will need
Gold wire-edged ribbon in two shades
Scissors
Organza ribbon in three colours
Bead-edged ribbon, 5cm/2in wide
Tape measure
Double-sided adhesive tape
Gold corded ribbon
Thin card (stock)
Stapler

1 Wrap a length of wire-edged ribbon around the gold parcel and tie in a single knot on top. Tie a length of another shade in the other direction and knot as before. Tie all four ends together in a bow. Open out and adjust the loops, then cut the free ends into fishtails.

2 For the multicoloured bow, place organza ribbons in three colours one on top of the other and tie around the parcel together. Open out the loops and cut the free ends into fishtails.

3 To make the pompom, cut a length of bead-edged ribbon 126cm/49in long and fold into seven concertina (accordion) pleats, each 18cm/7in long. Trim the ribbon ends diagonally. Holding the pleats together, carefully make a 2cm/¾in cut in the centre of each long edge.

4 Cut a second length of ribbon long enough to wrap around the parcel plus 15cm/6in. Tie this length around the centre of the pleats, then wrap it around the parcel and secure the ends underneath with double-sided adhesive tape. Open out the folds of the pompom to form puffed loops.

5 Make the rosette from a 3cm/1¼in circle of cardboard and 110cm/43in of ribbon. Fold under one end of the ribbon, make a pleat and staple to the centre of the circle. Continue pleating and stapling in a spiral. Staple the raw end underneath. Wrap the parcel in ribbon and tape the rosette to the top.

It's easy to make ribbon roses and they always look gorgeous. You simply wrap, roll and tweak. Here, they are randomly applied to a plain lampshade to add splashes of colour.

Rosy Lampshade

1 Cut a 40cm/16in length of wire-edged ribbon. Ruche the ribbon by pulling up the wire along one edge from both ends.

2 Keep pulling until the ribbon is evenly ruched and the wire ends even.

3 Fold the ribbon in half and roll it up loosely, starting at the raw ends. Fan out the ribbon edge to create the rose, and secure the base with a few small slip stitches.

4 Make enough roses to cover the surface of the lampshade. To give it an informal look, fix them in place at random, but regularly spaced, intervals.

5 Cut a length of ribbon to fit the lower edge of the lampshade, allowing a 2cm/¾in overlap. Glue in place with strong glue or a glue gun.

The pleasure given by your gifts will be doubled when they are presented in these gorgeous wrappings. Plain boxes – new or recycled – can be painted brightly and adorned with ribbons to suit any occasion.

Gift Boxes

you will need
Wire-edged shot-taffeta ribbons
in various widths
Gift boxes
Scissors
Tape measure
PVA (white) glue
Needle and matching threads

Red gift box

1 Cut a 105cm/41in length of 4cm/ 1½in ribbon and fold into seven 15cm/6in concertina pleats. Trim the ribbons into chevrons. Carefully cut a small nick in the centre of each long side and tie a small piece of ribbon around the middle to secure the loops.

2 Open out each fold to make a rounded loop. Hold the bow in place on the gift box lid. Tuck the ends of the ribbon under the box lid and glue in place. Cut off the excess ribbon.

Large purple gift box

Green gift box

Cut four lengths of green ribbon. Wrap each length around one side of the box and tie in a single loop bow at one corner. Slip each new ribbon under the previous bow. Cut the end of each ribbon into a chevron.

1 Wrap a length of purple wire-edged shot-taffeta ribbon around the gift box and cut off, leaving a little extra for tying a knot. Fold the ribbon into small pleats widthways at regular intervals. Secure the pleats with neat stitches in matching thread.

2 Wrap the ribbon around the box, gluing in place at the points where the ribbon is tied. Tie the ribbon in a knot close to one corner of the box and cut the ribbon ends in chevrons.

Small purple gift box

Dark purple gift box

1 Glue a length of pink ribbon around the edge of the lid. Cut two equal lengths of ribbon and glue one end of each to the inside of the lid on opposite sides. Cut three 38cm/15in lengths of ribbon and twist together in the middle. Place the twist in the centre of the lid and tie the two glued ribbons together over the twisted ribbons.

2 Making sure that the ends are all level, tie all eight ribbons together with an overhand knot. Cut the ends at a diagonal angle and ease the ribbons apart to give depth to the trim.

Cut two lengths of pink ribbon. Tie one length around the box in one direction and the other ribbon in the opposite direction. Holding the ribbons together in pairs, fasten in a single-loop bow. Pull the loops and tails apart. Cut the extending ribbon ends into chevrons.

Pamper yourself with these coordinating accessories – easily and quickly made by adding pretty ribbons to bathroom basics – but don't forget to check that both the ribbon and accessory are washable.

Bathroom Set

you will need

White hand towel:

Dressmaker's pins

Tape measure

Crewel needle

Red double-face satin ribbon,
3.5m x 3mm/4yd x ⅛in

Scissors

Black mesh container:

Dressmaker's pins

Tape measure

Red spotted double-face satin ribbon,
11.75m x 3mm/13yd x ⅛in

Red double-face satin ribbon,
1.5m x 3mm/1⅔yd x ⅛in

Small red starfish

PVA (white) glue

Scissors

Crewel needle

Needle and matching threads

Wash mitt:

Black spotted double-face satin
ribbon, 25cm x 1cm/10 x ½in

Scissors

Needle and matching thread

Black spotted ribbon,
1.5m x 2.5cm/1½yd x 1in

White hand towel

Place pins 2.5cm/1in apart along all four edges of the towel. Thread a crewel needle with the red ribbon. Insert the needle at one pin and bring it out at the next. Knot the ends of the ribbon together neatly so that the ribbon lies flat against the towel. Cut off the excess ribbon, leaving short tails.

Black mesh container

1 Decorate the rim of the lid and base of the container with the spotted ribbon, as for the towel. Glue the starfish around the sides.

2 To make a tassel, bunch together 26 x 38cm/15in lengths of red spotted ribbon. Cut two 30cm/12in lengths of the red ribbon. Fold one length in half and wrap it around the middle of the bunch. Thread the ends through the loop and pull tightly.

Wash mitt

Cut a length of 1cm/⅓in black spotted ribbon to fit the strap, adding an extra 1cm/½in. Turn under 6mm/¼in at each end and stitch the ribbon to the strap. Cut three long lengths of 2.5cm/1in black spotted ribbon. Place them on top of each other and tie in a bow around the strap.

3 Thread a crewel needle with the remaining ribbon. Bind it tightly around the tassel, then slip the needle behind the binding ribbon and pull tightly. Trim the tassel ends level, then sew it to the centre of the lid.

This project uses simple ribbon-embroidered flowers to great effect. To vary the bag, embroider multi-coloured flowers directly on to striped cotton and tie with matching ribbon.

Ribbon-embroidered Bag

you will need

White loose-weave waffle fabric, 30 x 25cm/12 x 10in

Embroidery hoop

Deep blue, pink, purple and yellow satin ribbons, 1m x 3mm/ 1yd x ⅛in of each

Chenille needle

Iron

Scissors

Emerald green satin ribbon, 70cm x 3mm/27½ x ⅛in

Bright blue satin ribbon, 1.75m x 3mm/2yd x ⅛in

Green and white striped fabric, 25 x 13cm/10 x 5in

Dressmaker's pins

Matching thread

Pot pourri

1 Place the fabric in an embroidery hoop. Starting 10cm/4in in from one long edge, work a row of eight lazy daisy stitch flowers in deep blue, pink, purple and yellow ribbon (see page 275) over 20cm/8in. Space themevenly and make each flower 2cm/¾in in diameter. Work a French knot in the centre of each flower.

2 Press the fabric lightly and trim to 25 x 20cm/10 x 8in so the flowers lie 7.5cm/3in from the bottom. Thread the needle with emerald green ribbon and weave two horizontal lines through the top threads of the fabric to form a border on either side of the flowers. With bright blue ribbon, weave seven vertical lines.

3 Pin and stitch the green and white fabric along the top edge of the waffle fabric, right sides facing, with a 1cm/½in seam allowance. Open out and press the seam. Fold in half vertically, right sides of the lining facing. Pin and stitch a side seam along the edge.

4 Pin and stitch along the bottom edge. Clip the corners and turn right-side out. Push the green lining to the inside and press the top edge. Fill with pot pourri. Complete by tying the remaining ribbons into a bow around the neck of the bag.

Inspired by fond memories of 1950s raffia baskets, this design uses ribbon embroidery to emblazon a plain shopping basket with a scattering of simple coloured daisies.

Embroidered Basket

you will need
Thin card (stock)
Pencil
Craft (utility) knife
Fabric marker
Straw basket
Large-eyed tapestry needle
Narrow embroidery ribbons
Needle and matching threads
Matchstick (wooden match)

1 Cut out the template at the back of the book from card. Following the main picture as a guide, mark two rows of flowers around the basket, changing the angle of each one as you work, to give variety to the pattern.

2 Thread the tapestry needle with green ribbon, then make a long stitch from one end of the stem to the other. Finish off with a knot on the wrong side. Using a sewing needle and matching thread, couch down the ribbon along the marked line with small straight stitches.

3 To make the centre of the flower, thread the tapestry needle with a length of ribbon and make a small stitch over a matchstick. Do not pull the ribbon tight. Make a second small stitch over the matchstick and then remove it. Work five more "knots" around the centre.

4 For the petals, thread the tapestry needle with ribbon and knot the end. Insert the needle on the wrong side and bring it out next to the centre knots. Insert the needle at the same point and return to the wrong side leaving a loop about 2.5cm/1in long.

5 Thread a sewing needle with matching thread and, bringing it out to the right side at the tip of the petal, sew down the loop. Repeat all around the flower. Continue stitching the flowers until the bag is complete.

Trimming is the main function of ribbon, and here a plain place mat is transformed to brighten up a simple table setting. As with any other item that will be laundered, check the ribbon is washable.

Ribbon Table Mats

you will need

Woven table mats

Ruler

Contrasting grosgrain ribbon, 1cm/½in wide

Contrasting checked ribbon, 2.5cm/1in wide

Toning grosgrain ribbon, 15mm/⅝in wide

Scissors

Dressmaker's pins

Needle and contrasting and matching threads

Iron and damp cloth

1 Calculate the ribbon requirements by measuring all around the edges of the table mats, adding 20cm/8in for turnings. Cut each colour of ribbon into four lengths, one for each edge of the mat plus a 2.5cm/1in turning allowance at each end.

2 Starting from the outside edge, lay the ribbons in place around the mat. Use the ruler to ensure the ribbons are parallel to the edge. Pin each one in place, leaving the ends free.

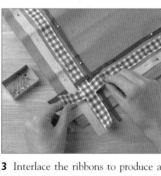

3 Interlace the ribbons to produce a woven effect where they meet and overlap at the corners and pin in place. Tack (baste) them down with contrasting thread and remove the pins.

4 Sew the ribbons down with matching thread using an invisible slip stitch along each edge, working the stitches closely together. Turn under the raw ends and sew to the back of the table mat. Press the piece under a damp cloth with the right side down.

Customize a child's denim jacket with this colourful sunflower. Ribbon appliqué is deceptively simple to work, as the woven edges mean no fussy hemming, and tricky curves and angles are easy.

Sunflower-motif Jacket

you will need

Denim jacket

Brown double-face satin ribbon,
1.5m x 1cm/1²⁄₃yd x ½in

Needle and matching threads

Yellow double-face satin ribbon,
1m x 4cm/40 x 1½in

Scissors

Leaf-green double-face satin ribbon,
50 x 4cm/40 x 1½in

Embroidery threads (floss)

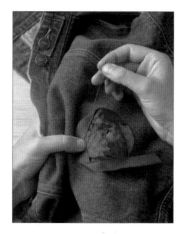

1 Mark the design area on the jacket as a rough guide for the appliqué work. Start by stitching the end of the brown ribbon to the centre of the design area. Sew the ribbon in a spiral, overlapping the coils and turning the ribbon over itself to form a circle. Sew along the inside edge of the ribbon as you make the spiral, using back stitch or running stitch to secure the outer edge of the previous coil (see pages 274–5). Leave the outer edge of the completed spiral unsewn.

2 Make 11 flower petal shapes from yellow ribbon, snipping a curve along each side of the tip without cutting the straight edges.

3 Stitch the petals around the flower centre, turning under the raw edges and tucking the base of each petal under the unsewn edge of the centre of the flower.

4 Continue adding petals around the centre, overlapping some of the edges. Leave a gap at the bottom for the last two flower petals to be added after the flower stem.

5 Cut the flower stem from the leaf-green ribbon. Tuck one end under the outer edge of the flower centre and sew the stem in place, using green embroidery thread. Turn under the bottom raw edge before stitching. Sew the last two petals over the stem.

6 Sew down the outer edge of the flower centre, securing the petals and the top of the stem. Decorate the centre with French knots of various sizes worked in brown embroidery thread.

7 To finish off, cut two leaves from the green ribbon and stitch to either side of the stem. Stitch veins on the leaves using a small running stitch and green embroidery thread.

A great advantage of ribbon is its versatility. Here pieces of richly patterned ribbon have been fashioned into a stunning necklace – an idea that could be extended to make a bracelet or earrings to match.

Ribbon Jewellery

you will need

Thin white card (stock)

Pencil

Ruler

Scissors

Wire-edged patterned ribbon,
40 x 5cm/16 x 2in

Super epoxy clear glue

Glue spreader or paintbrush

Needle and matching thread

Round and tubular beads,
15mm/⅝in wide

Plastic-coated garden wire

Toning ribbon, approximately
75cm x 3mm/30 x ⅛in

Small gold beads

Necklace clasp

1 Cut six 7 x 4cm/2¾ x 1½in rectangles from the card and roll each one carefully into a tube.

2 Cut six 7cm/2¾in strips of patterned ribbon, selecting the pattern area you want to use along the ribbon. Glue one end of each piece of ribbon on to the outside end of each tube of paper. Allow to dry.

3 Fold over the other end of the ribbon by 6mm/¼in. Roll the ribbon around the tube so that the edges of the ribbon meet. Stitch down the join. Push the wired edges of the ribbon into the tube. Apply glue to both ends of the tubes and press on a bead.

4 Hold the beads in place while the glue dries by threading a piece of wire through each tube and bending the end around. Thread the ribbon-covered tubes on to the 3mm/⅛in ribbon with gold and coloured beads arranged in a repeating pattern in between.

5 Thread a clasp on to the ends of the ribbon. Fold each ribbon end back on itself and stitch down, wrapping the thread over the stitching. Knot the end of the ribbon and wrap again with thread to cover the knot. Secure the thread firmly before cutting it off.

Fun to make and bound to be a conversation piece, these plaid roses can be adapted to suit many festive occasions: as part of a garland, as a table centrepiece or stitched to a bag, gown or satin slippers.

Tartan Ribbon Roses

you will need

For one rose:

Tartan ribbon, 60 x 4cm/24 x 1½in

Stub (floral) wire, 20cm/8in

Needle and matching thread

Craft scissors

Tartan wire-edged ribbon,
30 x 4cm/12 x 1½in

Fine florist's wire

Florist's tape (stem wrap)

1 Bend the end of a piece of stub wire to form a hook equal in depth to the ribbon width. Holding the tartan ribbon with the cut end to the right, hook the wire through the upper right-hand corner of the ribbon, approximately 6mm/¼in from the edge. Close the hook to hold the ribbon in place.

2 Roll the ribbon around the hook two or three times from right to left to enclose the wire. Stitch at the base to secure. Then, holding the wire stem in your right hand and the loose ribbon in your left, fold the ribbon so that it runs downwards, parallel to the wire.

3 Roll the covered hook end from right to left into the fold, turning tightly at the bottom and loosely at the top until the ribbon is once again horizontal to the wire.

4 With the wire stem facing towards you, stitch the base of the rose to secure the petal in place.

5 Continue folding the ribbon and rolling the rose in this way, stitching the base after each fold until you have the desired shape and size of rose. To complete the rose, cut the ribbon squarely, fold it back on to the rose and stitch in place.

6 To make a leaf, cut the wire-edged ribbon into 10cm/4in lengths. Cut three 20cm/8in lengths of florist's wire and make a small loop 2.5cm/1in from the end of each one. Fold two corners of a piece of ribbon down and forward into a triangle. Place a wire in the centre with the short end upwards and stitch it in place.

7 Fold the lower corners of the ribbon triangle under and backwards to create a leaf shape. Gather the lower part of the leaf neatly around the long wire stem and stitch to secure in place. Make two more leaves in this way.

8 Bind the wire stems of two leaves with florist's tape for 1cm/½in. Bind the wire stem of the third leaf for 2.5cm/1in. Join the three leaves together at this point and continue binding all three wires to create a single stem. Bind the rose stem, adding in the triple leaf about 10cm/4in down from the flower.

Give your prettiest clothes the care they deserve with these luxurious padded hangers, decorated with roses and bows made from exquisite silk and brocade ribbons in beautiful muted shades.

Ribbon-rose Coat Hangers

● ● ●

you will need
Polyester wadding (batting)
Scissors
Wooden coat hangers
Needle and matching thread
Satin ribbon, 8cm/3in wide
Selection of organza, silk,
petersham or grosgrain
and brocade ribbons

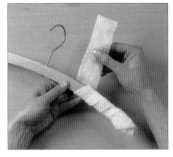

1 Cut a 5cm/2in wide strip of polyester wadding and wind it around the wooden part of a hanger. Secure it with a few stitches at each end.

2 Cut a long, narrow rectangle of wadding to cover the hanger. Fold it over the bound wadding and sew in place along the top edge, folding over and neatening the ends as you go.

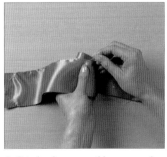

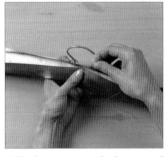

3 Cut two lengths of wide satin ribbon to make the cover for the hanger and, with right sides together, stitch each end in a gentle curve.

4 Stitch the two ribbons together along one long edge of the satin cover and turn to the right side.

5 Fit the cover over the hanger and slip stitch the top edges neatly, gathering the ends gently and easing in the fullness as you sew.

▶

6 To make a rose to decorate the hanger, fold a tiny piece of wadding into the end of a length of organza ribbon and secure with a stitch.

7 Fold and wind the rest of the ribbon around this central bud, stitching through the layers to secure. Tuck in the raw edge and stitch down. Make two roses for each hanger.

8 To make a rosette, cut a length of silk ribbon about five times its width and join the raw edges.

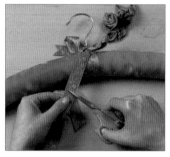

9 Gather the ribbon with a running stitch slightly above the centre. Pull up and secure. Flatten the ribbon out with your fingers to complete the rosette. Make two for each hanger.

10 To make a leaf, take a small piece of green petersham or grosgrain ribbon and fold both ends down to the side. Work a running stitch along this side and pull up the gathers tightly, securing with a stitch. Make four for each hanger.

11 Tie a length of brocade ribbon around the centre of each hanger to finish in a bow around the hook. Use this as a foundation to attach the roses, leaves and rosettes. Decorate with loops of ribbon to make a pleasing arrangement.

Hat boxes make ideal storage containers for all sorts of items beside hats. The basic boxes can be bought from stationery or gift shops and, with a little imagination, the decorative possibilities are endless.

Ribbon Hat Box

you will need

35cm/14in diameter hat box

Patterned fabric,
1.5m x 115cm/1⅔yd x 45in

Dressmaking scissors

Iron

Glue gun or contact adhesive

Heavy gold cord, 1.75m/2yd

Thin card (stock)

Lining fabric, 40 x 90cm/16 x 36in

Polyester wadding (batting), 38 x 75cm/15 x 30in

Matching sewing thread

Plain ribbon, 1m x 10cm/1yd x 4in

Wire-edged gilded ribbon,
1.8m x 10cm/2yd x 4in

3 bunches artificial grapes

2 gold tassels

1 Cut a length of patterned fabric slightly longer than the circumference of the box and 2½ times its height. Press under 1cm/½in along one short side, then glue the fabric to the box using a glue gun or impact adhesive. Overlap the folded edge to make a neat join.

2 With the point of a pair of scissors, make a small hole ⅔ of the way up each side. Cut a 75cm/30in length of gold cord, and insert through the holes to form a carrying handle. Knot securely on the inside and glue in position if necessary.

3 Cut a circle from card measuring 1cm/½in less in diameter than the base of the box. Cut out a slightly larger circle of lining fabric and use it to cover one side of the card. Smooth the fabric to prevent any wrinkles forming, then turn over and glue down the edges.

4 Fold the excess patterned fabric into the box to line the inside, smoothing the fabric so it lies neatly. Stick the covered circle to the base of the box, with the fabric-covered side uppermost. Any surplus lining fabric will be hidden underneath the card circle.

▶

5 Cut a circle of wadding to fit the top of the box lid and glue in place. Cut a circle of the remaining fabric, slightly larger than the radius and circumference of the box lid. Glue this around the outside of the lid, matching the edge of the material with the edge of the lid to leave excess for gathering.

6 Run a gathering thread through the fabric 18cm/7in from the rim, draw up and secure.

7 Cut the plain ribbon in half and stretch one piece across the lid, gluing the ends inside the rim. Knot the other piece to the centre and glue the ends inside the rim, at right angles to the first.

8 Glue gold cord around the outside of the rim. Butt the two ends together and cover with a narrow strip of fabric to neaten the join.

9 Make a bow from the wire-edged ribbon. Cut the ends in fishtails and shape the loops. Glue to the centre of the lid, then stick on the grapes.

10 Finish off by sewing a tassel to each end of the handle.

Although not difficult, lavender bottles are time-consuming to make. However, they do make charming drawer and cabinet scenters. As the smell dulls squeeze the bottle to release the scent.

Lavender Bottles

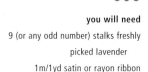

you will need
9 (or any odd number) stalks freshly picked lavender
1m/1yd satin or rayon ribbon

1 Take a bunch of lavender and, using the ribbon, tie the stalks together tightly just below the flowerheads.

2 Very carefully bend the stalks down one by one over the lavender heads, being careful not to snap them.

3 Weave the ribbon in and out of the lavender stalks. When you have covered the heads, wrap the ribbon around the stalks and bind them to their ends. Cover the ends of the stalks with the ribbon, then bind back up the stalks until you reach the heads again. Tie in a knot and a bow to fasten.

This pretty token, made of woven satin ribbon and finished with a lace edging, is a quick gift to make. Use colours that co-ordinate with the furnishing fabrics of the recipient.

Decorative Heart

you will need

Tissue paper

Pen, scissors and metal ruler

Double-sided tape

7mm/⅜in satin ribbon, 60cm/24in in 8 different colours

Needle and sewing cotton

15cm/6in square wadding (batting)

15 x 30cm/6 x 12in cream silk dupion (mid-weight silk)

1m/1yd of 2.5cm/1in lace

3mm/⅛in satin ribbon, 1m/1yd in 5 different colours

Beading needle and tiny beads

Masking tape

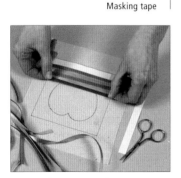

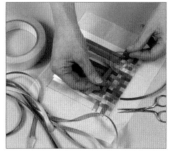

1 Trace the heart template on to tissue paper and draw a rectangle around it, 2cm/¾in away. Stick double-sided tape along the base and down the left-hand side. Cut four 13cm/5in lengths of each colour of 7mm/⅜in ribbon. Arrange half of the ribbons horizontally in random colours to cover the heart.

2 Weave another ribbon over and under the weft ribbons, sticking it to the tape at the bottom and securing it with tape at the top. Continue until the rectangle is covered.

Place a piece of tissue paper over the weaving. Turn the weaving over and backstitch along the heart line. Stitch again 3mm/⅛in outside the first line. Finish off and tear the paper away.

3 Cut two wadding hearts slightly smaller than the ribbon heart. Sandwich them between the silk and ribbon weaving and stitch the fabrics together between the backstitch rows. Trim to 5mm/¼in of the motif and oversew neatly. Stitch the lace to the right side.

These subtle ribbon decorations – a combination of earthy colours and natural textures – make a welcome change from glitzy baubles. Hang them from a tree or wreath, or string them along the mantelpiece.

Ribbon Christmas Decorations

you will need

Baubles:

Polystyrene (Styrofoam) balls, 7.5 or 5cm/3 or 2in diameter

Pencil

Tape measure

Gold, brown and cream ribbons, 1m x 3–9mm/40in x ⅛–⅜in

Dressmaker's pins

Scissors

Toning patterned ribbon, 2m x 3–10mm/2¼yd x ⅛–½in

Tiny gold beads

Gold-coin pendants

Brass lace pins

Large, ornate gold beads

Pine cone parcels:

Gold, lemon or brown ribbon, 4cm/1½in wide

Gold or brown ribbon, 3mm/⅛in wide

Pine cones

White (PVA) glue

Golden tassel:

Cotton-pulp ball, 2.5cm/1in in diameter

Scissors

Gold grosgrain ribbon, 10m x 3mm/11yd x ⅛in

Crewel needle

White (PVA) glue

Baubles

1 Draw lines on a polystyrene ball to divide it vertically into four segments, then mark horizontally round the sphere to divide it into eighths. Place a length of ribbon along one quarter, pin the ends on the lines and trim. Fill in the section with a patchwork of assorted ribbons, taking care to overlap the edges.

2 Fill in each section. Lay the patterned ribbon over the pins and ribbon ends, following the guidelines, and pin at each point where the lines cross. Fold under the ends to neaten. Make a hanging loop by slipping a 25cm/10in length of ribbon under one intersection and knotting the ends.

3 Slip a tiny gold bead and a coin pendant on to each of 15 brass lace pins. Pin them in a row around the centre. Thread a small and a large bead on to the last pin and stick into the base of the ball to complete. Make other baubles in the same way, using different ribbons.

▶

Pine cone parcels

Golden tassel

Tie the wide ribbon into a bow (see page 270). Wrap the narrow ribbon around a pine cone, as if wrapping a parcel, tying off at the tip. Dab with glue to secure. Make a hanging loop by tying the ends together 10cm/4in from the knot. Glue the bow to the top of the cone.

1 Use scissors to make a hole through the centre of the cotton-pulp ball. Pull out some of the fibre to enlarge the hole to 1cm/½in in diameter. Cut 25cm/10in grosgrain ribbon, then cut the rest into 30cm/12in lengths.

2 Put the 25cm/10in and a 30cm/12in length aside and use the crewel needle to thread the others through the hole. Allow 12.5cm/5in of each ribbon to hang below the ball. Spread glue thinly over the ball. Fold down the ribbons protruding from the top to cover the ball completely.

3 Thread the needle with the 25cm/10in length of ribbon. Glue one end around the ribbons close to the base of the ball. Wrap the ribbon tightly around the tassel.

4 Insert the needle behind the binding ribbon and pull tightly. Unthread the needle, allowing the ribbon end to hang down with the other ribbons. Do not trim at this stage.

5 To suspend the tassel, double the 30cm/12in length of ribbon and thread it through the needle. Insert the needle down through the hole in the ball. Remove the needle, knot the ends neatly together and trim. Gently pull the loop taut, hiding the knot among the ribbons. Trim the ends.

This luxurious little evening bag exudes style and elegance. The velvet is painted with luxurious gold stripes, then woven through with complementary coloured ribbons.

Classic Evening Purse

you will need
Black velvet, 40cm/16in square
Black lining fabric, 20cm/8in square
Scissors
Large sheet of paper
Masking tape, 2.5cm/1in wide
Gold fabric paint
Paintbrush
Thin card (stock)
Fabric marker
Small sharp-pointed scissors
Silver ribbon, 1.6m x 6mm/1³⁄₄yd x ¹⁄₄in
Green ribbon, 1.75m x 6mm/2yd x ¹⁄₄in
Maroon ribbon, 1.75m x 6mm/
2yd x ¹⁄₄in
Tape measure
Tapestry needle
Dressmaker's pins
Needle and matching threads
Iron

1 Enlarge the three pattern pieces at the back of the book to size. A seam allowance of 1cm/12in is included. Cut two of the larger rectangles from black velvet, two of the smaller rectangles from the black lining fabric and one circle from each fabric.

2 Place one rectangle of velvet fabric face up on a sheet of paper (to protect the work surface). Lay vertical strips of masking tape over the velvet, leaving a gap of 2.5cm/1in between them. Lay a double strip of masking tape across the centre of the fabric.

3 Apply gold paint lightly and evenly to the exposed areas of fabric with a dry brush. Leave to dry completely, then peel off the tape carefully. Follow the manufacturer's instructions for fixing the paint.

4 Make a template for the ribbon insertion, cutting points from a strip of card cut to the length of the painted stripes. Mark six evenly spaced points along one edge of the strip. Transfer these points to the velvet with a fabric marker along both sides of each painted strip. Mark only the bottom half of the whole piece of velvet.

▶

5 Use sharp scissors to cut 6mm/¼in slits in the fabric at the marked points. Cut the ribbons into 20cm/8in lengths. Use a tapestry needle to thread one through each row of slits, alternating the colour with each row. Thread the ribbon loosely, allowing it to fall naturally.

6 Secure the ends of each ribbon on the back of the velvet with a few stitches. Repeat steps two to six with the second rectangle of black fabric to make the other half of the bag.

7 With right sides facing, pin, tack (baste) and sew the long sides of the two rectangles together, leaving a space in each seam where indicated on the pattern. Sew both lining rectangles together along the short edges, leaving a gap in one seam for turning.

8 With right sides facing, pin, tack and sew the long sides of the lining to the upper edge of the bag, matching up the seam lines. Press lightly and stitch the seam.

9 Turn the bag inside out and, with right sides facing, pin, tack and sew the circle of velvet to the bottom edge of the bag. Join the circle of lining fabric to the bottom edges of the lining. Turn the bag through the opening to the right side. Fold along the fold line and press gently.

10 Tack along the stitching lines indicated on the pattern to form the drawstring channel, then stitch. Close the side opening with slip stitch (see page 275). Thread the remaining ribbon through the channel and tie the ends together to form a drawstring.

Join lengths of Fortuny-style pleated ribbon to make this sculptural bag, which is lined with iridescent fabric and, as a pretty finishing touch, embellished with sparkling beads.

Ribbon Evening Bag

●●●●

you will need

Pleated wire-edged ribbon,
1.6m x 5cm/1⅞yd x 2in

Scissors

Tape measure

Needle and matching thread

Pleated wire-edged ribbon,
40 x 6cm/16 x 2½in

Matching organza fabric

Plate, 14cm/5½in diameter

Pencil

Sewing machine

Dressmaker's pins

Fine matching cord, 38cm/15in

Decorative glass beads

1 For the main bag, cut eight pieces of 5cm/2in-wide pleated ribbon. Using a matching thread, oversew the long edges of the pieces of ribbon together to form a rectangle, then join the two outside edges together to make a cylinder.

2 To make the bottom of the bag, stitch the two ends of the 6cm/2½in wide ribbon together with a 1cm/½in seam. Run a gathering stitch along one edge and pull up tightly. Secure the ends on the wrong side.

3 Slip stitch the outer edge of the bottom of the bag to the lower edge of the side, turning in the raw edges.

4 For the lining, cut a rectangle 18 x 40cm/7 x 16in and a circle with a 7cm/2¾in radius from the organza, using a plate.

5 Machine stitch the side seam, and pin and tack (baste) the side to the bottom of the bag. Machine stitch together.

6 With the wrong sides facing, fit the lining into the bag. Fold in the top edges of both the lining and the ribbon and slip stitch the two together.

7 To make the carriers for the tie, cut two 6cm/2½in lengths of cord and poke the raw ends through a side seam on either side of the bag, 4cm/1½in from the top. Stitch in place. Cut a piece of cord 25cm/10in long, fold it in half and knot the ends.

8 Thread the loop through the carriers and pass the knotted ends through the loop. Hand stitch decorative glass beads around the top edge of the bag at regular intervals.

Whether containing a collection of drawings, school project, or college thesis, this beautiful folder is bound to enhance its contents. The book cloth and lining paper are available from good craft suppliers.

Woven Ribbon Folder

●●●●

you will need
2 pieces of stiff board,
36 x 25cm/14 x 10in
Sheet of artist's black lining paper
PVA (white) glue
Glue spreader or paintbrush
Book cloth or stiffened fabric,
1m x 50cm/1yd x 20in
Pencil
Ruler
Scissors
Wood chisel
Hammer
Piece of wood
Black ribbon, 90cm x 6mm/36 x ³⁄₈in
Iron-on interfacing, 35 x 23cm/14 x 9in
Masking tape
Burgundy fleur-de-lis ribbon,
4.6m x 4cm/5yd x 1¹⁄₂in
Iron

1 Line the two boards with black paper, glueing it in place. To make the gusset, cut an 86 x 10cm/34 x 4in strip of book cloth or stiffened fabric and line it with artist's black paper. Fold the strip in half lengthways, then fold the two halves in half again to create a concertina.

2 Mark a point 27cm/10½in from each end of the strip. Fold the strip lengthways at the first point so that you have a double layer. Carefully cut a triangle out of each corner. Open out, then fold and cut the strip at the other 27cm/10½in point in the same way.

3 Fold the strip at the two 27cm/10½in points so that the two end sections of the gusset strip are at right angles to the middle section.

4 Glue the two boards inside the gusset so the edges lie within the two outermost folds. Press all the creases firmly. Cut two pieces of cloth 5cm/2in longer than the boards and slightly narrower. Stick these to the outside of the boards, leaving the excess at the open edge to be turned over later.

5 Chisel two holes into each side of the top edge of the folder. Protect the boards while you do this by placing a piece of wood between them. Cut the 6mm/¼in ribbon into four equal lengths and thread one through each hole. Turn over the excess lining and glue down to secure the ribbons inside the folder.

6 Tape the interfacing to a weaving board, glue side up. Cut the fleur-de-lis ribbon into eight 27cm/10½in strips and six 40cm/16in strips. Place the eight shorter ribbons side by side over the interfacing and hold them in place with masking tape.

7 Weave the six longer ribbons, plain side up, through the fleur-de-lis ribbons, following the plain-weave technique (see pages 272–3). Make sure the weaving is even and tight. Press with a dry moderate iron when complete to fuse the ribbon to the interfacing.

8 Trim the edges of the weaving to 2cm/¾in. Fold this allowance over the interfacing and iron carefully. Glue down the edges as necessary, then glue the woven panel to the front of the folder to complete.

This handy case brings together types of needlework: patchwork, embroidery and sewing. The crazy design will be unique for every case made and requires only a little planning to create a stunning look.

Roll-up Needlework Case

●●●●
you will need
Lightweight canvas, 60 x 30cm/
24 x 12in
Pencil
Ruler
Dressmaking scissors
5 different toning ribbons,
1m/1yd of each
Needle and matching threads
Toning embroidery threads (floss)
Dressmaker's pins
Ribbon for binding, 1.5m x 2.5cm/
1²⁄₃yd x 1in
Ribbon for ties, 50cm x 6mm/
20 x ¼in

1 Cut the canvas into four rectangles, two measuring 30 x 20cm/12 x 8in and two 30 x 10cm/12 x 4in. Cut the toning ribbons into various lengths between 2.5 and 7.5cm/1 and 3in.

2 Use running stitch or back stitch (see pages 274–5) to sew the ribbon pieces on to one of the 30 x 20cm/12 x 8in canvas rectangles, turning under the raw edges. Continue until the entire panel is covered. Don't worry about any small gaps: these add to the crazy patchwork look and can be filled with embroidery stitches.

3 Oversew the edges of the patchwork pieces using three or four different embroidery threads and a range of stitches. Cross stitch, running stitch and chain stitch all work well.

4 Work blanket stitch around three edges of one of the 30 x 10cm/12 x 4in rectangles, leaving one of the long edges unsewn.

5 Draw lines across the second small rectangle to mark the pockets. Blanket stitch along the top edge and position the panel along one edge of the second large rectangle. Join the two together by stitching along the pocket lines.

6 To assemble the case, place the patchwork panel face downwards. Place the pocket piece on top, right side up. Tack together and bind the side and bottom edges with the 2.5cm/1in ribbon. Use a small running stitch to secure the ribbon, stitching through all the layers.

7 Place the remaining rectangle above the pocket piece to form a flap, with the unsewn edge at the top. Pin in place and bind the top edge with ribbon as described in step 6.

8 Fold the length of 6mm/¼in ribbon in half and at the centre point stitch it inside one side edge of the case. Use this ribbon to secure the needlework case, when rolled up.

The beautiful blooms that make up this romantic coronet will require special care to keep them pristine: give them a long drink before use and mist the finished headdress lightly with a water spray.

Flower and Ribbon Headdress

●●●●

you will need

12 small clusters of *Aronia melanocarpa* berries

Scissors

Stub (floral) wire, 0.38mm/28g

12 small clusters of hydrangea florets

12 *Leycesteria formosa* flower heads

Small garden roses

12 *Lizianthus* flower heads

12 single *Antirrhinum* florets

Florist's tape (stem wrap)

Burgundy sheer ribbon, 8m x 23mm/ 8¾yd x ⅞in

Tape measure

Stub wire, 0.71mm/22g

1 Trim the berry stems. Cut short lengths of fine stub wire to double leg mount them. Holding the stem between finger and thumb, place a wire behind and at a right angle to the stem, one-third of the way up. Bend it into a "U" so that one leg is twice as long as the other.

2 Holding the short leg against the stem, wrap the long leg twice around both the stem and the other wire. Straighten both legs, which should now be about equal and in line with the stem. Mount the roses, hydrangeas and *Leycesteria* in the same way.

3 Wire each *Lizianthus* flower head by piercing the seedbox with a length of stub wire. Push it about one third of the way through, then bend the wire legs down and wrap the legs around the stem as described for double leg mounting in step 1.

4 Remove the flower heads of the *Antirrhinum* from the main stem and cut two short stub wires for each one. Fold one wire in half and twist into a loop at the bend. Push the legs down through the throat of the flower and out at the base to create a stem.

▶

5 The loop will sit in the narrowest part of the flower, preventing the wire from pulling all the way through. Use the second piece of wire to double leg mount the protruding wires and any natural stem that remains, as shown in steps 1 and 2.

6 Cover all the stems and wires with florist's tape. Hold the end against the top of the stem. With the other hand, hold the rest of the tape at an angle to the stem. Slowly rotate the stem and, keeping the tape taut so that it stretches slightly, wrap it in a downwards spiral, overlapping and pressing it in place.

7 Make 14 three-loop ribbon bows, each with two tails. For each bow, cut a 55cm/22in length of ribbon and divide it into six equal sections. Fold the ribbon accordion-style, pinching the folds together at the base. Double leg mount each bow using stub wire.

8 Cut several equal lengths of heavy stub wire to make the headdress foundation. Group four wires together so each overlaps the next by 3cm/1¼in. Starting at one end, bind them together with florist's tape. As the tape reaches the end of the first wire, add in another length.

9 Continue in this way until the wire measures 3cm/1¼in more than the circumference of the wearer's head. Tape the wired flowers and ribbons to the foundation in your chosen arrangement. Continue to within 3cm/1¼in of the end, curving the wire as you work.

10 Overlap the undecorated end of the stay wire with the decorated beginning. Tape the wires together under the flowers.

A project for a dressmaker, this lined waistcoat will fit a medium adult: adjust the ribbon requirements accordingly for another size. Choose a paper pattern without any darts in the front panels.

Woven Ribbon Waistcoat

●●●●●

you will need

Iron-on interfacing

Commercial waistcoat pattern

Scissors

Pencil or fabric marker

Ruler

Masking tape

Gold ribbon, approximately
20m x 2.5cm/22¼yd x 1in

Steam iron or dry iron and damp cloth

Needle and matching threads

Small gold beads

Blue lining fabric, 1.5m x 115cm/
1²⁄₃yd x 45in

Dressmaker's pins

Sewing machine, with zip foot

Three buttons

1 Lay the iron-on interfacing, glue side down, on top of the waistcoat front pattern piece. Cut the interfacing around the pattern. Transfer the markings to the interfacing. Turn the pattern piece over and repeat to cut out the second waistcoat front. Draw two crossing diagonal lines as a guide for weaving.

2 Tape the interfacing, glue side up, on a board. Following the pencil lines, lay and cut ribbons side by side in one diagonal direction, overlapping the edges. Tape one long ribbon on the opposite diagonal at both ends and weave in further lengths of ribbon (see pages 272–3). Adjust the ribbons to keep the weave neat as you work.

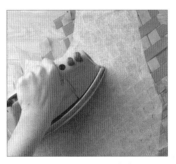

3 Continue weaving until the interfacing is covered. Press with a dry iron. Remove the tape, turn over and press again with a steam iron or under a damp cloth.

4 Trim the ribbons to the edge of the interfacing. Iron an extra strip of interfacing to the front edge of each piece to provide a firm base for the buttonholes and buttons. Overlap the seamline slightly. ▶

5 Using a double thread with a knot at the end, sew a small gold bead to each point where the ribbons cross. Work along the diagonal and keep the seam allowances free of beads. Secure each bead with a double stitch before going on to the next bead.

6 Cut an outer back, a back lining, and two front pieces from the blue lining fabric. Mark the position of the back ties and buttonholes. Pin and machine stitch the front lining and woven fronts together, right sides facing. Fit a zip foot, and machine stitch around the front edge, along the bottom and around the armholes, leaving the shoulder and side seams open. Trim the seams and corners, clipping the curves. Turn right-side out.

7 Cut two 60cm/24in lengths of ribbon for the back ties. Fold in half and sew down both sides, stitching in the same direction to avoid puckering. Hand sew in place on the waistcoat back, trimming the raw ends to 6mm/¼in and folding them neatly under.

8 Join the waistcoat back to the back lining with right sides facing. Stitch around the neck and armholes. Trim and clip the seam allowances and turn to the right side. With right sides facing, sew the front and back together along the shoulder seams.

9 Stitch through one layer, leaving the linings free. Trim and press the seam open. Fold the lining seam allowance inside and slip stitch closed. Sew the side seams in the same way. Slip stitch the bottom edge of the waistcoat back closed.

10 Make three buttonholes, using gold thread on top of the machine and blue in the spool case, so that the thread matches the fabric on both sides. Snip the buttonholes and sew the buttons in position.

Ribbonwork
Furnishings

Ribbons are the perfect material with which to accessorize home furnishings and make them unique. They are available in such a vast range of colours, materials and textures that there is almost always sure to be a ribbon that will suit the theme of your home furnishing scheme. Used in small quantities as trimmings, ribbons add accent colours and a touch of luxury. On a grander scale, whole fabrics can be woven from ribbons and then made into cushions, a headboard and even a deckchair.

Glamorize plain bedlinen by edging a pile of pillows with ribbon bands and bows. Bright ginghams work well in a child's bedroom, but you could adapt the idea using cooler colours for a more sophisticated look.

Pillowcase Edgings

you will need

Plain white cotton pillowcases

Plain and gingham ribbons of
various widths

Tape measure

Scissors

Fusible bonding web

Iron

Needle and matching thread

Dressmaker's pins

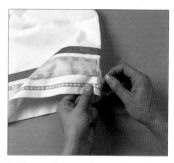

1 For the banded pillowcase, cut lengths of three different ribbons about 5cm/2in longer than the width of the pillowcase. Cut three lengths of fusible bonding web to size and use to attach each of the ribbons.

2 Turn in the raw edges and stitch the ribbons to the pillowcase at each end. Hand sew with tiny stitches along each long edge of the pillowcase.

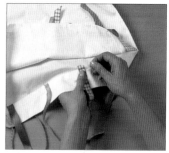

3 For the pillowcase with ties, cut two 30cm/12in lengths from each of five different narrow ribbons and pin one of each pair at regular intervals along the folded edge of the pillowcase opening. Stitch in place at the ends.

4 Use fusible bonding web to attach a length of wide ribbon to conceal the stitched ends of the ties. Hand or machine stitch around all four edges.

5 Attach the matching ribbon lengths to the other side of the pillowcase opening, folding in the raw edges and stitching neatly to secure.

6 To decorate the pillowcase with ties, cut lengths of ribbon of differing widths and pin them across the corners. Slip stitch to secure.

7 Fold the loose ends to the back of the pillowcase. Cut a second length of each ribbon, tuck under the ends to conceal the raw edges and slip stitch in place.

8 Finish the corner with a small ribbon bow, stitched through the knot to prevent it from coming undone.

Let fresh air in and keep flies out with a brilliant Mexican-style curtain. Each length ends with a large glass bead to add weight and substance: the number required depends on the width of the door frame.

Ribbon Door Curtain

you will need
Tape measure
Length of 2.5 x 2.5cm/1 x 1in wooden batten (furring strip)
Hacksaw
Drill and drill bit
Ruler
Pencil
Double-face satin ribbon in six bright colours, 15mm/⅝in wide
Scissors
Coloured glass disc-shaped beads
Staple gun
2 long woodscrews
Screwdriver

1 Measure the width of your door frame. Mark the distance on the wooden batten, then use the hacksaw to cut it to the correct length. It should fit snugly inside the top of the door frame.

2 Draw a pencil line along the centre of the batten. Make a mark every 2.5cm/1in along the batten to indicate the positions where the ribbons will be attached. Drill a hole through the mark closest to each end to hold the screws.

3 Cut a length of satin ribbon for each point marked on the batten, about 15cm/6in longer than the door measurement to allow for attachment and tying on the glass beads. Trim one end of each length into neat points.

4 Fold the trimmed end over for about 10cm/4in, then push the folded end through the hole in the centre of a glass bead. Pull the whole length of the ribbon through the loop and pull taut to hold the bead securely. Repeat with all the ribbon lengths.

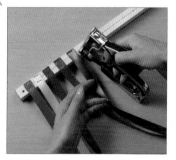

5 Fold under 15mm/⅝in at the other end of each ribbon and staple to the batten at a pencil mark, checking they are all the same length as you go. Follow the same colour sequence all across the curtain. Finally, attach the batten to the door frame with two long woodscrews.

Bring instant colour and a touch of Asian opulence to your home with this dazzling cushion. The richly textured woven metallic braids have a luxurious feel and many interesting combinations can be achieved.

Golden Braid Cushion

you will need

Approximately 18 different patterned gold braids, 1m/40in of each

Red and green satin ribbons, 1.75m x 15mm/2yd x ⅝in

Tape measure

Scissors

Striped ticking, 75 x 40cm/30 x 16in

Dressmaker's pins

Needle and matching threads

Iron

Co-ordinating backing fabric, 60 x 30cm/24 x 12in

Cushion pad, 60 x 30cm/24 x 12in

Heavy gold furnishing cord, 1.75m/2yd

1 Cut the braids and ribbons into 40cm/16in lengths. Starting at the centre and using the woven lines of the ticking as a guide, pin the braid and ribbon in place. Arrange the colours for dramatic effect, interspersing the gold braid with red and green satin ribbons. Sew down using a narrow zigzag stitch, working slowly and carefully to avoid puckering.

2 When the ticking is completely covered, press from the back with a cool iron. Trim the edges so that the piece measures 60 x 30cm/24 x 12in. Turn under a 1cm/½in allowance on one short edge and hem. Make a 1cm/½in hem along one short edge of the backing fabric. With right sides facing, pin then sew the front and backing together around the three raw edges.

3 Clip the corners, turn through and press lightly. Insert the pad and slip stitch the opening (see page 275).

4 Slip stitch the furnishing cord around the edge of the cushion, making a small decorative loop at each corner.

A relatively small amount of expensive ribbon makes a big difference to this natural linen throw. Antique-style crushed velvet ribbon applied diagonally across the throw brings an element of real luxury.

Ribbon-decorated Throw

you will need
Natural linen, 1.5m/5ft square
Fabric marker
Ruler
Iron
Crushed velvet ribbons, 3cm/1¼in
and 15mm/⅝in wide
Scissors
Dressmaker's pins
Tape measure
Sewing machine
Matching thread
Silk lining, 167cm/5ft 7in square
(widths joined if necessary)
Needle

1 Lay the linen flat, then use a ruler and fabric marker to mark a border all around the square, 7cm/2¾in from the edge. Fold two opposite corners together and press along the crease to make a diagonal fold across the centre.

2 Using the picture as a guide, pin the velvet ribbon diagonally across the linen following the direction of the fold and alternating the widths. Cut the ribbon to overlap the border by 2.5cm/1in at each end.

3 Machine stitch the ribbons in place, stitching close to the edges. To ensure that the ribbon lies flat, stitch both edges in the same direction.

4 With right sides together, match two opposite edges of the lining fabric to the border line marked on the linen. Pin and machine stitch the seams, starting and finishing 2cm/¾in from each end of the marked lines.

5 Match the two remaining edges in the same way. Machine stitch the edges together, leaving a 30cm/12in gap on one side.

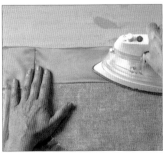

6 Turn the fabric through to the right side. Centre the linen to give an even border 7cm/2¾in wide and press with a warm iron.

7 Turn in the lining along the opening edge and press. Slip stitch the gap closed. At the corners, trim and tuck in the excess fabric to form a mitred seam. Press and ladder stitch or slip stitch the folded edges together.

Bands of satin, velvet and taffeta ribbon across this silk cushion make up a symphony of rich textures. Though all the tones are similar, light plays on the ribbons in different ways, creating dramatic contrasts.

Striped Ribbon Cushion

1 For the cushion front, cut a 45cm/18in square from the silk fabric. Fold diagonally through the centre and press. Arrange lengths of ribbon side by side across the fabric, using the fold as a guide, and pin in place. When you are satisfied with the ribbon positions, tack (baste) the ribbons to the front of the cushion.

2 Using stranded embroidery thread in a range of colours to complement the ribbons, work rows of feather stitch to join the edges, varying the direction of the stitches. Fold the velvet diagonally and cut 4cm/1½in wide strips parallel with the diagonal.

3 Stitch the short edges together with a 6mm/¼in seam allowance and press open to make a length of bias binding. Pin the binding around the piping cord and machine stitch in place.

4 Pin the covered cord all around the cushion front with the raw edges matching. Clip the seam allowance at the corners so that it lies flat. Tack, then machine stitch close to the cord.

7 Using a zip foot on the sewing-machine, top stitch around the zip. Unpick the temporary seam. Undo the zip. With right sides together, pin and machine stitch the cushion back and front together, following the line of piping. Clip the corners, turn through and insert the cushion pad.

5 Unpick 2cm/¾in of the machine stitching from the beginning of the piping. Trim the cord so the ends butt together and lap one end of the casing over the other, turning under the raw edges. Pin to the cover and machine stitch. Slip stitch the casing edge.

6 For the cushion back, cut two pieces of silk 23 x 45cm/9 x 18in. With right sides together, match the two long edges and machine stitch using a long stitch setting. Press the seam open. Centre the zip over the back of the seam and tack in place.

Lantern frames are available in many different shapes and sizes, so this idea is very versatile. Measure the four sides of the frame and select a width of ribbon that can be multiplied to fit into this length exactly.

Ribbon Lantern

1 Cut pieces of ribbon to twice the finished frame length. To mitre one end of each ribbon, turn in 1cm/½in along the raw edge and press lightly with a dry iron to hold in place.

2 Fold in one corner to the centre of the ribbon, then fold in the other corner to make a triangular, mitred point. Iron to hold in position.

3 Thread a needle and tie a knot in one end. Pass the needle through the point of the mitre, then thread a small bead followed by a large bead and a rocaille. Pass the needle back through the large and small bead so the rocaille forms a stopper. Secure with a small stitch on the inside of the point.

4 Starting close to the final stitch, slip stitch along the central join of the mitre, keeping a neat point at the end of the triangle (see page 275).

5 Turn the other end of the ribbon over, and loop the ribbon over one side of the frame. Fold under and slip stitch the other end of the ribbon to the top of the mitre, making sure that the wrong sides of the ribbon will be inside the frame. Make all the other ribbons in this way.

The cover for this striped lampshade consists entirely of ribbons, allowing you to introduce a rich variety of colour and texture. They are simply stuck side by side on to a piece of lampshade backing material.

Satin and Velvet Ribbon Shade

● ● ●

you will need

Graph paper

Pencil

Drum-shaped lampshade frame
with reversible gimbal,
top diameter 18cm/7in,
bottom diameter 20cm/8in,
height 20cm/8in

Scissors

Self-adhesive lampshade
backing material

Satin bias binding

Selection of coloured velvet and
satin ribbons

White (PVA) glue

Clothes pegs (pins)

Needle

Matching thread

Ceramic lamp base

Spray enamel paint and face mask

1 Make a paper pattern to fit the frame. Cut a piece of self-adhesive backing material to the size of the pattern. Remove the backing paper from the lower edge of the backing material to expose the adhesive. Cut a piece of satin bias binding to the length of the lower edge plus 2cm/¾in. Press one edge of the bias binding to the lower edge of the backing material.

2 Cut lengths of satin and velvet ribbon to fit the circumference of the shade, leaving a 1cm/½in overlap at one end. Lay a length of ribbon alongside the bias binding, following the curve of the pattern. Lay more lengths of ribbon across the backing until the last one is 6mm/¼in from the top edge. Alternate velvet with different coloured satin, and remove the paper.

3 Cut a piece of binding to fit the top edge, with a 2cm/¾in allowance. Lay one edge of the bias binding along the top edge. Apply glue to the wrong side of the backing at top and bottom. Fold over to the wrong side.

4 Apply glue to the side edge and fold the raw ribbon ends to the wrong side. Leave to dry. If the ribbons begin to curl away from the backing, place under a heavy object. Neaten untidy edges or hanging threads with scissors.

5 Apply a thin line of glue to the underside of the same edge. Take care to wipe away any glue that squeezes on to the ribbons. Roll into a drum shape and lap the glued edge over the opposite edge, matching up the stripes of colours perfectly. Use two clothes pegs to hold the edges together firmly at the top and bottom until the glue is completely dry.

6 Where the raw edges of the bias binding meet, turn under 1cm/½in of one raw edge and stick it down so that it overlaps the other raw edge. Use the clothes pegs to hold the bindings together until the glue is dry. Slip stitch the folded edge in place. Apply a line of glue to the outside edge of the frame and insert it into the cover.

7 Working in a well-ventilated space, and wearing a face mask, spray the lamp base with a thin coat of pink enamel paint. Leave to dry before applying a second coat. Spray the shade with flame retarder if necessary, before attaching to the base. Use a medium-wattage bulb.

Shocking pink ribbon in a variety of styles – embroidery, satin, velvet and wire-edged – makes up this pretty tie-back. A satin band holds the curtain in place, while the tassel hangs decoratively to one side.

Ribbon Tassel Tie-back

you will need
Large-eyed tapestry needle
Narrow embroidery ribbon
Wooden beads in two sizes
Scissors
Selection of satin, velvet and wire-edged ribbons
Needle and strong thread
2 brass rings

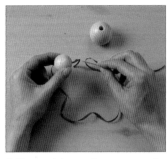

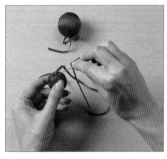

1 Using a large-eyed tapestry needle, thread narrow embroidery ribbon around two large wooden beads to make the tassel head.

2 When the beads are completely covered, tie off the ends securely. Create a hanging loop at the top of the smaller bead.

3 To make a rosette, cut a length of satin ribbon and join the ends neatly together, turning in the raw edges. Work a running stitch along both edges of the ribbon.

4 Gather up the edges tightly to make a puff shape and secure the threads. Make a second rosette, using ribbon of a different width and colour.

▶

5 To make a loop rosette, cut two pieces of narrow velvet ribbon: 30cm/12in lengths will make a rosette that is 15cm/6in across – cut longer lengths for a larger rosette. Fold the raw ends of the first to the centre and secure with a few stitches.

6 Fold and stitch the second length in the same way. Place this loop at right angles across the centre of the first to form a cross, then stitch through all the layers to form the rosette.

7 Select satin and wire-edged ribbons for the skirt of the tassel, cutting them to twice the finished length: this will depend on the size of the tassel head, so experiment until the tassel looks right. Arrange the ribbons in a star shape and secure by stitching through all the layers in the centre.

8 To assemble the tassel, thread the large needle with several lengths of strong thread and stitch through the centre of each element, starting with the skirt. Fasten off securely when you reach the top of the smaller bead.

9 To make the tie-back, cut a suitable length of wide satin ribbon. Neaten the raw edges and stitch a brass ring securely to each end. Cut a second piece of the same ribbon twice the length of the tie-back and gather by working a line of running stitches along the centre.

10 Draw up the fullness to fit the foundation ribbon and stitch down the centre. Sew the tassel's hanging loop to one end of the tie-back, so that it will hang at the side of the curtain.

Ruched organza ribbons, sewn on to translucent voile in a fine tracery of delicate spirals, give an interesting, three-dimensional effect to this light and airy curtain.

Appliquéd Ribbon Café Curtain

●●●

you will need
Tape measure
Voile
Dressmaking scissors
Dressmaker's pins
Sewing machine
Matching thread
Iron
Thin card (stock)
Pencil
Fabric marker
Needle
Organza ribbons in green and pink

1 Calculate the width and drop of the curtain and cut out the voile, adding 5cm/2in to the width and 15cm/6in to the length. To make the facing, cut a second piece of voile to the same width by 30cm/12in. Turn under and machine stitch a 6mm/¼in hem along the lower edge of the facing. Press. With right sides together, pin the facing to the curtain, matching the top edges.

2 Cut a scallop template out of thin card. Add the width of the template to the proposed width of each fabric loop (4–7cm/1½–2¾in) and divide the finished curtain width by this figure to calculate the number of scallops required. Allow for a strip at each end of the curtain. Draw around the template along the top of the curtain, using a fabric marker.

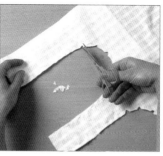

3 Machine stitch the facing to the curtain along the marked lines. Cut out the scallops, leaving a 1cm/½in seam allowance. Clip the corners and snip into the curves.

4 Turn the curtain through to the right side and press. Topstitch around the seams, 4mm/⅕in from the edge.

▶

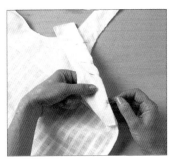

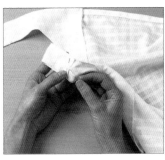

5 Turn under and press a double hem 1cm/½in wide down each side edge of the curtain. Turn under and press a 5cm/2in double hem along the bottom edge.

6 Mitre the corners and slip stitch them neatly in place. Turn under and press a 1cm/½in single hem down both side edges of the facing. Slip stitch the facing and all the hems in place.

7 To make the fabric hanging loops, turn 5cm/2in of each strip to the wrong side of the curtain. Pin and slip stitch them to the facing, taking care not to let the needle pass through to the right side.

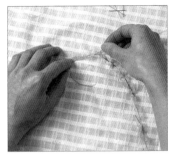

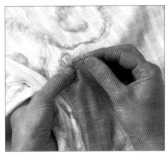

8 Cut the green ribbon into 1m/1yd lengths. Set the machine to a long straight stitch and sew down the centre of each length. Pull up the bobbin thread from each end to gather the ribbon, then adjust the ruffles so that they lie evenly.

9 Draw a series of freehand spirals randomly across the curtain, using a fabric marker. Pin the ruched ribbons along the lines. Machine stitch along the gathering threads, being careful not to trap the ribbon under the stitches.

10 Gather the pink ribbon as before and cut a strip 15cm/6in long for each flower. Fold each one into three small loops and pin the flowers to the curtain in the spaces between the spirals. Machine stitch, securing the loops in place. Insert a narrow pole through the hanging loops and fix it in place at the window.

An old deckchair can be transformed with a new cover and an interesting way to make this is with grosgrain ribbon. Here, two contrasting colours have been interwoven to make a chequerboard effect.

Deckchair Cover

●●●

you will need

Deckchair

Claw hammer or pliers

Medium-grade abrasive paper

Large sheet of card (stock)

Tape measure

Pencil

Grosgrain ribbon in white and blue, 4cm/1½in wide (10m/11yd is sufficient for a small chair)

Scissors

Drawing pins (thumb tacks)

Dressmaker's pins

Needle and tacking (basting) thread

Sewing-machine and matching thread

Staple gun

1 Remove the existing canvas from the chair frame, setting it aside to use as a template and carefully prising out any old fabric fixings with a claw hammer or pliers. Sand down any rough edges on the frame and repaint if necessary.

2 Mark the dimensions of the cover on the sheet of cardboard. Cut lengths of white grosgrain ribbon to the length of the measured rectangle, plus about 10cm/4in for fixing. Pin the ribbons to the board side by side along the top of the rectangle to form the "warp".

3 Cut lengths of blue ribbon to fit across the rectangle and form the "weft". To weave the cover, pin a blue ribbon to the warp length at one side, weave it under and over the warp until you reach the other side, then pin securely again.

4 Continue weaving until you have the size required. When complete, tack (baste) across the edges of the woven piece to hold the warp in place. Cut two lengths of blue ribbon to fit down each side of the new cover. Lay one length over the raw edges of the weft at each side and tack in position.

5 Remove the cover from the board and machine-stitch the blue and white ribbons together, stitching very close to both edges. Attach the new cover to the wooden frame by wrapping the ends of the ribbons around the horizontal rungs and stapling them securely in place.

The openweave effect used to make this plush cover allows the dark blue moiré taffeta backing fabric to show through the complementing richness of the brocade, velvet and jacquard ribbons.

Basket-weave Cushion

● ● ●

you will need

Dark blue moiré taffeta,
1m x 38cm/1yd x 15in

Dressmaking scissors

Ruler

Black rosebud brocade ribbon,
1.15m x 2cm/1¼yd x ¾in

Claret rosebud brocade ribbon,
1.15m x 2cm/1¼yd x ¾in

Dressmaker's pins

Claret velvet ribbon,
1.15m x 23mm/1¼yd x ⅞in

Purple marble-print ribbon,
1.15m x 23mm/1¼yd x ⅞in

Dark red ribbon,
1.15m x 25mm/1¼yd x 1in

Claret jacquard ribbon,
1.15m x 7mm/1¼yd x ⅜in

Green velvet ribbon,
2.5m x 2cm/2¾yd x ¾in

Needle and matching threads

Iron and pressing cloth

Cushion pad, 36cm/14in square

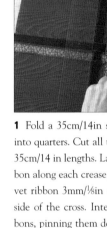

1 Fold a 35cm/14in square of taffeta into quarters. Cut all the ribbons into 35cm/14 in lengths. Lay a brocade ribbon along each crease, then put a velvet ribbon 3mm/⅛in away from each side of the cross. Interweave the ribbons, pinning them down at the ends and the crossing points.

2 Using a ruler to ensure that all the lines are straight, continue to weave in the other ribbons, following the design of the completed cushion. When the weave is complete, pin all the loose ribbon ends to the backing fabric.

3 Starting at one edge, sew the ribbons to the taffeta by making two small, neat overstitches across each point where the ribbons overlap. Sew the ribbons firmly in place but avoid pulling the thread too tightly across the back, as this will distort the weave.

4 Cut two 35 x 25cm/14 x 10in taffeta rectangles. Hem one long side of each. Right sides facing, pin to the cushion front so the hems overlap in the centre and the cut edges match. Stitch all round 2cm/¾in from the edge. Clip the corners, turn through, press and insert the cushion pad.

Ribbon is ideal for weaving, and wonderful effects can be achieved with subtle combinations of colour and texture. This headboard sets the tone for a minimalist bedroom in neutral shades.

Woven Ribbon Headboard

you will need

Length of 25 x 25mm/1 x 1in
wooden batten (furring strip)

Hacksaw

Medium-grade abrasive paper

Drill and bit

Tape measure

Pencil

Wood glue

Dowels

4 right-angled fixing brackets

Screws

Screwdriver

Grosgrain ribbon in blue, brown and beige, 5m x 12mm/5$\frac{1}{2}$yd x $\frac{1}{2}$in

Cream satin or taffeta ribbon, 20m x 2.5cm/22yd x 1in

Satin striped ribbon in blue, brown and beige, 5m x 3cm/5$\frac{1}{2}$yd x 1$\frac{1}{4}$in

Grosgrain ribbon in blue, brown and beige, 5m x 15mm 5$\frac{1}{2}$yd x $\frac{5}{8}$in

Scissors

Staple gun

1 Using the hacksaw, cut the softwood batten into four lengths, each measuring 90cm/36in. This will make a headboard to fit a single bed: increase the width of the board for a larger bed and increase the amount of ribbon proportionately. Sand the cut edges.

2 Use a drill with a bit to fit the dowels to make a hole at each end of the two battens that will form the horizontal pieces of the frame. Drill a hole 1cm/$\frac{1}{2}$in from the top of each side piece and a second hole 60cm/24in down. Glue the dowel joints and assemble the frame.

3 Screw four right-angled fixing brackets to the reverse side of the headboard frame to reinforce the joints and hold the frame rigid while you work. This will help to keep the woven pattern symmetrical.

4 Cut the ribbons into 70cm/28in lengths. Lay them vertically on the frame in a symmetrical pattern: start at the centre with a wide grosgrain overlaid with a light satin striped ribbon, then work outwards with alternate narrower satin and grosgrain ribbon.

5 Repeat the sequence to fill the frame. Staple the ribbons to the frame, pulling each piece taut. Cut two short pieces of cream satin or taffeta ribbon and staple to cover the wooden batten at the top two corners.

6 Interweave ribbons horizontally across the headboard in a pattern sequence similar to the warp. Turn the headboard over and staple the raw ends securely to the frame as before, making sure that the ribbons are pulled quite taut.

Create an heirloom gift for a new baby by combining the freshness of pure white cotton and broderie anglaise with the silky soft appeal of floral ribbon embroidery in delicate pastels.

Ribbon-embroidered Baby Pillow

●●●●

you will need

White cotton piqué,
90 x 30cm/36 x 12in

Dressmaking scissors

Tape measure

Lightweight iron-on interfacing,
23cm/9in square

Iron

Fabric marker

Embroidery hoop

Chenille needle

Satin ribbon in pale pink, dusky pink,
pale mint green, pale lime green
and pale aqua, 1.75m x 3mm/
2yd x $\frac{1}{8}$in of each

Narrow broderie anglaise insertion,
1.4m/1$\frac{1}{2}$yd

Broderie anglaise edging,
1.4m x 7.5cm/1$\frac{1}{2}$yd x 3in

Dressmaker's pins

Needle and matching and
contrasting threads

Ribbon, 1.4m x 6mm/1$\frac{1}{2}$yd x $\frac{1}{4}$in

Tapestry needle

Cushion pad, 30cm/12in square

1 Cut a 23cm/9in square of cotton piqué and iron the interfacing to one side. Trace the template at the back of the book and mount in a hoop. For the rose centre, sew a star of four pale pink straight stitches. In dusky pink work a ring of stitches around the star.

2 Work the leaves in straight stitch with the green ribbons and the rose-buds in lazy daisy. Complete the rest of the design using a range of random stitches, and add a bow to the space at the bottom edge. Trim the fabric down a 15cm/6in square.

3 Cut four 9cm/3$\frac{1}{2}$in squares and four 15 x 9cm/6 x 3$\frac{1}{2}$in pieces of piqué. From the broderie anglaise insertion, cut four 9cm/3$\frac{1}{2}$in, two 15cm/6in and two 33cm/13in lengths. Position the pieces and the lace around the embroidered square, following the diagram opposite.

4 Make the front panel by joining the pieces together in three rows with the short lengths of lace insertion, leaving a 1cm/$\frac{1}{2}$in seam allowance. Use the two long strips to join the three rows together. Press the seams away from the insertion. Join the two ends of the broderie anglaise edging and run a gathering thread along the raw edge.

5 Fold the edging into four equal sections, marking each quarter division with a small scissor cut. Pin each of these cuts to one corner of the front panel on the right side. Draw up the gathering thread to fit the front panel. Distribute the gathers evenly, allowing a little more fullness at the corners. Pin the broderie anglaise around the outside edge so that it lies on top of the cushion.

6 Tack (baste) and sew in place. Thread the 6mm/¼in ribbon through the insertion using the tapestry needle. Secure each end with a few tacking stitches.

7 Cut a 30cm/12in square of cotton piqué for the panel back. Pin to the right side of the front panel, ensuring that the lace is free of the seam line. Sew around three sides then turn to the right side. Insert the cushion pad and slip stitch the fourth side closed.

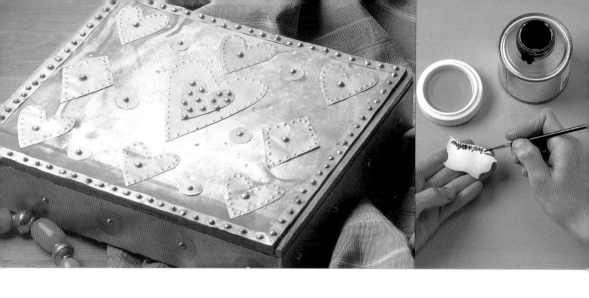

Enamelling and
Metalwork

As soon as early people learnt how to work metal, they valued it as much for its beauty as its practical uses: the creation of jewellery, from delicate silver filigree to magical iron rings, has been an important skill in every civilization. Enamelling also has a long history of decorative use and early craftspeople used it in jewellery to imitate precious stones. Learning to use these materials in new designs continues a beautiful art and an ancient tradition.

Enamel is a form of glass, and enamelling is the process of fusing it to metal with heat. Like metalwork and wirework, enamelling is a craft steeped in tradition.

History

Enamelling

The technology of enamelling – using heat to fuse a vitreous material on to a metal base – has obscure beginnings, but it is thought to have originated in Europe around 1400BC.

The craft of enamelling has been practised for centuries. Early civilizations used enamel in imitation of precious stones. The Greeks and Romans then developed and continued the craft of enamelling. Some of the earliest examples of enamel can be found on buckles, swords, coins and helmets from as early as the 5th century BC.

Enamel, like glass, has the qualities of brilliance and permanence: the colours of the earliest known examples of enamelling remain as rich today as when they were created. Its fluidity of application, using a variety of techniques, has allowed it to be adapted to many different decorative traditions over at least 3000 years. Many of these techniques are still in use today.

To contain molten enamel on a metal surface during firing, there are various methods of creating a raised order around it. In champlevé work, it is achieved by hammering, engraving, etching or stamping the surface to form recesses. The powdered enamel, mixed with water, is applied using a quill or brush and allowed to dry out before firing.

The Romans preferred to decorate their jewellery with gemstones and canes and used enamel to embellish medallions and larger objects. In the Classical period, around 500BC–AD500, enamel was contained in cells made by attaching narrow strips of metal at right angles to the metal base. This type of work became known as cloisonné. The colours used are jewel bright and opaque. The enamel shrinks on firing and when it has cooled its surface is lower than the outline. In the 8th–12th centuries Byzantine cloisonné rose to great artistic heights and religious ornaments

Above: This beautiful bowl is decorated with delicate wire motifs and then enamelled in bright colours in the style of cloisonné work.

and icons made from it found their way into religious houses all over Europe.

A radical development in the art of enamelling occurred during the Renaissance, in the 15th–16th centuries when the mastery of firing at controlled temperatures enabled enamellers to produce pictures on copper. This technique was refined in France, specifically at Limoges.

Right: Traditional wirework has a charm of its own. Once widely used, wire has now been replaced with newer materials.

Metalwork

The Romans are known to have mined tin, one of the most popular and widely used metals. Its value in its pure form was quickly recognized. It was also mixed with copper to form bronze and to plate other metals.

Tinware flourished with the production of candle holders, sconces, boxes and sieves. The basic product was left unadorned or decorated by punching and piercing. Punching the tin with a nail could leave purely decorative indentations, or could make actual holes which were also functional: punched tin cabinets, for example, were used to keep food ventilated while protecting it from flies and other pests.

Tinware was also decorated to look like Japanese lacquerware with stencils and paints. The most popular forms were toleware including trays, boxes and caddies. The tin was painted a dark colour, then decorated with stencilled and handpainted designs such as fruits and flowers.

Wirework

Wirework is an ancient art form, probably practised by the Egyptians around 3000BC. The wire was originally made by chiselling thin strips from a sheet of metal. The strips were either twisted and then rolled between two flat surfaces to smooth them, or spirally wound around a mandrel.

Today wire is made by drawing rods of metal through conical holes in a drawplate. In early history the ironware trade was mainly for chain mail, but wool carders, girdles, chains, fish hooks and needles were also made. Because iron is easily corroded, few examples of the broad range of objects once made have survived. By the early 19th century, tinning and black-japanning had become popular ways of protecting the wireworker's craft. These treatments prevent rusting and help to cement items made from unsoldered wire.

The industry reached its peak in Europe and America at the turn of the 20th century, when an impressive range of products was available. The craft of wireworking was applied to every possible household device until the advent of plastic gradually led to its demise.

Wirework is still alive and well in many countries around the world.

Left: Tinware was once used to make an enormous range of simple, functional objects.

Metal and wirework are often associated with old industries, and products made from them have the charm of a bygone era. Enamelling, though steeped in tradition, is still a contemporary craft.

Gallery

For contemporary craftspeople working with age-old crafts offers the opportunity to recreate products that are often more attractive than their modern equivalents, or to learn crafts in a traditional way. While metal and wirework were once dying crafts, their materials replaced with more convenient, rustproof lighterweight alternatives, the crafts continue to thrive, with the reproduction of antique-style items with nostalgic qualities or with bespoke and contemporary pieces.

Enamelling too continues to thrive in the traditional way, but with all the convenience of modern technology. Such crafts that add colour and beauty to everyday objects, or elevate them to become luxury items will always have a place in the world.

Above: TOY CARS
These brightly printed toys were made in India from scrap tin. The toys are made in small workshops and commercially manufactured. The decoration may be printed on the recycled tin.

Left: TOASTING FORK
Traditional toasting forks were once used to toast English muffins and bread over an open fire. This fork is cleverly made from four coathangers.
ANDREW GILMORE

Above: NECKLACE AND
ENAMELLED BOX
The necklace is made up of silver
enamelled beads with pure gold foil
decoration. The unusual cone-shaped
box uses the cloisonné enamel technique.
RUTH RUSHBY

Below: EMBOSSED BOOK JACKET
The panel covering this book imitates
the ornate leather and metal bindings
adorning early bibles and prayer books.
Gold lacquer paint has been used to
imitate the look of semi-precious stones.
MARY MAGUIRE

Above: ABSTRACT ART KEYRING
This unusual design is composed of tiny
pieces of coloured enamel threads and
silver cloisonné wire lightly fused on to
an enamel base.
ALEX RAPHAEL

Below: FLEUR DE LIS
BOOK MARK
This heraldic design has been achieved
using a silver foil motif against a rich
blue enamel background.
LISA HAMILTON

Enamel is a form of glass and enamelling is the process of fusing it to metal using heat. Most materials need to be obtained from a specialist supplier: start by buying what you need for the simplest projects.

Enamelling Materials

Acids and pickles
Dilute solutions of various acids are used to degrease and de-oxidize metal before or after firing.

Ceramic fibre
This can be moulded to support awkwardly shaped pieces during firing.

Enamels
Jewellery enamels are available in lump or powder form, with or without lead. Leaded and non-leaded cannot be used together. Use transparent, translucent or opaque enamels to create different effects.

Enamel gum solution
Various organic gum solutions are available, some as sprays. Dilute solution is used to position cloisonné wires; a weak solution is used to hold powder enamel before firing. Use sparingly.

Etchants
Solutions of nitric and other acids are painted on metal to produce etched designs for filling with enamel.

Foil
Fine gold (23.5 ct) and silver (.995 ct) foil are available in a variety of thicknesses. Gold leaf is usually too thin for enamelling purposes.

Kaolin (ballclay, batwash)
This helps prevent enamel adhering to the firing support or the kiln floor.

Mica
In the technique called *plique-à-jour*, "windows" of translucent enamel are created in a pierced metal form. A sheet of mica can be used to support the enamel when firing such items.

Pumice powder
A pumice and water paste is used to polish enamel and metal after firing.

Resists
Stopping-out varnish can be painted on to areas of metal to be protected during etching. PnP blue acetate film produces a photographic resist.

Sheet metal
Copper and silver sheets come in various thicknesses and sections. Silver should be at least .925 (Sterling) quality. Avoid beryllium-containing copper.

Solder
Hard (4N, "IT" grade) silver solder should be used prior to enamelling.

Washing soda crystals
Use a soda solution to neutralize acids.

Water
In hard-water areas use bottled water or rainwater, as limescale and additives can impair the clarity of enamels and the finished result.

Wire
Copper, fine silver and fine gold wire are available in rectangular section, pre-annealed, for cloisonné.

The main piece of equipment needed for enamelling is a domestic-sized gas or electric kiln. This and other specialist items are available from enamellers' and jewellers' suppliers.

Enamelling Equipment

Artist's brushes
Pure sable paintbrushes are the traditional tools for applying wet enamel.

Brass brush
Use a suede or other brass brush to clean metal after pickling.

Diamond-impregnated paper
This is a cleaner and faster abrasive than carborundum, the traditional abrasive for enamel, and is invaluable for concave surfaces.

Doming block, swage block, mandrel and punches
These blocks of steel, brass or hardwood are used to shape metal. Use a hammer with steel and brass blocks and a mallet with wood.

Felt polishing mop
Impregnated with pumice powder and water, a felt mop is used to polish fired enamel, either by hand or connected to an electric polishing motor.

Files
Use hand files to remove burrs after cutting metal. Diamond files can be used with water to abrade fired enamel.

Glass fibre brush
This will not scratch metal and can be used to clean enamel. Avoid contact with the hands.

Kiln
Electric kilns take longer to heat up to firing temperature than gas-fired kilns but are comparatively inexpensive. A regulator (thermostat) is needed to

prevent overheating and a pyrometer gives an accurate temperature reading. Use ready-made firing supports or make them from stainless-steel mesh.

Pestle and mortar
Use only vitrified porcelain to grind and wash enamels.

Quills
Goose quills, from calligraphers' suppliers, are used to apply wet enamel.

Rolling mill
Use to impress textured designs on sheet silver for *champlevé* enamel.

Sieves (strainers)
Use to apply dry enamel. Match the size of the mesh to that of the ground enamel fragments.

Soldering equipment
You need solder, charcoal, a gas blowtorch and borax-based flux (auflux).

Tongs and tweezers
Brass or plastic tongs or tweezers must be used to move metal in and out of pickle or etchants.

Enamelling involves high temperatures and hazardous substances. Work in a well-ventilated place, wear protective clothing, follow all manufacturers' instructions and turn off the kiln when not needed.

Enamelling Techniques

Preparation of Metal

Metal must be degreased and de-oxidized (pickled) before enamelling. To make it more malleable, anneal it by heating with a blowtorch to cherry-red. Allow it to return to black then quench in cold water and pickle to remove oxidation.

1 To degrease, abrade metal with emery paper. Treat copper by placing in a general pickle solution (a 10 per cent solution of sulphuric acid, safety pickle or alum).

2 Cover sterling or Britannia silver in neat nitric acid and swill gently until the metal appears white. (Fine silver does not need de-oxidizing.)

3 Brighten all metals with a brass brush and washing-up liquid (dishwashing) solution. Dry on a clean cotton cloth, taking care not to touch the area to be enamelled with your fingers.

Soldering

When designing a piece, aim to have as little soldering as possible under enamelling, to avoid the enamel discolouring or bubbling. During soldering, support the work with binding wire or tweezers if necessary, so that the sections do not move while you work.

1 Apply borax-based flux (auflux) to the joint. Cut a length of solder into small pieces and apply them to the joint using a brush laden with flux.

2 Play a flame over the whole piece to dry the flux without letting it bubble. When it is crystalline, direct the flame on the joint to heat both sides evenly until the solder melts.

3 Cool the piece then immerse in general pickle solution to remove fire stain and flux. Rinse the metal under running water, dry and remove any excess solder using a file.

Acid Etching

After metal has been pickled and brightened, the surface can be etched ready to take enamel. Wear protective gloves and goggles when working with etchants, and use only brass or plastic tweezers.

1 To protect the back and edges of the prepared metal from the etchant, paint on three coats of stopping-out varnish. Leave to dry.

2 Paint the design on the front in varnish. The acid will etch away any areas that are not covered by varnish. Alternatively, cover the whole surface then remove the varnish from areas to be etched using a fine steel point.

3 Place the piece in a solution of 1 part neat nitric acid to 3 parts cold water in an open plastic container. Stroke away bubbles using a feather. Remove the piece when the required depth of etching is achieved (not more than one-third of the thickness of the metal).

4 Rinse the metal under running water, using a glass fibre brush to clean off the etchant. Remove any remaining varnish with brush cleaner and brighten the surface by cleaning with a brass brush and washing-up liquid (liquid soap) solution.

Photo-etching

Instead of painting the design on the metal, you can create a resist photographically. Draw a high-contrast black and white design, twice final size, with all lines at least 0.7mm/0.03in thick. (The black areas represent the metal and the white the enamelled areas.) Reduce the design to actual size on a photocopier.

Photocopy the reduced image at high contrast on a sheet of PnP blue acetate film, emulsion side up. Iron the resist on to the prepared metal, using a cotton/dry iron setting, to fix the image. Paint the back and edges of the piece with stopping-out varnish and etch with nitric acid as above.

Preparing Enamel

Intricate designs and curved surfaces usually require the enamel to be more finely ground than large, flat pieces. To start, break up enamel nuggets by wrapping them in a cotton cloth and hitting with a hammer.

1 In a clean mortar, cover a small piece of enamel with purified water and hit it with the pestle until it resembles granulated sugar. Add another piece and repeat until you have enough for your project, adding water to cover if necessary.

2 Hold the pestle upright and grind firmly with a circular action until the enamel feels soft and powdery. Allow to settle, then pour off the water. Rinse until the water runs clear and the enamel is uniform in colour.

Wet Application of Enamel

Pour the rinsed enamel into a palette and keep covered with water. It should be applied in several thin layers rather than one thick one, using a fine artist's brush, goose quill or stainless-steel point.

1 Pour off excess water and tip the palette so the waterline lies across the enamel. Pick up the enamel from just above the water. Apply evenly to the metal, pushing it well into any corners as it will draw back during firing.

2 Draw off any excess water by touching the edge of the metal with a clean cotton cloth. Do not touch the enamel itself as this will impair the finish of the fired surface. Fire the piece as soon as possible.

Dry Application of Enamel

Once the enamel is ground and cleaned, pour off as much water as possible then spread the paste on cooking foil, cover and leave to dry on top of the kiln or a radiator.

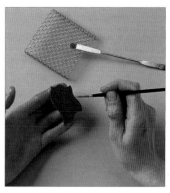

1 Having prepared the metal by degreasing and de-oxidizing it, cover the area to be enamelled with a layer of enamel gum, applying it thinly with a brush. Place it on a sheet of paper.

2 Place the enamel powder in a sieve (strainer), hold it about 5cm/2in above the metal and tap gently. Lift the metal and clean any excess enamel from the sides with a fine brush. Place the piece on a trivet ready for firing.

3 On subsequent layers, if you wish, you can paint a design in the enamel gum, or use a stencil, before sifting the enamel. Alternatively, you can scratch a design in the enamel before firing, using a paintbrush or steel point.

Kiln Firing   The temperature of the kiln should be about 900°C/1,650°F for small items. Place the piece to be fired near the kiln to remove any moisture. Put it in the kiln when the surface looks crystalline and no more steam rises.

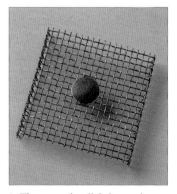

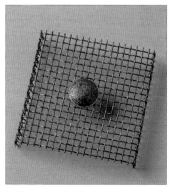

1 The enamel will lighten when it is first placed in the kiln and the metal will oxidize. Later the enamel will darken, still appearing matt (flat) and granular.

2 The enamel will then start to melt and look uneven but shiny.

3 Fully fired enamel looks smooth and shiny. If it pulls away from the edges and discolours, then it is overfired. It is best to underfire the first layers slightly and keep the highest firing for the last.

Finishing   In order to achieve a smooth finish, the enamel needs to be abraded and polished after it has been fired. Depending on the shape of the piece you can use carborundum stones, diamond-impregnated paper or silicon carbide (wet and dry) paper, all of which are readily available in a range of grades.

1 Abrade the enamel using plenty of water and working in all directions. The surface will appear matt, showing up any low spots that may need to be filled with enamel and re-fired. Remove the residue with a glass fibre brush and water. Dry with a cotton cloth and do not touch the surface.

2 Re-fire the piece. When it is cool, place in a general pickle solution. Polish the enamel and metal with a paste of pumice powder and water, using a felt polishing mop either by hand or using a polishing motor running at 900–1200 rpm.

This stylized – and stylish – bird, who carries a heart in his beak, is enamelled on silver to make an attractive lapel pin. In this project, the opaque enamel colours create a matt (flat) surface.

Bird Lapel Pin

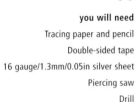

1 Trace the template at the back of the book. Stick the tracing on to the silver sheet using double-sided tape and cut out with a piercing saw. Drill a hole so that you can thread the saw blade through to reach the area between the heart and the bird.

2 Cut and file a piece of silver tube 5mm/¼in long. Solder it in an upright position on to the back, using hard solder. For the pin, cut a 6cm/2½in length of silver wire. Bend with pliers 5mm/¼in in from one end to make a right angle.

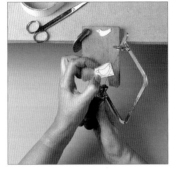

3 Burnish the edges of the bird to provide a "grip" for the enamel to adhere to. Grind and clean the enamels then add a drop of enamel gum to each and water to cover.

4 Degrease the silver using a glass fibre brush and water. Place the bird on a trivet and apply the enamel using a paintbrush or quill.

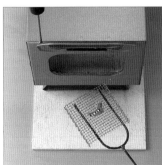

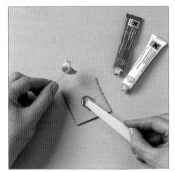

5 Place the bird on top of the kiln to dry, then fire it. Apply two more layers of enamel, firing each layer.

6 Abrade the enamel with diamond-impregnated paper and water. Smooth with damp silicon carbide paper and rinse. Leave the enamel surface matt (flat). Buff the plain silver side of the bird. Glue the pin into the tube using epoxy resin glue.

Make a set of these wonderful buttons in any size, to suit a special garment. They are decorated with a delicate scattering of tiny gold or silver shapes and dabs of brightly coloured enamel.

Multicoloured Buttons

you will need

Drill

20 gauge/0.8mm/0.03in copper discs, size as required

Pumice powder

Toothbrush

Pestle and mortar

Enamel gum

Artist's brushes

Sieve (strainer)

Opaque enamels in various colours

Kiln and firing equipment

Stilts to fit buttons

Scissors

Flat gold or silver *cloisonné* wire

Hole punch

34 gauge/0.16mm/0.006in silver sheet

1 Drill two large holes side by side in the centre of each copper disc.

2 Clean the copper with pumice powder and water, using a toothbrush.

3 Grind and clean the enamels. Lightly apply enamel gum to the back of each button. Using a sieve, apply enamel, using different colours. Leave to dry, then fire in the kiln. Clean the fronts and repeat, supporting the buttons on stilts. Apply a second layer of enamel if necessary.

4 Using scissors, cut tiny squares and triangles off the end of the gold or silver wire. Punch holes in the silver sheet to make tiny circles.

5 Decorate the buttons with the metal shapes, secured with enamel gum. Moisten a little enamel powder with enamel gum to make a paste, then apply to the buttons in small dots using a fine paintbrush.

6 Support the buttons on stilts and fire in the kiln until the enamel dots have fused. When cool, remove oxidation by cleaning with pumice powder and water, using a toothbrush.

Embellish a variety of enamelled silver beads with tiny scraps of gold foil for a really opulent effect. Instead of a chain, you could thread a few beads on to a leather thong or a silk cord.

Gold Foil Beads

you will need

Selection of silver beads

18 gauge/1mm/0.04in silver wire

Scissors

Metal rod of diameter to match holes in beads

Piercing saw

Soldering equipment

Hard solder

Pliers

Glass fibre brush

Trivet

Pestle and mortar

Turquoise transparent enamel

Enamel gum

Fine artist's paintbrush or quill

Kiln and firing equipment

Diamond-impregnated paper

Gold foil

Nail buffer

Necklace chain

Assorted silver and semi-precious beads

Necklace findings and clasp

Easy solder or epoxy resin glue

1 Assemble a collection of silver beads in different shapes and sizes to add interest to the necklace.

2 Cut a length of annealed round silver wire. Spiral it around a metal rod of the same diameter as the holes in the beads.

3 Remove the rod then cut down the length of the spiral, using a piercing saw, to make jump rings. Bend the rings to close the join and solder with hard solder.

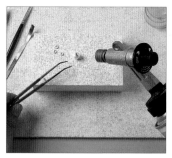

4 Using hard solder, solder a jump ring around the hole at the top and bottom of each bead. Remove the firestain and rinse, then clean the beads with a glass fibre brush and water.

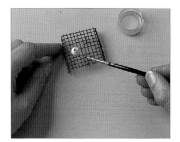

5 Cut and bend a piece of wire up from the trivet and place a bead on it to hold it during enamelling. Grind and clean the enamel then add a few drops of enamel gum and water to cover. Using the wet enamel as dry as possible, apply it to the bead with a fine paintbrush or quill. Dry out the enamelled beads on top of the kiln.

6 Fire the beads in the kiln. Repeat with two more layers of enamel, firing each layer. Abrade the enamel smooth with diamond-impregnated paper and water. Rinse.

7 Cut up small pieces of gold foil into geometric shapes with a pair of sharp scissors. Now, using a fine paintbrush dipped in a little enamel gum, attach these pieces of foil to some of the enamelled beads. Dry on top of the kiln and then fire.

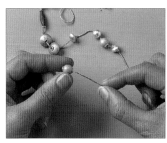

8 Polish the silver edges of the beads with a nail buffer. Thread on to the chain, mixing the enamelled beads with plain silver and semi-precious beads.

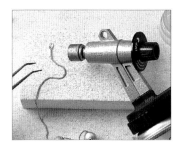

9 Attach the findings to the chain using easy solder. Solder or glue on the clasp. The clasp can be glued if using a leather thong or silk cord.

The subtle etched design resembling snakeskin on this handsome ring is enamelled in two shades of grey. Engrave a matching design around the side. The dimensions given here will make a medium to large ring.

Reptilian Ring

you will need

Half-round jeweller's pliers

8.5mm x 58mm/³/₈in x 2¹/₄in strip of 12 gauge/2mm/0.08in silver, for the ring

Soldering equipment

Hard solder

General pickle solution

Ring mandrel

Mallet

File

Emery paper

Graver

17mm/²/₃in diameter circle of 18 gauge/1mm/0.04in silver, for the domed top

Doming block

Doming punch

Drill

2mm/³/₃₂in x 6cm/2¹/₂in strip of 14 gauge/1.6mm/0.06in silver, for the bezel

2cm/³/₄in diameter circle of 18 gauge/1mm/0.04in silver, for the base

4mm/³/₁₆in square of 22 gauge/ 0.6mm/0.025in silver

14BA ³/₁₆th cheesehead brass screw and matching nut

Stopping-out varnish

Fine artist's paintbrush or quill

Nitric acid

Glass fibre brush

Brush cleaner

Brass brush

Washing-up liquid (liquid soap)

Easy solder

Pumice powder

Toothbrush

Pestle and mortar

Transparent enamels: mid-grey and dark grey

Kiln and firing equipment

Carborundum stone or diamond file

Silicon carbide (wet and dry) paper

Epoxy resin glue

1 Using half-round-nosed pliers, bend the strip of 12 gauge silver into a ring smaller than the finger size. Solder the joint, using hard solder. Pickle and rinse.

2 Check that the ring is circular by placing it on the mandrel and correcting it with a mallet. File, then sandpaper inside and out.

3 File the sides parallel. Scribe a light centre guideline around the outside. With the joint at the top, file a taper on both sides from a width of 8.5mm/⅜in at the bottom to 4mm/³⁄₁₆in at the top. Engrave a reptilian design around the outside, using a graver, or etch with acid.

4 For the top, place the annealed 17mm/²⁄₃in silver circle in the doming block. Using a doming punch and a mallet, tap into a hemispherical shape.

5 Mark the centre of the domed top and drill a small hole to take the decorative brass screw.

6 Using the half-round-nosed pliers, bend the strip of 14 gauge silver into a collar, or bezel, so that it will fit snugly around the base of the domed top. Now solder the joint with hard solder. Check that the shape of the bezel is a circle on the ring mandrel, as described in step 2.

7 Solder the 2cm/¾in circle of silver to the bezel with hard solder to make the base. File the edge of the circle flush with the bezel, then file both to create an angled profile. Drill a 1mm hole through the centre of the 4mm/³⁄₁₆in silver square, then dome it to match the profile of the domed top. Thread the brass screw through the hole from the top and secure with hard solder underneath. File the top of the screw to make a decorative feature. ▶

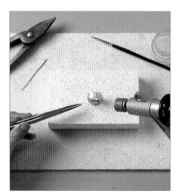

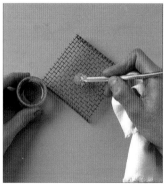

8 Clean and degrease the silver. Apply stopping-out varnish to the back, edges and hole of the domed top. Leave to dry, then paint a reptilian design in varnish on the front. Place in nitric acid diluted with 3 parts water for 3–3½ hours to etch the design. Rinse with water and a glass fibre brush and remove any remaining varnish with brush cleaner. Brighten the top using a brass brush and washing-up liquid solution.

9 Solder the bezel to the narrowest point of the ring strip at the joint, using easy solder. File and sand then apply pumice powder with a tooth-brush. Brighten the silver with a glass fibre brush and washing-up liquid solution.

10 Grind and clean the enamels. Wet-apply the mid-grey enamel to the entire top surface, checking that it does not run into the hole. Fire in the kiln and leave to cool. On the next three to four layers, emphasize the etched recesses with dark-grey enamel to suggest scales. Use mid-grey for the rest of the design.

11 Use a carborundum stone or dia-mond file and silicon carbide paper to abrade the enamel. Use a glass fibre brush to rinse under running water, then fire for the final time. When cool, scrub with a paste of pumice powder and a toothbrush. Thread the decorative brass screw through the central hole of the dome and secure using the 14BA nut. Glue into the bezel using epoxy resin glue.

Wet-applying enamel on round objects is easier if it is ground very finely and you control the amount of water carefully. For a frosted finish, place the beads in matting salts for 2–3 minutes before pickling.

Striped Necklace

●●●

you will need
Dividers
50cm/20in length of thick-walled, silver joint tubing, 4mm/³/₁₆in diameter
Square or triangular needle file or lathe
Piercing saw with fine blade
Tube cutter or pin vice
File
Silicon carbide (wet and dry) paper
Ball fraize
Copper or silver wire
Brass brush
Washing-up liquid (liquid soap)
Pestle and mortar
Transparent enamels
Stainless steel wire
Fine artist's paintbrush or quill
Clean cotton cloth
Kiln and firing equipment
Diamond file or carborundum stone
General pickle solution
Nylon thread and beading needle or fine silver chain
Co-ordinating beads (optional)
Necklace clasp

1 Using dividers, mark unequal stripes at random along the silver tubing.

2 Using a needle file, carefully make straight-sided grooves around the circumference of the tubing to a depth of 0.3mm. Try to keep them as even in depth as possible. Alternatively, turn the grooves on a lathe.

3 Using a piercing saw, carefully cut off unequal lengths of silver tubing between the recesses to make the actual beads. ▶

4 File the ends of each bead and smooth with silicon carbide paper. Countersink the central hole of each bead using a ball fraize.

5 Temporarily thread several beads on to a loop of wire and scrub with a brass brush and washing-up liquid solution.

6 Grind the enamels very finely. Make several stainless-steel wire spirals to hold each bead firmly, as shown. Wet-apply the enamel, using a fine artist's paintbrush or quill. Draw off excess water with a clean cloth before firing.

7 Keeping each bead on its wire spiral, fire in the kiln and leave to cool, still on the wire. Apply further layers of the same colour until each recess is full. Fire between each layer of enamel.

8 Thread each bead on a cranked length of stainless steel. Abrade each bead and smooth with silicon carbide paper, rotating the wired bead. Temporarily thread several beads on to a length of copper or silver wire. Rinse before and after pickling.

9 String the enamelled beads, perhaps interspersing them with coordinating beads. Alternatively, thread them on their own on to a fine silver chain. Attach a clasp.

Create your own design for these earrings, using transparent enamels in pale, clear colours. The holes should be large enough to allow the light to shine through but small enough to hold the wet enamel.

Plique-à-jour Earrings

●●●

you will need
Pencil and paper
16 gauge/1.2mm/0.05in silver sheet
Piercing saw
Drill
Tweezers
Brass brush
Washing-up liquid (liquid soap)
Pestle and mortar
Transparent enamels in pale colours
Fine artist's paintbrush
Trivet
Kiln and firing equipment
Sheet of mica (optional)
Diamond-impregnated paper
Pumice powder
Jeweller's rouge
Earring wires

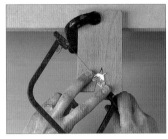

1 Draw your design on paper and attach it to the silver sheet. Using a piercing saw, cut out the shapes. Drill holes where the enamel will appear, then insert the saw into each hole and cut out. Use the saw to smooth the edges from front and back.

2 Shape the silver with a pair of tweezers. Clean the silver with a brass brush and washing-up liquid solution. Grind and wash the transparent enamels.

3 Using a fine paintbrush, apply the wet enamel into the spaces in the earrings. Practise getting the right consistency – if the enamel is too wet, it will fall through the holes.

4 Fire while the enamel is still damp. Beginners may find it easier to fire on a sheet of mica. Remove from the kiln as soon as the enamel begins to melt. Refill the holes if the enamel has pulled to the side, and re-fire.

5 When the holes are completely filled, abrade the earrings with diamond-impregnated paper. Rinse and fire again. Polish with pumice powder and water, then jeweller's rouge. Attach the earring wires.

A central band of enamel with a simple photo-etched design makes an elegant decoration for this silver ring. You can omit the final firing if you would prefer a matt (flat) finish to the enamel.

Banded Ring

you will need
Silver ring blank
PnP blue acetate film and iron
Ring clamp
File
Emery paper
Pliers
Binding wire
Soldering equipment
Hard solder
General pickle solution
Ring mandrel
Wooden or hide mallet
Nitric acid
Brass brush
Washing-up liquid (liquid soap)
Pestle and mortar
Transparent enamels
Enamel gum
Fine artist's paintbrush
or quill
Kiln and firing equipment
Diamond-impregnated paper
Pumice powder or felt
polishing mop

1 Photocopy the template provided at the back of the book to produce a high contrast black-and-white design for photo-etching on to the ring blank (see page 365). Place the ring blank in a clamp and shorten it to the required finger size by filing the ends. Smooth the sides with a file and then emery paper.

2 Using a pair of pliers, carefully bend in the ends to form a ring. The shape doesn't need to be perfectly round at this stage. Now file the ends of the ring so that they will meet exactly and make a good joint.

3 Twist binding wire around the ring. Solder the joint with hard solder, then quench in cold water and dry. Remove the wire, then pickle the ring.

4 File off the excess solder. Place the ring on a ring mandrel and tap with a mallet until it is perfectly round. Remove firestain by placing the ring in nitric acid, and then rinse. Now, using a brass brush, brush the silver with water and washing-up liquid solution until it is shiny.

5 Grind and clean the enamels, then add a drop of enamel gum and water to cover. Apply carefully to the etched band using either a fine paintbrush or a quill. Leave the enamel to dry, then fire in the kiln. Now leave to cool.

6 Using medium-grade diamond-impregnated paper and water, abrade the enamel until you expose the silver design. Rinse the ring and apply more enamel to any shiny areas of the design then repeat the firing and abrading. Polish with fine-grade diamond-impregnated paper, rinse then fire again to glaze the surface if you wish. Leave to cool then pickle, rinse and polish the ring.

Choose transparent enamels in watery colours for these fish, set against a deep blue sea. The photo-etched design needs to be reversed for the second blank so that the cufflinks make a symmetrical pair.

Fishy Cufflinks

⬤⬤⬤⬤

you will need

Silver cufflink blanks to fit the template
or 17 gauge/1.1mm/0.045in
silver sheet

PnP blue acetate film and iron

Piercing saw

Ring clamp

File

Emery stick (board)

Wooden doming block

Wooden doming punch

Mallet

Nitric acid

Brass brush

Washing-up liquid (liquid soap)

Pestle and mortar

Transparent enamels

Enamel gum

Fine artist's paintbrush or quill

Trivet

Kiln and firing equipment

Diamond-impregnated paper

Emery paper

Soldering equipment

Easy solder

Cufflink findings

General pickle solution

Pumice powder or felt polishing mop
(optional)

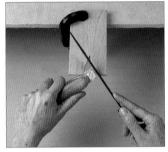

1 Photocopy the template at the back of the book to produce a high contrast black-and-white design. This needs to be photo-etched on to the cufflink blanks or silver sheet (see page 365). Cut out the cufflink shapes with a piercing saw, place each one in a clamp and file the edges straight. Polish the edges with a fine emery stick.

2 Place each cufflink in the doming block. Tap the silver with a doming punch and mallet to create the desired domed shape.

3 De-oxidize the silver by placing each piece in nitric acid for a few minutes and then rinsing in cold water. Using a brass brush, scrub with washing-up liquid solution until the metal is shiny.

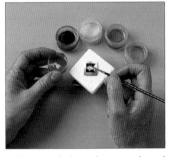

4 Grind and clean the enamels and add a drop of enamel gum to each. Apply the wet enamels to the design, using a paintbrush. Do not mix the colours. Leave to dry, then fire in the kiln until molten. Leave to cool.

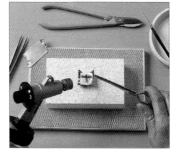

5 Using a medium-grade diamond-impregnated paper and some water, abrade the enamel to expose the silver design, and then rinse. Apply more enamel and repeat. Polish with fine-grade paper, then fire again. Leave to cool. Remove the oxidation with emery paper.

6 Melt easy solder on to the foot of each finding and solder to the back of the cufflink. Cool, then pickle and polish the cufflinks.

The design for these jolly earrings is transferred to a pair of silver blanks using the photo-etching technique. Remember to apply it to the second earring in reverse so that the finished pieces are symmetrical.

Stargazer Earrings

you will need

Silver earring blanks, to fit the template, or 17 gauge/1.1mm/0.045in silver sheet

PnP blue acetate film and iron

Piercing saw

Ring clamp

File

Fine emery stick (board)

Masking tape

Centre punch

Drill

Wooden doming block

Wooden doming punch

Mallet

Nitric acid

Brass brush

Washing-up liquid (liquid soap)

Pestle and mortar

Transparent enamels

Enamel gum

Fine artist's paintbrush or quill

Trivet

Kiln and firing equipment

Diamond-impregnated paper

Emery paper

General pickle solution

Pumice powder or felt polishing mop (optional)

Earring wires

Pliers

◀ **1** Photocopy the template provided at the back of the book to produce a high contrast black-and-white design the size of the finished earrings. This design needs to be photo-etched on to the earring blanks or silver sheet (see page 365). Now cut out the earring shapes with a piercing saw, place each earring in a clamp and file the edges straight.

2 Polish the edges of the earrings with a fine emery stick to remove any scratch marks left after filing.

3 Secure each earring in turn on your work surface with masking tape. Centre punch and drill a hole in the top edge for the wires.

4 Place each earring in the doming block. Tap the silver with a doming punch and mallet to create the desired domed shape.

5 De-oxidize the earrings by placing them in nitric acid for a few minutes, then rinsing in cold water. Using a brass brush, brush with washing-up liquid solution until shiny. Hold by the edges only.

6 Grind and clean the enamels, then add a drop of enamel gum and water to cover. Apply the wet enamels, using a paintbrush or quill. Take care not to mix the colours.

7 Leave the earrings to dry, then fire in the kiln until the enamel is molten. Leave to cool. Apply further layers of enamel and fire each time until the cells of the design appear full.

8 Using medium-grade diamond-impregnated paper and water, abrade the enamel until you expose the silver design. Apply more enamel to any shiny areas, then repeat the firing, abrading and rinsing. Refire to glaze the surface.

9 Leave to cool. Abrade the back of the earrings with emery paper, and then place in pickle solution to remove oxidation.

10 Polish both sides of the earrings if desired. Carefully open the ear wires with the jewellery pliers and insert through the drilled holes. Squeeze the wires gently together to close.

This jaunty character is created by photo-etching the design on to a square brooch, leaving a generous frame of silver, then filling the etching with enamel. Follow the colours shown here or choose your own.

Pet Brooch

you will need

Silver brooch blank, to fit the template, or 17 gauge/ 1.1mm/0.045in silver sheet

PnP blue acetate film and iron

Piercing saw

Ring clamp

File

Fine emery stick (board)

Wooden doming block

Wooden doming punch

Mallet

Nitric acid

Brass brush

Washing-up liquid (liquid soap)

Pestle and mortar

Transparent enamels

Enamel gum

Fine artist's paintbrush or quill

Trivet

Kiln and firing equipment

Diamond-impregnated paper

Emery paper

Soldering equipment

Brooch catch, joint and pin

Easy solder

Pickle solution

Toothbrush

Pumice powder

Parallel (channel-type) pliers

◀ **1** Photocopy the template at the back of the book. The design needs to be photo-etched on to the brooch blank or silver sheet (see page 365) and the template should be copied at the actual size of the finished brooch. If you are using sheet silver, cut out the brooch shape with a piercing saw, place the silver in a clamp and file the edges straight.

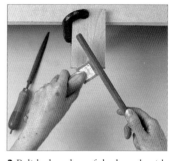

2 Polish the edges of the brooch with a fine emery stick to remove any scratch marks left by the file.

3 Place the annealed brooch blank in the doming block. Tap lightly with the punch and mallet until the piece is slightly domed.

4 De-oxidize the silver by placing in nitric acid for a few minutes then rinsing in cold water. Using a brass brush, brush with water and washing-up liquid until shiny. Hold by the edges only.

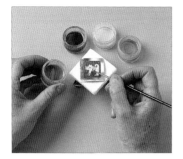

5 Grind and clean the enamels, then add a drop of enamel gum and water to cover. Apply the wet enamels using a paintbrush or quill. Leave to dry on top of the kiln. Fire in the kiln until the enamel is molten. Leave to cool. Apply further layers of enamel, firing in between each layer, until the cells appear full.

6 Using medium-grade diamond-impregnated paper and water, abrade the enamel until you expose the silver design. Apply more enamel to any shiny areas, then repeat the firing, abrading and rinsing. Refire to glaze the surface.

7 Leave to cool then remove the oxidation from the back of the brooch with emery paper.

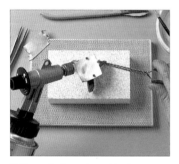

8 Place the brooch upside down on a trivet so that only the edges touch. Solder on the brooch catch and joint with easy solder. Leave to cool, then place in pickle solution. Rinse and clean using a toothbrush and a paste of pumice powder.

9 Polish the brooch if desired. Cut the brooch pin to length and place it in the ball joint. Using parallel pliers, squeeze the joint carefully to hold the pin in place.

Decorate this photo-etched pendant with as many transparent enamel colours as you like, including several shades of green, to evoke the atmosphere of a sunny summer garden in full bloom.

Flower Pendant

●●●●

you will need

Silver pendant blank, to fit the template, or 17 gauge/1.1mm/0.045in silver sheet

PnP blue acetate film and iron

Piercing saw

Ring clamp

File

Emery stick (board)

Wooden doming block

Wooden doming punch

Mallet

Nitric acid

Brass brush

Washing-up liquid (liquid soap)

Pestle and mortar

Transparent enamels

Enamel gum

Fine artist's paintbrush or quill

Trivet

Kiln and firing equipment

Diamond-impregnated paper

Fine-grade emery paper

Small piece of silver wire

Soldering equipment

Easy solder

Tweezers

Pickle solution

Pumice powder or felt polishing mop (optional)

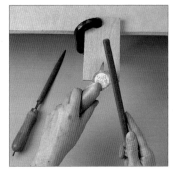

1 Photocopy the template at the back of the book to produce a high contrast black-and-white design. Photo-etch the design on to the silver. Cut out the shape with a piercing saw and file the edges until circular, then smooth with an emery stick.

2 Shape the pendant in a doming block, using a doming punch and mallet. To de-oxidize the silver, place it in nitric acid for a few minutes then rinse with water. Scrub with a brass brush and washing-up liquid solution.

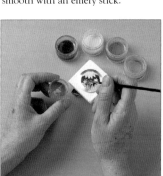

3 Grind and clean the enamels, then add a drop of enamel gum to each and water to cover. Apply the wet enamels using a paintbrush or quill. Take care not to mix the colours. Leave to dry, then fire in the kiln. Leave to cool.

4 Using diamond-impregnated paper and water, abrade the enamel to expose the silver design, then rinse. Apply more enamel to the shiny areas, then repeat. Abrade the enamel and fire again.

5 Leave to cool, then remove the oxidation from the back of the pendant by rubbing with fine-grade emery paper.

6 Bend the wire into a loop and melt easy solder on to the ends. To attach the loop to the pendant, hold it in tweezers against the back of the pendant and heat the ends until they join. Leave to cool, then pickle and polish the pendant as desired.

A delicately textured surface is created by impressing silver with watercolour paper then applying two enamel colours and flux to create a marbled effect. Small shards of silver foil are fired between the layers.

Shield Earrings

⬤⬤⬤⬤⬤

you will need

Scissors

Rough-textured watercolour paper

20 gauge/0.8mm/0.03in silver sheet

Blow torch

General pickle

Rolling mill

Tracing paper and pencil

Double-sided tape

Piercing saw

File

Drill

Burnisher

Brass brush

Washing-up liquid (liquid soap)

Clean cotton cloth

Pestle and mortar

Transparent enamels: mauve and pale yellow-green

Fine artist's paintbrush or quill

Borax-based flux (auflux)

Trivet

Kiln and firing equipment

Craft (utility) knife

Scraps of fine silver foil

Diamond file or carborundum stone

Silicon carbide (wet and dry) paper

Earring wires

Round-nosed (snub-nosed) pliers

2 small domed silver discs

2 frosted beads

2 bead pins

1 Cut a piece of watercolour paper slightly larger than the silver sheet. Anneal the silver and remove the oxidation (see page 364). Place the silver sheet on top of the paper and run them together through the rolling mill, with the rollers tightly clamped down.

2 Trace the templates at the back of the book to create the main body of both earrings. Attach the tracings to the silver with double-sided tape.

3 Using a piercing saw, cut out the shield shapes. File the edges. Drill small holes in two matching diagonally opposed corners of each shield. ▶

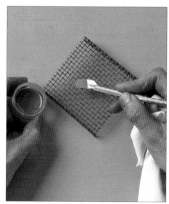

4 Burnish around the sides to raise an edge to contain the enamel. Now scrub the shields with a brass brush and washing-up liquid solution, rinse and dry.

5 Grind and clean the enamels. Using a fine paintbrush or quill, wet-apply the flux and mauve enamel randomly to create a marbled effect. Ensure that they do not run into the drilled holes.

6 Draw off any excess water with a clean cotton cloth. Fire the first layer in the kiln and leave to cool.

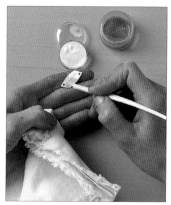

7 Using a craft knife, cut small jagged pieces of silver foil. Moisten the fired enamel with water and apply the pieces of foil in a broken S-shaped line, using a damp paintbrush. Draw off any excess water with a cloth. Wet-apply a spot of flux to one corner of each shield and fire. When the flux has fused, the foil will have adhered to the enamel.

8 When cool, wet-apply the yellow-green enamel over the foil. Apply flux to all other areas and fire. Finally, fire a last layer using flux only.

9 Abrade the fired surface using a diamond file, then rinse and fill in any low spots with more enamel, and re-fire. Remove excess enamel from the edges then finish all sides of the shields with fine-grade silicon carbide paper and rinse. Attach the earring wires to the holes at the top of the earrings and add discs, frosted beads and bead pins to the bottom.

This modern brooch is made in three layers, sandwiching copper between sheets of silver. The design is accentuated by stencil-rolling waves on the silver before enamelling to create a textured effect.

Wave Brooch

●●●●●

you will need

Scissors

Rough-textured watercolour paper

4 x 2.5cm/1 $^1/_2$ x 1in piece of 18 gauge/ 1mm/0.04in silver sheet

Pencil

Craft (utility) knife

Nitric acid

Rolling mill

Graver

Tracing paper

4 x 6cm/1 $^1/_2$ x 2 $^1/_2$ in piece of 18 gauge/1mm/0.04in copper sheet

Piercing saw

Scriber

4 x 6cm/1 $^1/_2$ x 2 $^1/_2$ in piece of 20 gauge/0.8mm/0.03in silver sheet

File

Drill

4 x 14BA $^3/_{16}$ th cheesehead brass bolts and matching nuts

Burnisher

Glass fibre brush

Washing-up liquid (liquid soap)

Pestle and mortar

Transparent enamels: turquoise and blue

Fine artist's paintbrush or quill

Flux

Trivet

Kiln and firing equipment

Carborundum stone or diamond file

Silicon carbide (wet and dry) paper

Pumice powder

Toothbrush

Stopping-out varnish

Brush cleaner

Blowtorch

Soldering equipment

Hard solder

Brooch catch, joint and pin

Pickle solution

1 Cut the watercolour paper larger than the piece of 18 gauge silver sheet. Draw stylized wave shapes on the paper and cut out carefully with a craft knife to make a stencil.

2 Anneal the silver sheet. Remove the firestain by placing it in nitric acid until it whitens. Place the paper stencil on top of the sheet. Run them together through the rolling mill, with the rollers tightly clamped down. Emphasize the waves by engraving a few lines around them with a graver.

3 Trace template 1 from the back of the book on to the copper sheet and cut out with a piercing saw. Using a scriber, draw round this shape on to the 20 gauge silver sheet.

▶

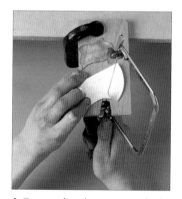

4 Cut out the silver just outside the marked line so that it is slightly larger than the copper shape. Next, trace template 2 on to the rolled, textured silver and cut out. File the edges of all the pieces.

5 Drill a small hole in each corner of the rolled silver to fit the brass screws. Burnish the edges to provide a lip to contain the enamel. Scrub thoroughly with a glass fibre brush and washing-up liquid solution, and then rinse.

6 Grind and clean the enamels. Wet-apply the turquoise enamel, using a paintbrush or quill. Make sure it does not flow into the holes. Fire this layer.

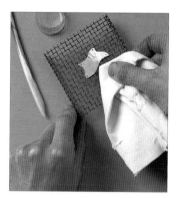

7 For the next three to four layers of enamel, emphasize the wavy lines by shadowing with blue and highlighting them with the flux, applied with a clean, dry cloth.

8 Abrade the fired enamel using a carborundum stone or diamond file. Rinse, fill in low spots and re-fire if necessary. Abrade again, smooth with silicon carbide paper, then scrub with a glass fibre brush under running water. Scrub the back and sides with a paste of pumice powder and water, using a toothbrush.

9 Scrub the copper with pumice powder, then de-grease with a glass fibre brush and washing-up liquid solution. Cover the back and edges with stopping-out varnish and paint a "breezy" border on the front. When the varnish is dry, place the brooch in nitric acid diluted in 3 parts water for about 5 minutes. Rinse, then remove any varnish with brush cleaner. File the edges.

10 Gently shape the silver and copper backing pieces to match the curve of the enamelled piece. Colour the copper iridescent purple by gently heating it with a blowtorch. Drill holes in both pieces to match the enamelled piece.

11 Solder the brooch fittings on to the backing piece using hard solder. Pickle and rinse. Abrade thoroughly with silicon carbide paper, then with a toothbrush and pumice powder that has been mixed to a paste with water.

12 Clean with a glass fibre brush and washing-up liquid solution. Rivet the brooch pin. Assemble the brooch using brass screws and nuts.

In *cloisonné* work, fine wires are laid down in a pattern to make cells for the enamels. The triangles in this design echo the outline of the silver mounts, and small curls of silver wire add a final flourish.

Cloisonné Earrings

●●●●●

you will need

Piercing saw

18 gauge/1mm/0.04in silver sheet

Tracing paper and pencil

24 gauge/0.5mm/0.02in silver sheet

Double-sided tape

File

Fine emery stick (board)

Metal snips

16 gauge/1.2mm/0.05in round silver wire

Pliers

Soldering equipment

Hard solder

Swage block

Wooden doming punch

Mallet

Silver earring posts and backs

Burnisher

Glass fibre brush

Scissors

28 gauge/0.3mm/0.013in silver *cloisonné* wire

Fine artist's paintbrush

Enamel gum

Trivet

Pestle and mortar

Transparent enamels: turquoise, light amber, bright blue

Quill (optional)

Kiln and firing equipment

Diamond-impregnated paper

Silicon carbide (wet and dry) paper

Nail buffer

1 Cut two 16 x 22mm/⅝ x ⅞in rectangles from the thicker silver sheet. To create the earring tops, trace template 1 from the back of the book. Attach the tracing to the thinner silver sheet with double-sided tape. Cut out twice, using a piercing saw.

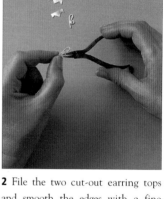

2 File the two cut-out earring tops and smooth the edges with a fine emery stick. Cut two lengths of round silver wire and bend into matching curls with pliers, following the shape of template 2.

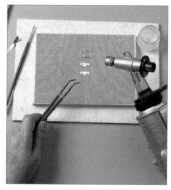

3 Melt hard solder on to the back of the earring tops and the straight part of the wire design.

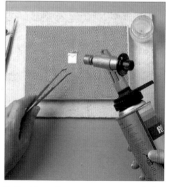

4 Position the earring tops and the wire designs, solder side down, in place on top of the silver rectangles. Flux the metal and rerun the solder with the blowtorch.

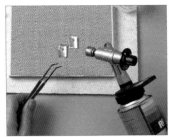

5 Place each earring face down in a swage block. Lay a wooden doming punch along its length and tap with a mallet to create a curved shape.

6 Solder the earposts to the earrings with hard solder. Burnish the edges of the earrings to provide a "grip" for the enamel to adhere to. Clean the metal with a glass fibre brush and water.

7 Cut the required lengths of *cloisonné* wire and lay on each earring in a geometric pattern, using a fine paint-brush dipped in a little enamel gum. Place on a trivet.

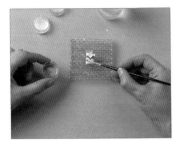

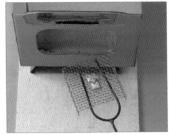

8 Grind and clean the enamels. Add a few drops of enamel gum and water to cover. Using a fine paintbrush or quill, apply the enamel to the cells between the *cloisonné* wires.

9 Allow to dry on top of the kiln, then fire. Apply two more layers of enamel, firing twice more. The enamel should now reach the top of the wire.

10 Abrade the enamel with diamond-impregnated paper and water to expose any covered *cloisonné* wire. Rinse and re-fire. Smooth the silver with silicon carbide paper and finish with a buffer.

In this brooch, the enamel is applied within *cloisonné* cells and is also enclosed within a wire rectangle, which acts as a frame. The piece shows how this traditional technique perfectly suits a modern design.

Cloisonné Brooch

●●●●●

you will need

Metal snips

18 gauge/1mm/0.04in square silver wire

Square needle file

Soldering equipment

General pickle solution

Hard solder

18 gauge/1mm/0.04in silver sheet

Piercing saw

Swage block

Wooden doming punch

Mallet

Brooch catch, joint and pin

Glass fibre brush

28 gauge/0.3mm/0.013in fine silver *cloisonné* wire

Scissors

Fine artist's paintbrush

Enamel gum

Pestle and mortar

Transparent enamels: turquoise, black, grey and light amber

Opaque enamel: bright red

Quill (optional)

Trivet

Kiln and firing equipment

Diamond-impregnated paper

Silicon carbide (wet and dry) paper

Nail buffer

Parallel (channel-type) pliers

1 Cut two 5cm/2in lengths of 18 gauge square silver wire. Holding a square needle file at an angle, file a triangular groove 18mm/³⁄₄in from one end of each wire, three-quarters of the way through the wire's thickness. Anneal the wires (see page 364), and bend to right angles at the filed points. Solder the mitre on each wire, using hard solder.

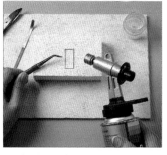

2 File the ends of the two L-shapes at 45 degrees so that they will fit together to make a rectangular frame. Solder together with hard solder.

3 Place the wire rectangle on the silver sheet. Lay pieces of hard solder around the outside of the wire frame and solder it to the silver sheet. Cut off the excess silver sheet but do not file the edges until the enamelling is complete.

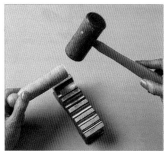

4 Place the piece in a swage block, with the side to be enamelled face down. Using a wooden punch and mallet, create a curved shape.

▶

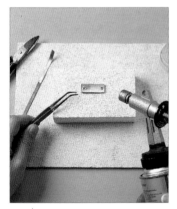

5 Solder the brooch fittings on to the back, using hard solder.

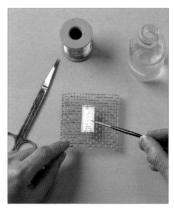

6 Remove firestain and clean the front of the brooch thoroughly with a glass fibre brush and water. Cut the *cloisonné* wire into the required lengths and place on the brooch to make the geometric pattern, using a fine paintbrush dipped in enamel gum.

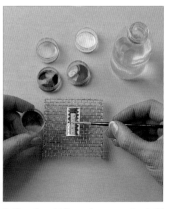

7 Grind and clean the enamels. Add a few drops of enamel gum to each colour, with water to cover. Using a fine artist's paintbrush or a quill, apply the enamel to the cells created by the *cloisonné* wires.

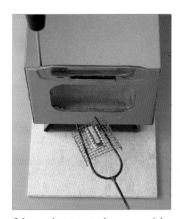

8 Leave the piece to dry on top of the kiln, then fire the enamel. Apply two more layers of enamel, firing each layer. The enamel should now reach the top of the wire.

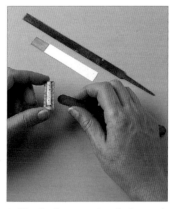

9 Abrade the enamel with diamond-impregnated paper and water until it is even, exposing any *cloisonné* wires that have been covered. Rinse thoroughly with water and a glass fibre brush and re-fire. File the silver around the outer edges of the brooch.

10 Clean and polish the edges of the silver with silicon carbide paper and a nail buffer. Attach the brooch pin using parallel pliers.

The slender elegant shape of this pendant is reminiscent of Art Deco jewellery. A little *cloisonné* detailing has been added within the delicate silver frame, matching its geometric design.

Triangular Pendant

●●●●●

you will need

Tracing paper, pencil and ruler

24 gauge/0.5mm/0.02in silver sheet

Double-sided tape

Piercing saw

Drill

File

Soldering equipment

Hard solder

18 gauge/1mm/0.04in silver sheet

Swage block

Wooden doming punch

Mallet

Doming block

Silver chain

Glass fibre brush

Trivet

Small, sharp scissors

28 gauge/0.3mm/0.013in fine

silver *cloisonné* wire

Fine artist's paintbrush

Enamel gum

Pestle and mortar

Transparent enamels: turquoise, light

amber, bright blue and grey ·

Quill (optional)

Kiln and firing equipment

Diamond-impregnated paper

Silicon carbide (wet and dry) paper

Nail buffer

Silver necklace clasp

1 Trace the template from the back of the book on to tracing paper. Attach the tracing to the 24 gauge silver sheet with double-sided tape.

2 Cut out the outer shape with a piercing saw. Drill holes to allow access for the saw blade and cut out the inner parts of the design. File and smooth the inside edges.

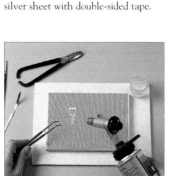

3 Melt some small pieces of hard solder on to the back of the pierced pendant shape.

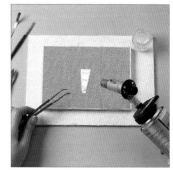

4 Place the pierced shape, solder side down, on the 18 gauge silver sheet. Place hard solder around the outside and solder the pierced shape to the sheet. If any solder runs into the areas that are to be enamelled, it should be removed.

▶

5 Following template 2, saw off the excess silver sheet, leaving a tab at the top for a loop and a circle at the bottom. Do not file the edges. Drill a hole in the centre of both tab and circle.

6 Place the pendant face down in a swage block. Using the doming punch on its side, tap it into a curved shape using a mallet.

7 Cut out a circle of silver sheet fractionally larger than the circle at the bottom of the pendant. Place in a doming block and create a small dome. File the base of the dome flat.

8 Solder the dome on to the circle at the bottom of the pendant with hard solder. Use a piercing saw to make the opening in the tab large enough to take your silver chain. Clean the metal with a glass fibre brush and water. Place on a trivet.

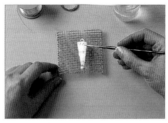

9 Cut the required lengths of *cloisonné* wire and place in the recesses in the pendant to form a geometric pattern, using a fine paintbrush dipped in enamel gum.

10 Grind and clean the enamels. Add a few drops of enamel gum and water to cover. Apply the enamel to the cells, using a fine paintbrush or quill.

11 Leave the enamel to dry on top of the kiln, then fire. Apply two more thin layers of enamel, firing each time.

12 Abrade the enamel with diamond-impregnated paper and water. Clean with a glass fibre brush and water. Re-fire. File the pendant edges. Smooth the silver areas with silicon carbide paper. Finish with a buffer. Thread the chain through the loop. Solder on a clasp and polish.

Fine wire and metal foils can be obtained from craft suppliers as well as hardware stores, but look out for containers such as oil cans and other unusual sources of metal that you can recycle.

Metal and Wirework Materials

Brass shim

Thin brass sheet is available in a range of thicknesses, as flat sheets or in rolls.

Copper wire

Soft copper wire has an attractive, warm colour and is easy to work with. It is available in a wide range of gauges and different tempers (hardnesses).

Epoxy resin glue

Strong, two-part glue can be used to join metal items such as brooch backs.

Galvanized wire

A coating of zinc on steel wire prevents it rusting. Galvanized wire is springy and fairly hard to bend in thicker gauges.

Paints

Use hardwearing enamel paints to add bright, opaque colours to pieces of metal jewellery.

Pipe cleaners and paper clips (fasteners)

These quirky wire products are fun to work with. Both are available in many different colours and styles.

Silver-plated copper wire

This pretty wire is particularly well suited to jewellery making. It can be manipulated easily.

Solder

This is designed to melt and then harden to form a joint between pieces of metal. You should therefore always use a solder that has a lower melting point than the metals you are joining, and various alloys are available.

Tin plate

This is mild sheet steel coated with tin to stop it tarnishing. Biscuit tins are a useful source of recycled tin plate.

Wired tape

This thin, flat plastic tape with a wire core is designed for household and garden use and is available in various colours, such as green for tying plants.

Zinc sheet

Thin zinc sheet has a matt (flat) surface and is fairly soft and easy to cut.

You may already have many of the tools you will need as they are fairly basic. For coiling and shaping wire accurately it is essential to invest in some good pliers.

Metal and Wirework Equipment

Bench vice
Use a vice to clamp pieces of metal to a workbench or table when filing, drilling and hammering edges.

Centre punch
Use a punch or nail (with a hammer) to make decorative holes in metal.

File
A hand file can be used to remove burrs of metal from the edges after cutting out a shape from sheet metal.

Hammer
A medium ball hammer is used with a punch or nail to decorate tin plate, or alone to create a hammered texture.

Pliers
Use round-nosed (snub-nosed) or half-round pliers to coil wire and to bend it into curves, and parallel (channel-type) pliers to flatten coils.

Protective clothes
Heavyweight gloves and a thick work shirt should always be worn when working with metal.

Silicon carbide (wet and dry) paper
Damp fine-grade paper is good for finishing filed metal edges. Wrap the paper around a small wooden block.

Soldering iron
A soldering iron is used to heat solder when joining pieces of metal. The job should always be done on a fireproof soldering mat.

Tin snips
These are very strong shears, designed especially for cutting metal. They are available with either straight or curved blades (the latter type are used to cut curves and circles more easily).

Wire cutters
Always choose wire cutters that have good leverage and are an appropriate size for the wire to be cut. Don't be tempted to use scissors to cut wire as it will ruin their blades.

Neat wire coils and twists will make all the difference to the appearance of your finished pieces. Practise on a few spare lengths of wire to get the feel of your tools and the tension required.

Wirework Techniques

Making Coils The coil is the most commonly used decorative device in wirework. If you are making a symmetrical ornament it will take some practice to create open coils of matching sizes.

1 Using a pair of round-nosed (snub-nosed) pliers, make a small loop at the end of the wire. Hold the loop in the pliers, place your thumb against the wire and draw the wire across it to form a curve. Hold the pliers still and use your thumb to supply the tension needed as you bend the wire down.

2 After the first round has been formed, hold the middle of the coil flat with parallel (channel-type) pliers and continue to pull the wire round in a curve with your other hand. Use your eye to judge the space between the remaining turns of the coil.

3 Begin a closed coil in the same way as an open coil, by making a small loop in the end of the wire.

4 Hold the loop securely with parallel pliers and keep bending the wire around it, adjusting the position of the pliers as you work, until the coil is the required size.

Twisting Soft Wire A hand drill can be used to twist soft wire neatly and quickly. You can use wires with different finishes and twist multiple strands in this way.

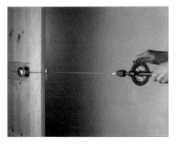

◀ Double the length of wire and loop it around a door handle. Wrap the ends in masking tape and secure them in the chuck of the drill. Keep the wire taut as you rotate the drill. Start slowly so that you can gauge the tension needed and continue until the wire is twisted to the degree required.

Thin sheet metal is not difficult to work with but the edges can be sharp, and tools such as tin snips and soldering irons should be treated with respect. Always wear protective clothing, even for small projects.

Metalwork Techniques

Cutting Metal

The cutting of any sheet metal produces small razor-sharp shards. Collect up these scraps as you go and keep them all together so that you can dispose of them safely when you have finished.

1 To avoid creating jagged edges, never close the blades of the shears completely. Keep the blades in the cut until the line is complete.

2 When cutting a curved shape, don't attempt to turn tin shears or snips: cut as much as you can then turn the metal to continue.

3 Large cans provide an excellent source of tin plate. Use a hacksaw blade to make a cut just below the top so that you are able to insert a blade of the tin snips and then cut around the drum. Cut straight down the side, then around the base, pushing back the panel as you go.

Finishing Edges

The cut edges of a piece of sheet metal are very sharp and should be smoothed immediately with a file to prevent them causing harm to you or anyone else.

1 Small shapes should be firmly clamped in a vice for filing. Smooth all edges using a hand file, moving the file forwards at a right angle to the metal in one light stroke, then lifting it to repeat.

2 After the rough edges have been filed, make them completely smooth by finishing with fine-grade silicon carbide (wet and dry) paper. Dampen the paper and wrap it around a small sanding block.

Adorn patch pockets with these highly original and decorative clips. Galvanized wire has been used here; if you wish, the wire can be sprayed with metallic car paint to change its colour.

Pocket Clips

you will need
Wire cutters
18 gauge/1mm/0.04in and 22 gauge/
0.6mm/0.025in galvanized wire
Ruler or tape measure
Round-nosed (snub-nosed) pliers
Half-round jeweller's pliers

1 Cut a 1m/40in length of 18 gauge galvanized wire. Make a coil at one end with the round-nosed pliers. Bend the wire to make an S-shape, referring to the diagram above. Square off the loop below the coil with half-round pliers.

2 Using half-round pliers, nip in the wire to form one side of the neck, then make a large loop in the wire. From top to bottom the large loop measures 11.5cm/4½in. Make a mirror-image loop and coil on the other side of the large loop, cutting off any excess wire.

3 Fold the structure in half and bend the top of the large loop at both sides to make shoulders. Nip in the bottom of the large loop to make a scallop. Using the 22 gauge wire, bind the coils together and bind the neck for 12mm/½in.

This necklace is great fun to create and is the perfect project to make with children. You could also make matching accessories using clip-on earring backs and headband bases.

Furry Flower Necklace

you will need
Round-nosed (snub-nosed) pliers
Plain, furry and thick, bumpy pipe cleaners
Coloured paper clips (fasteners)
Wired tape
Wire cutters

1 Using round-nosed pliers, make small flowers from plain pipe cleaners. Make the centres of the flowers by straightening paper clips and coiling them into spirals. Bend a pipe cleaner into a five-petalled flower and twist the ends together.

2 Coil a plain pipe cleaner and a striped paper clip into a tight, neat spiral to make the centre of the largest flower. Tie a knot in a length of wired tape and thread it neatly through the flower centre so that the knot sits at the front.

3 Bend a thick, bumpy pipe cleaner to form the necklace. Bind the small flowers to the pipe cleaner necklace with the wired tape, tucking in the tape ends behind the flowers. Bind the large flower to a paper clip and clip on to the pipe cleaner necklace.

4 Form a loop at each end of the pipe cleaner. Attach wired tape to each loop. Coil two paper clips into cones and slide them on to the ends. Bend straightened paper clips into coils and join them together to make two chains. Attach the chains to the ends of the pipe cleaner. Make a "hook-and-eye" fastening from paper clips.

A good way to use up small scraps of tin is to make brooches. These can be simple in construction and made special with some painted decoration. Enamel paints are opaque and look stunning.

Painted Tin Brooch

you will need

30 gauge/0.25mm/0.01in tin sheet
Felt-tipped pen
Protective gloves
Tin snips
Bench vice
File
Silicon carbide (wet and dry) paper
Chinagraph pencil
Enamel paints
Fine paintbrushes
Clear gloss polyurethane varnish
Epoxy resin glue
Brooch fastener

1 To make the brooch front, draw a circle 5cm/2in in diameter on a piece of tin with a marker pen. Now, making sure first that you are wearing protective gloves, cut out the circle using tin snips.

2 Clamp the tin circle in a bench vice and file the edges. Finish off the edges with damp silicon carbide paper so that they are smooth.

3 Draw a motif on one side of the brooch using a chinagraph pencil. Paint around the outline with enamel paint, then fill in the design. Leave the brooch to dry thoroughly.

4 Paint in the background, then add any features on top of the first coat of paint, using a fine paintbrush and enamel paint. Leave to dry. Seal the surface with two coats of clear gloss polyurethane varnish. Leave to dry thoroughly between coats.

5 Mix some epoxy resin glue and use it to stick a brooch fastener on to the back. Let the glue dry thoroughly before wearing the brooch.

Reproduce the delicate texture of a web in glittering copper and silver wire. The resident spider is resplendent in blue and gold and not at all threatening, especially as she has only six legs and a curly tail!

Spider's Web Brooch

you will need

18 gauge/1mm/0.04in copper wire

Ruler

Wire cutters

Round-nosed (snub-nosed) pliers

22 gauge/0.6mm/0.025in silver wire

Self-hardening clay

Modelling tool

Two small glass beads

Brooch pin

Epoxy resin glue

Turquoise acrylic paint

Paintbrush

Clear varnish

Gold powder

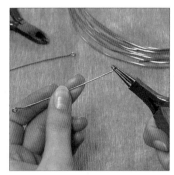

1 Cut four 7.5cm/3in lengths of copper wire. Curl both ends of each piece into a loop using round-nosed pliers.

2 Arrange the pieces to form a star. Wrap the silver wire round the centre. Working outwards in a spiral, twist the silver wire once round each copper wire. Secure and trim.

3 Cut six 6cm/2½in lengths of copper wire. Curl one end of each into a tight loop then bend the rest of the length into the shape of the spider's legs.

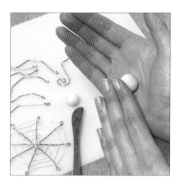

4 Cut a 7.5cm/3in length of wire and bend it into a spiral for the tail. Roll two balls of self-hardening clay for the body and head.

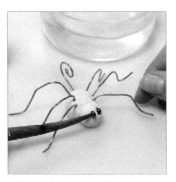

5 Press the two clay balls together, joining securely with the help of the modelling tool. Smooth the surface of the clay with wet fingers or the modelling tool.

6 Insert the looped ends of the wire legs and tail into the spider's body. Press two glass beads into the head to make the eyes.

7 Press the spider's body on to the wire web. Flatten a small piece of clay and attach it to the spider from underneath the web, using the modelling tool to join it securely. Leave the clay to harden.

8 Glue the brooch pin to the back of the spider, and secure the legs and tail with drops of glue. Paint the body and head turquoise and leave to dry. Apply a coat of varnish to seal the paint. Mix gold powder with a little varnish and apply swiftly with a dry brush to leave some of the turquoise paint showing through.

This jewel box is made from a combination of thin zinc sheet, which has a subtle sheen rather like pewter, and brass shim, which is a fairly soft metal used mostly by sculptors.

Tinware Jewel Box

●●●

you will need
Protective gloves
Tin shears and snips
Thin zinc sheet
Cigar box
File
Pencil, stiff card (stock) and
scissors (for templates)
Brass shim
Sheet of chipboard (particle board)
Hammer and nail
Soldering equipment
Solder
Epoxy resin glue

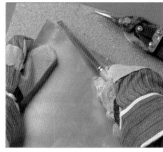

1 Wearing protective gloves, use tin shears to cut a piece of zinc to cover the lid of the cigar box. The zinc should be slightly larger than the box lid, to allow for a rim to cover the edges of the lid. File the rough edges. Draw a diamond and two different-sized hearts on a sheet of stiff card and cut them out.

2 Place the templates on a piece of brass shim and draw around them – six small hearts, one large heart and two diamonds. Draw some small circles freehand. Draw one small heart on a scrap of zinc. Cut out all the shapes and file the edges smooth. Place the hearts and diamonds on the chipboard and stamp dots around the edge of each using a hammer and nail. Do not stamp the circles or the zinc heart.

◀ **3** Cut four strips of shim to make a border around the zinc lid cover. Place all the pieces on a soldering mat and drop a blob of liquid solder in the centre of the circles, small hearts and diamonds. Cover the zinc heart with solder blobs. Add a line of blobs to each piece of the shim border.

4 Turn down a narrow rim around the zinc panel at 90 degrees to fit over the sides of the lid. Glue all the shapes and the borders to the panel.

5 Cut a strip of zinc the width of the box side and long enough to fit all round it. File the edges smooth. Cut circles of shim, decorate each with a blob of solder and glue in place.

6 Glue the zinc strip around the sides of the box. Glue the zinc panel to the top of the lid. Gently tap the edges of the panel to make them flush with the sides of the lid.

Clay and
Shells

Modelling clay is an ideal medium for intricate ornaments such as buttons, earrings and beads. You can roll it, coil it and shape it in fancy moulds, and a host of different surface textures are possible. This chapter also includes ideas for making jewellery using shells, though ideally you should buy these from a craft store, with holes ready drilled in them, rather than taking them from the beach.

Polymer clay is a marvellous modern medium for moulding brightly coloured and detailed jewellery and accessories. Shells have been used throughout history for personal adornment and to beautify objects.

History

Clay

Polymer clay originated in Germany in the late 1930s. It was an accidental biproduct created by the daughter of a doll maker, who used it to make doll's heads and mosaics. The product became widely available in the 1960s when other brands were introduced into the market. Each was a slightly different version of the product with regard to consistency or texture. Each brand introduced its own colour range.

Because polymer clay is a relatively new product the artists who work with it have borrowed techniques from other disciplines, notable the glass cane work technique of millefiori. Though imitating a very skilled art, making canes in polymer clay requires

Above: This mirror was made using a plain wooden picture frame as a base, hardboard and tile adhesive into which shells have been embedded. Once dry the entire surface has been varnished to bring out the natural qualities of the shells.

Left: This box decorated with shells and glitter looks as if it is modelled on a wedding cake. The base is an antique wooden box and the small shells have been precisely positioned.

Right: These polymer clay beads are unique handmade creations that show the skill and artistry of the craftsperson.

attention to detail. The canes are crafted like sticks of rock and the image is sliced from the cane and applied to a central ball of clay. The canes are fused together by rolling to remove any seams, and the resulting bead is hardened by baking it in an oven set at a low temperature.

Shells

Unlike polymer clay, shells have a long history and have been collected for vessels, tools, weapons, personal adornment, and even musical instruments. They appear in the oldest jewellery, shaped into beads or worn as bracelets with their centres ground out. Patterns have been etched into them in all manner of ways. Their greatest use was for mosaics and inlays. with shell grottoes once being an important feature of grand and landscaped gardens. Grottoes were cave-like places in which to ponder on philosophy and poetry. Originally decorated with oyster shells, pumice chips and volcanic ash in Italy, they became works of art with shell marquetry becoming an important feature.

Sophisticated craftworking techniques have been applied to shells including etching, engraving, lapidary and the carving of cameos, with stunningly intricate results. In the 18th century sailor's valentines were very popular.

During Victorian times shellcraft was recommended as a genteel pastime for ladies. Arrangements of shells

Above: These millefiori beads have been individually crafted from canes of polymer clay. The canes are built up in layers to produce a single pattern. Large and complicated patterns make very large canes. As the cane is rolled to a narrow sausage the polymer clay retains the pattern without distortion.

were made and placed under glass domes. As the seaside holiday became an established event a lucrative cottage industry developed, with all manner of knick-knacks made to sell to holiday makers as souvenirs. The craft continues to this day in seaside holiday resorts.

Below: A chandler's rope fashioned into a wreath and decorated with shells is a perfect decoration for a door of a house situated by the sea.

Claycraft and shellcraft are two media that have keen followers, who have raised their craft to a level of art. Beautiful and unique pieces can be created with both media.

Gallery

Shellcraft once had a bad press, associated with tacky seaside trinkets and old-fashioned designs. Today's crafts people appreciate the innate qualities to be found with shells of all kinds and use these natural materials to fashion small- and large-scale inspiring pieces that bring out the best colours and textures of the materials available.

Below: PEOPLE BEADS
These tiny people are made by layering tiny pieces of polymer clay on to a basic bead and incorporating cane work into the costumes. Each is a labour of love.
CYNTHIA TROOP

Polymer clay and modelling clay have huge potential as craft media. The malleability of the material and for polymer clay, the huge range of colours that are available are the best qualities. The unique features of clay have been recognised by several craftspeople, who have each developed their own styles of working.

Right: GROTTO FRAME
This grotto frame has been made using a picture frame covered with tile adhesive. Different coloured shells are embedded in the adhesive.
MARY MAGUIRE

Below: HEART BROOCH AND FLOWER JEWELLERY
Nature, pop art and kitsch culture are the inspiration for this craft artist's work.
LARA BOHNIC

Right: CANE WORK AND
MILLEFIORI BEADS
*Ancient glasswork techniques are the
inspiration behind these millefiori beads.
Long rods of pictures are made and slices
are then taken from the rod and adhered
to a small ball of clay. To remove the
seams between the slices, the beads are
rolled until smooth.*
INGRID PROUDFOOT

Below: MARY'S JEWELLERY
*This set of jewellery is made from shells
recycled from old necklaces. The brooch
and earrings are formed from small
abalone shells with rock crystal pebbles.*
MARY MAGUIRE

Below: CLAY POMANDER
*Modelling clay, unlike polymer clay, has
a porous quality, making it a good choice
for decorative and modern pomanders.
Scented oil can be added to the
pomander and then used to freshen the
contents of a drawer or cupboard.*
PENNY BOYLAN

Choose from self-hardening modelling clay – which does not require firing and can be painted, varnished or gilded once dry – or colourful polymer clay, which is hardened by baking in a domestic oven.

Clay Materials

Bronze powder
This is a fine metallic powder that is available in gold, silver, copper and other colours. Mix the powder with varnish and brush on to produce a gilded effect.

Button backs
Self-cover buttons are useful for making clay buttons.

Clay hardeners
Powdered hardeners can be mixed into modelling clay before the clay is shaped and they harden the clay throughout. Liquid hardeners seal and harden the outside only.

Glass gemstones and beads
Beads for embedding in clay should be flat-backed. If beads are mounted in clay that is to be fired, they must be made of glass.

Glue
PVA (white) glue will be suitable for holding hardened clay, but epoxy resin is stronger. Diluted PVA glue is commonly used as a sealant on modelling clay.

Jewellery wire
Use this fine wire to connect clay pieces for jewellery items such as earrings and necklaces.

Metallic leaf
Both modelling clay and polymer clay can be gilded. Dutch metal leaf, in gold, silver, copper and aluminium, is easier to apply than real gold.

Modelling clay
Clay comes in many brands and qualities. Air-dried modelling clay needs no firing, but you can strengthen some brands by baking or adding hardeners. Follow manufacturer's instructions.

Paint
Artist's acrylics or acrylic craft paints are suitable for decorating modelling clay and can also be applied to polymer clay. Many effects are possible with special paints: metallic or pearlized colour, verdigris and crackle glaze.

Polymer clay
Actually a plastic (polyvinyl chloride), polymer clay is clean to work with, does not shrink and needs only a low-temperature firing. Already coloured, it needs no further decoration except for special effects such as gilding. It is available in many colours, plus translucent and glow-in-the-dark effects.

Varnish
Gloss or matt (flat) varnish specially formulated for polymer clay is available. Acrylic spray varnish is convenient for small projects.

The most important tools required for working with modelling and polymer clay are your hands. Many ordinary items such as knitting needles, dough cutters and knives can be used for shaping clay.

Clay Equipment

Airtight boxes and bags

Polymer clay goes crumbly if exposed to heat and daylight. Wrap it in greaseproof paper before storing it in a box. Spare modelling clay should be kept soft inside a plastic bag – moisten the inside of the bag if necessary.

Baking parchment

A sheet of parchment taped to the work surface gives a smooth surface for modelling. Finished models can also be placed on it for baking.

Brayer

This small roller is used to smooth clay and for applying metal leaf.

Knives

A very sharp slim-bladed craft (utility) knife is needed when working with small pieces of polymer clay, and a surgical tissue blade can cut very thin slices without distorting patterns.

Mirror

Placed behind the work, a mirror helps you to see all round the clay for accurate cutting and shaping.

Modelling tools

Many different shapes are available for shaping and smoothing clay. Dental probes make excellent precision tools for modelling. Cocktail sticks and toothpicks are often useful.

Oven

Polymer clay can be hardened in a domestic oven. Accurate temperature control is important as clay burns easily but is fragile if undercooked.

Paintbrushes

Artist's brushes are needed for applying paints and bronze powders.

Pasta machine

Use this to roll out polymer clay to precise, even thicknesses and to mix colours together. Keep a machine just for use with clay, and wipe it clean when changing colours.

Pastry cutters and moulds

Cake decorating suppliers are a good source of modelling tools. A wheeled pastry cutter can be used to make zigzag edges. Skewers are useful for shaping clay and for holding clay beads during baking.

Plexiglass

This rigid clear plastic makes a smooth modelling surface and a small sheet is used to roll polymer clay canes to reduce their diameter uniformly.

Rolling pin

A vinyl or straight-sided glass roller is best for rolling out clay.

As polymer clay picks up any dirt and dust around, your hands must be scrupulously clean and you should wash them each time you change from one colour to another, to avoid discolouring the clay.

Polymer Clay Techniques

Preparing Polymer Clay

The clay must be kneaded before it is worked. As it is responsive to temperature the warmth of your hands contributes to the conditioning process. Work small amounts, about one-eighth of a block, at a time. Roll the clay into a sausage between your palms then bend it over and roll again, until it is soft and pliable. Try to avoid trapping air bubbles. A pasta machine can be used to knead the clay and to mix colours.

Mixing Colours

Although polymer clay is available in many colours, you can mix more subtle shades yourself. When mixing dark and light colours add tiny bits of the dark clay to the lighter colour to avoid overpowering it.

Rolling out

A pasta machine can be used to produce sheets of uniform thickness, or you can roll the clay out by hand on a smooth clean surface.

To achieve an even thickness throughout the sheet, place two equal-sized pieces of wood, metal or plastic, matching the required depth, on either side of the clay.

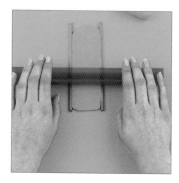

1 Twist together two or more sausages of clay in different colours.

Making Beads

A basic round bead is made by simply rolling a ball of clay between the palms of your hands. You may find that it is quite difficult to make a hole in soft clay without distorting it, so an effective alternative method is to drill the hole after the clay has been baked.

2 Roll the twisted clay into a smooth log then twist, stretch and double over, excluding any air. The clay can be used in this marbled state. Continue to work it to blend colours completely.

1 Make a hole in an unbaked bead using a drilling action with a tapered tool such as a darning needle. When it emerges, remove it and push it through from the other side to neaten the hole.

2 To prevent beads distorting during baking, support them on skewers or wire, suspended across a baking tray.

Clay Cane Work

Clay sheets of different colours can be stacked or rolled together with gentle pressure and then sliced to create a variety of patterns. Derived from glassworking techniques, cane work creates a roll with a design running along its length from which slices can be cut.

Jelly Roll

This technique creates a log that is sliced to create a simple spiral pattern.

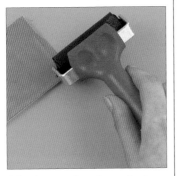

1 Stack two or three sheets of polymer clay together and trim the edges to form a rectangle. Roll a brayer over one of the shorter edges to taper it.

2 Starting at the tapered end, roll up the layers tightly and evenly. Roll the cane to smooth the seam and trim each end flat.

Picture Cane

Simple images can be made into canes. Choose a strong shape and use boldly contrasting colours so that the picture stays clear when the size is reduced.

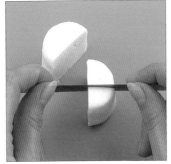

1 Roll a cane of white polymer clay about 3.5cm/1½in in diameter. Cut it in half lengthways using a tissue blade. Curve one half to make the duck's body and cut the other half in two to make two quarters.

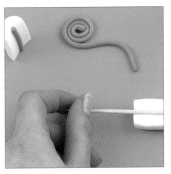

2 Roll one quarter into a round and cut in half again. Make a groove down the middle of one flat side and run a thin sausage of blue clay down it. Groove the other half and sandwich together to make the head and eye.

3 Place the head on the body. Cut a triangular wedge from a 1cm/½in diameter yellow cane and press it against the head to form the bill.

4 Pack the gaps around the duck with wedges of blue clay to make a circular shape and wrap with a thin sheet to hold it together. Roll to consolidate the pieces and surround with a sheet of dark blue. Roll the cane to smooth the join and trim the concave ends.

Flower Cane

Choose colours that contrast strongly to give the design clarity. Slices are best cut using a tissue blade: chill the cane if necessary to avoid distorting the pattern.

Complex Canes

Rolling the canes under a small sheet of plexiglass reduces their size.

1 Roll one cane for the flower centre, five for the petals and two for the leaves, each about 2cm/¾in wide. Wrap the centre cane in a thin sheet of a contrasting colour, and the petals in a different colour. Roll the canes to smooth the seams.

2 Cut the leaf canes lengthways into quarters. Roll out a thin sheet of a new colour. Arrange the canes to form a flower and wrap the bundle in the prepared sheet. Roll the cane to compact it, and trim the ends.

To make canes of different diameters, stop rolling at each size required and cut the cane in half. Reserve one half and continue to roll the other. Different canes can be joined and rolled together to create complex designs.

Metallic Finishes

Polymer clay can be decorated by brushing on metallic powders, or metal leaf can be applied to a sheet of clay before it is shaped.

1 Lay a sheet of Dutch metal leaf, metal side down, over a sheet of clay. Roll over it with a brayer as you lay it down to exclude air bubbles. Rub all over the backing paper then gently and slowly peel it off.

2 For a crackle finish, cover the applied metal leaf with another piece of paper and roll a brayer over the paper until the required amount of cracking is achieved.

3 Any mould can be used to shape polymer clay or impress a texture in the surface. To gild a moulded piece, lightly brush the mould with metallic powder before embossing the clay.

Brighten up a child's coat (or your own) with these friendly spiders. Use self-cover buttons, matching the size to your buttonholes, and snap the fronts on to the backs before you start to decorate them.

Spider Buttons

you will need
Polymer clay: bright green,
black and white
Self-cover metal buttons
Rolling pin
Craft (utility) knife
Self-healing cutting mat
Gloss acrylic varnish
Paintbrush

1 Roll the green clay out thinly and cut out a circle large enough to cover one of the buttons. Mould the clay over the button.

2 Using black clay, roll very thin strands for the legs and press them on to the button. Roll a finer strand for the spider's thread.

3 Roll a pea-sized ball of black clay and press it into the centre of the button for the spider's body.

4 Create eyes from two balls of white clay and two tiny balls of black clay. Bake in a low oven following the clay manufacturer's instructions. Apply two coats of gloss varnish when cool.

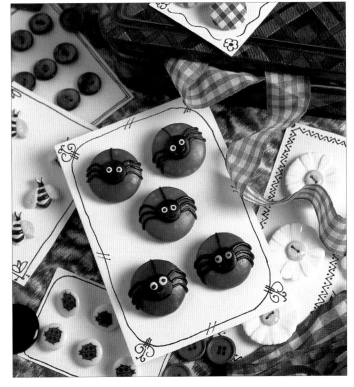

Glow-in-the-dark polymer clay covered with silver leaf is embossed with spiral patterns to create an intriguing effect on this hair slide (barrette). In the dark, a subtle glow emanates from tiny cracks in the silver leaf.

Abstract Hair Clasp

●●●

you will need
½ block glow-in-the-dark polymer clay
Rolling pin
Pencil, thin card (stock) and scissors (for template)
Craft (utility) knife
Silver leaf
Brayer
Old jewellery or buttons
Dark blue bronze powder
Artist's brush
Hair slide (barrette) clip
Varnish
Epoxy resin glue

1 Roll out some polymer clay to a thickness of 3mm/⅛in. Draw the shape required on card, and cut this template out. Place the card on the clay and cut round it with a craft knife.

2 Apply silver leaf to the clay shape. Roll over the backing sheet with a brayer until the leaf has adhered, then gently peel off the backing.

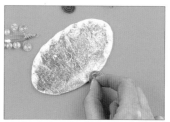

3 Create a regular pattern around the edge of the silvered clay by pressing interestingly shaped jewellery or buttons into it to leave indentations.

4 Fill in the central area with a random pattern applied in the same way as in step 3 but using different shapes if you wish.

5 Lightly brush the surface around the edge with dark blue bronze powder.

◄ **6** Slip a small piece of thin card through the full width of the hair slide clip then place the clay shape on top. The clay will mould itself to the curved shape of the slide but the card will prevent it sagging too much. Bake in this position, following the clay manufacturer's instructions. When cool, varnish the surface and glue the clip on to the back.

Polymer clay simplifies the craft of jewellery-making because stones can simply be pushed into the clay. Metal leaf and powders readily adhere to the surface of unbaked clay to give it a lustrous richness.

Burnished Bronze Necklace

●●●●

you will need

1 block black polymer clay
Rolling pin
Craft (utility) knife
Bronze powders: various colours
Artist's brush
Leaf pastry cutter
Modelling tool
Jewellery wire
Wire cutters
Glass cabochon stones
Varnish
Round-nosed (snub-nosed) pliers
Glass beads
Necklace clasp

1 Roll out a piece of black clay, about 4mm/³⁄₁₆in thick, and cut in half. Dust lines of bronze powders in various colours on to the surface of one piece.

2 Now carefully mark vertical lines between the colours and then cut out leaf shapes in such a way that your vertical lines form the leaf's central veins. Create the smaller veins on the leaves by using a modelling tool.

3 Roll the remaining clay slightly thinner and cut it into five or six 5cm/2in squares. Place a length of jewellery wire centrally on each square and place a cabuchon stone over it. Cut strips 3mm/⅛in wide from the remaining bronzed clay and wrap these round each stone, cutting off the excess.

4 Arrange three leaves to one side of the stone. The wire should consistently project from the same side of the middle leaf on each square, to allow the necklace to hang in a tight-fitting curve when assembled.

5 Press the leaves and stone surround gently but firmly enough to meld them together and to hold the stone securely in place. Cut out the black clay around the shape using a craft knife and smooth along the joins at the sides to obliterate them. Bake following the manufacturer's instructions.

◀ **6** Carefully varnish the bronzed areas and allow to dry. Using round-nosed pliers, make loops in the wire ends and trim off the excess wire. Hook the pieces together and close up the hooks. Attach glass beads at each end of the necklace in the same way to achieve the correct length. Finally, wire on a clasp.

It's hard to believe that this exotic-looking piece of jewellery is made from a piece of plastic pipe covered in polymer clay. Gold leaf and embedded stones help to effect a magical transformation.

Egyptian Bangle

●●●●

you will need

4cm/1½in length of plastic drainpipe

1 block black polymer clay

Rolling pin

Dutch gold leaf

Brayer

Craft (utility) knife and ruler

Self-healing cutting mat

Smoothing tool

Modelling tool

Gemstones

Epoxy resin glue

Acrylic craft paints

Fine artist's brush

Gloss acrylic varnish

1 Roll out a strip of clay large enough to cover the section of plastic pipe. Apply the gold leaf and crackle the surface using a brayer (see page 434).

2 Cut the clay exactly to size and wrap it carefully round the pipe, making sure there are no air bubbles.

3 Join the clay, taking care not to rub off any gold leaf when smoothing over the seam where the ends meet.

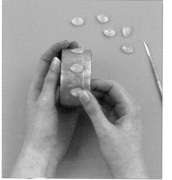

4 Using a modelling tool, mark a faint line around the circumference 1cm/½in from one edge. Measure the circumference, divide the figure by the number of stones you wish to use and mark their positions along the line. Press the stones into the clay.

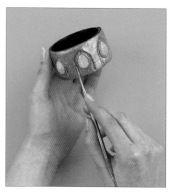

5 Draw a line round each stone then impress an arch around it.

6 Draw a line around the bangle joining the tops of the arches.

7 Erch a narrow petal shape between the arches all round the bangle to form the centre of the stylized flower.

8 Draw a pointed petal on either side of the central one then add smaller petals in between.

9 Carefully remove the stones and bake the bangle following the clay manufacturer's instructions. When cool, glue the stones back in place.

10 Paint the flowers and background sections in colours of your choice. Finish with several coats of gloss varnish to protect the paint and gilding.

The tiers of these glamorous but lightweight earrings swing when you move and glisten as they catch the light. Gold leaf scrolls, gemstones and droplet beads all contribute to the opulent effect.

Shimmering Earrings

you will need

Jewellery wire

Ruler

Wire cutters

Round-nosed (snub-nosed) pliers

½ block black polymer clay

Rolling pin

Craft (utility) knife

Dutch gold leaf

Brayer

Gemstones: oval 1cm/½in long;

rectangular 1.5cm/⅝in long;

round 5mm/¼in diameter

Dressmaker's pins

Palette knife (metal spatula)

Eyelet or similarly shaped object

Smoothing tool

Gloss acrylic varnish

Paintbrush

Large clip-on earring backs

Epoxy resin glue

10 droplet beads

1 Cut 12 x 2cm/¾in wire lengths; form a loop in one end of each. Cut two 3cm/1¼in lengths and two 6cm/2½in; loop all ends. Roll out the clay, cut in two and gild one half. Cut backing sheets from ungilded clay: two 3cm/1¼in squares (for the top tiers); two 4 x 3cm/1½ x 1¼in oblongs (central tiers); two 1.5cm/⅝in squares (bottom tiers).

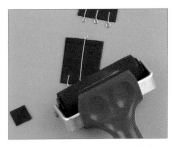

2 Lay three short wires along the bottom of each middle-sized backing sheet and press them in with the brayer. Lay a long wire down the centre of each large backing sheet with a short, single-hooked wire on either side, and press in. Lay the remaining short, single-looped wires one on each of the small backing sheets and press in.

3 Press an oval stone on to each of the middle-sized backing sheets. Cut two strips 3mm/⅛in wide from the gilded clay and wrap securely round each stone, trimming off any excess. Add more strips to decorate.

4 Cut two 3cm/1¼in lengths of gilded clay. Pinch both ends to taper, shape into scrolls and press on to the mid-sized backing sheets to cover the wires. Cut two small squares of gilded clay, cut in half diagonally and place above the scrolls. Press decorative marks and lines around the border with a pin. Trim off the excess backing sheet. ▶

5 Press the square stones centrally on the two large backing sheets. Cut a 1.5cm/⅝in square and a 1cm/½in square from gilded clay, then cut across to make four triangles. Press a large triangle above each stone and a small one beneath. Cut thin strips of gilded clay to fit each side of the stones.

6 Using a palette knife, press in all the pieces to make a tight fit round the stones (avoid distorting the shapes). Cut two thin strips 4.5cm/1¾in long from the gilded clay, curl them into scrolls and place one under each bottom triangle. Use an eyelet to stamp a circular design on the top triangles.

7 Make six tiny beads, roll them in gold leaf and use them to decorate the tops of the middle tiers. Trim off the excess backing sheet.

8 Place one of the remaining stones on each of the small backing squares. Cut two strips of gilded clay 3cm/1¼in long and wrap them round the stones. Trim off the excess backing sheet.

9 Using a smoothing tool or your finger go round the edges of each piece to make sure all the surfaces are melded together. Bake following the manufacturer's instructions and allow to cool.

10 Varnish all the gold leaf surfaces and allow to dry. Glue the clip-on earring backs to the backs of the first tier.

11 Join all the tiers of the earrings together, using round-nosed pliers to close up the wire hooks.

12 Hang droplet beads from the free hooks, closing up the hooks. The droplets at the bottom can be slightly bigger than the others.

Once you have mastered the art of making millefiori canes (see pages 427–8), you can use them in some exciting ways. Here, slices from different canes are applied to partially baked polymer clay beads.

Composite Beads

●●●●●

you will need

1 block white polymer clay

Rolling pin

Craft (utility) knife

Tissue blade

¼ block yellow polymer clay

1 block green polymer clay

Plexiglass

½ block fluorescent orange polymer clay

¼ block pale blue polymer clay

6cm/2½in of 3cm/1in diameter picture cane (see Polymer Clay Techniques)

20cm/8in flower cane

½ block coral polymer clay

Polymer clay beads in various shapes (see Polymer Clay Techniques)

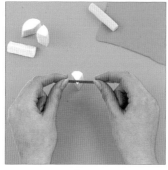

1 Roll a 3cm/1¼in diameter log of white clay. Cut it into five wedges from the centre and slice off the sharp angle of each wedge. Roll out a 6cm/2½in yellow cane and a flat sheet of green clay.

2 Arrange the white triangular wedges, separated by 3mm/⅛in slivers of green, around the central yellow cane to form a flower. Roll, using a sheet of Plexiglass to smooth.

3 Make a jelly roll with 4 x 10cm/1½ x 4in strips of yellow and fluorescent orange clay (see page 427). Wrap it in a sheet of pale blue clay about 1mm/¹⁄₁₆in thick.

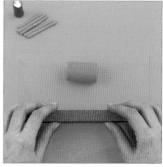

4 Reduce the picture cane to a diameter of 1cm/½in and the flower cane and jelly roll to about 5mm/¼in (see page 427–8). Reserve the trimmings to make beads. Cut the jelly roll into 7.5cm/3in lengths. Cut a 7.5cm/3in length from the duck cane. ▶

5 Cut the flower cane into four lengths of 7.5cm/3in. Arrange them in a cross pattern around the picture cane, interspersed with four lengths of jelly roll cane.

6 Roll the assembled canes carefully between your hands to meld them together then wrap in a 3mm/⅛in thick sheet of green clay.

7 Cut the cane in half using a tissue blade, rocking while you cut to avoid distorting the picture. Wrap one of the halves in a 3mm/⅛in thick sheet of coral clay, cut off the surplus and roll under Plexiglass to smooth the sides.

8 Make up several compilation canes then reduce them further to different sizes. Shave off thin slices to cover the surface of previously prepared disc beads and roll them smooth. It is a good idea to make the canes and the beads compatible sizes.

9 Use some of the surplus picture and flower cane to make borders or sides for the beads. Press them on firmly so they will adhere, then smooth over.

10 Cover previously prepared round beads, filling any triangular shaped gaps with slices of the surplus small flower or picture cane. If you cover any bead holes, pierce through again after you have rolled the surface smooth. Bake all the beads following the clay manufacturer's instructions.

These jolly earrings, made using the cane technique, will suit the mood of a hot summer's day or cheer up a dull one. Have fun making the orange slices as realistic as you can – these even have pips.

Orange-slice Earrings

you will need

Polymer clay: pearl, pale orange and dark orange

Rolling pin

Craft (utility) knife

Self-healing cutting mat

Bamboo skewer

Cheese grater

2 eye pins

Round-nosed (snub-nosed) pliers

2 large rings

2 earring hooks

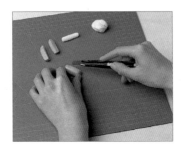

1 Roll a 5mm/¼in diameter sausage of pearl clay. Roll the pale orange clay into a short 1.5cm/⅝in diameter sausage and cut it lengthwise into four triangular segments.

2 Cut lengthways into two of the triangles and insert a skewer. Press the clay together to form a tunnel. Fill the tunnel with the sausage of pearl clay and reform the triangular shape.

3 Roll out a piece of dark orange clay thinly and cut strips 1cm/½in wide to fit between the segments. Arrange the pieces together to make a half cylinder. Roll out a 3mm/⅛in layer of pearl and a 2mm/¹⁄₁₂in layer of dark orange for the peel and mould these around the curved side of the cylinder.

4 Make two 1cm/½in balls in dark orange and roll on a cheese grater to make them look like small oranges. Fit an eye pin through the centre of each. Trim any overlapping edges from the half cylinder and roll the peel on a grater.

5 Cut two 5mm/¼in slices from the cylinder and make a hole in each for a ring. Bake the pieces following the clay manufacturer's instructions. To assemble each earring: using round-nosed pliers, loop the wire extending from the eye pin in each small orange and snip off any excess. Put a large ring through the orange slice and attach to the loop below the small orange. Attach the earring hook to the loop above the small orange.

Provided it is kept damp and soft when not in use, modelling clay is easy to handle and shape. Always keep spare clay covered with plastic wrap or in a plastic bag.

Modelling Clay Techniques

Preparing Clay Knead the clay until it is soft and malleable and all air bubbles are eliminated. Colour can either be kneaded into the clay before modelling or painted on once the finished model has hardened.

Mixing Clay with Colour

Use a concentrated colouring agent such as paste food colouring, which will produce intense colours without making the clay too wet.

1 Add colour gradually to achieve the shade you want. Remember that the shade will change slightly when the clay dries out.

2 Roll the clay into a long sausage, fold over and repeat. Add more colour as necessary and repeat until the colour is evenly distributed.

Mixing Clay with Hardener

This treatment makes the clay more difficult to work with, so keep it in a plastic bag. You can soften it slightly by kneading in a little hand cream.

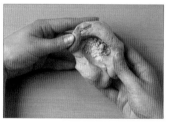

1 Make an indentation in the clay and add powder hardener. Fold the clay over the powder and knead a little before rolling into a sausage.

2 Fold the sausage over and add more hardener. Continue to knead until you have used all the powder you need.

Decorating Clay

A wide variety of decorative techniques, such as sponging and gilding, can be used on modelling clay.

Some types of self-hardening clay have a tendency to flake, so it is a good idea to seal the surface with one or two coats of diluted PVA (white) glue.

Apply paint to modelling clay with a brush or sponge, and spray or brush on a minimum of two coats of varnish.

Drying Clay

To avoid cracking, dry clay gradually, covering it with a damp cloth to slow the process.

Tape small, flat clay pieces to a board in order to prevent them from curling, adding a weight if necessary. Remove any rough edges when dry with some fine abrasive paper.

An easy-to-make clay mould is used to model these eye-catching silver earrings, so it's easy to produce as many pairs as you want – you can make them as gifts for everyone who admires them on you!

Moulded Star Earrings

you will need
Self-hardening modelling clay
Rolling pin
Tracing paper, pencil, paper or thin card (stock) and scissors (for template)
Modelling tools
Pair of earring studs
Bonding adhesive
Black acrylic paint
Paintbrushes
Silver powder
Varnish

1 Roll out a small piece of clay to a thickness of 8mm/⅜in.

2 Trace the template from the back of the book on to thin card or paper. Cut the star shape out of the clay.

3 Mark a line from the centre of the star to each point where two rays meet and use the flat side of the modelling tool to mould each point to a 90 degree angle. Smooth the star with water, tuck the edges in neatly and leave to dry.

4 Take a small ball of clay and press with your palm until it is about 2cm/¾in thick. Press in the hardened clay star then lift out carefully without distorting the mould. Leave to dry.

5 Use the mould to make further clay stars. Lift them out of the mould and place face up on the work surface. Trim off the excess clay with a modelling tool. Allow to harden.

6 Glue an earring stud to the back of each star.

7 Paint the stars with black acrylic paint and leave to dry completely.

8 Mix silver powder with varnish and brush this over the stars to complete.

Formalized leaves and gilded scroll-work turn simple square boxes into encrusted Renaissance-style treasures. You could line the inside of each little box with sumptuous fabric to hold small pieces of jewellery.

Florentine Boxes

you will need
Square and rectangular cardboard
craft boxes
Tracing paper
Hard and soft pencils
Masking tape
Modelling clay
Modelling tools
PVA (white) glue
Medium and fine artist's brushes
Acrylic craft paints: white, pale lilac
and pale blue
Dark and pale gold metallic paint
Matt (flat) acrylic spray varnish

1 Enlarge the templates provided to fit the top and sides of the box lid. Trace the outline with a hard pencil, then rub over the reverse with a soft pencil. Tape the paper to the lid. Draw over the lines again using a hard pencil to transfer the design.

2 Make the four leaf shapes from small rolls of modelling clay and press them into position on the box lid. Use modelling tools to add the details, and smooth the clay with a damp finger.

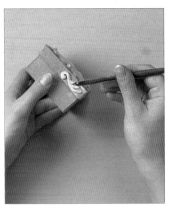

3 Make the dots from small balls of clay. Press them in place with the point of a pencil.

4 Finish the design on top of the lid by adding the four trefoil motifs on the corners.

5 Make the scrolls and leaves for each side of the lid. Allow the clay to dry thoroughly.

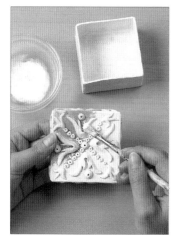

6 Paint the lid with PVA glue diluted with an equal quantity of water. When the glue is dry, paint the lid and box with white acrylic paint.

7 Now paint the lid of your box with a base coat of pale lilac.

8 Add a stippling of pale blue paint, applied with an almost dry brush.

9 Using a fine brush, paint the motifs in dark gold. When dry, add pale gold highlights as desired.

10 Give a textured look to the lid by brushing lightly over the surface with a dry brush loaded with a small amount of gold paint.

11 Paint the bottom of the box to match, adding a small amount of gold paint to each edge. Finish with a protective coat of matt varnish.

▶

These very striking earrings shimmer with a distressed black and gold paint effect that looks stunning but is actually quite simple to achieve. The faces are easily modelled out of clay.

Sun and Moon Earrings

you will need
Modelling clay
Rolling pin
Jar lid
Modelling tools
Earring posts and butterfly backs
Strong clear glue
Fine-grade abrasive paper
Black acrylic paint
Artist's brushes
Gold powder
Matt (flat) acrylic varnish

1 Roll out two pieces of clay, each to a circle about 5mm/¼in thick and 7.5cm/3in in diameter. Use a jar lid as a template to mark an inner circle. With a modelling tool, build up the central area so it is higher than the outer area but still flat.

2 Model the features of your sun on the raised central area with a modelling tool. Mark the rays around the face and cut away the excess clay. Pierce some dots in the face and rays and leave to dry for 1–2 days. Model a moon in the same way.

3 Glue the earring posts in position. Sand between the rays for a smoother look. Paint black. Mix the gold powder with the varnish, then paint. With a semi-dry brush, go over the face up and down quickly, so that the black underneath shows through and accentuates the features of the face. Paint the moon in the same way.

Shells are found in an amazing variety of shape, size, colour and texture, making them a fascinating craft medium. Stylish modern jewellery designs are an ideal setting for their natural, subtle beauty.

Shells

Assorted shells

Beautiful shells have been keenly collected for centuries, and their desirability has inevitably led to their exploitation in trade. Taking attractive and sometimes rare shells from a natural habitat – perhaps with their original owners still inside them – can result in the depletion of marine species. Consequently, shell-collection and export has now been made illegal in some parts of the world. It's important to make sure that any shells you use have been gathered in a responsible way.

Beachcombing is an enjoyable activity when you are at the seaside, and huge drifts of small shells can be found washed up. In these circumstances a small number can safely be collected as long as you make sure they are empty when you pick them up.

Other environmentally sound sources of shells include fish dealers and restaurants and old shell necklaces and other craft items. If you eat shellfish such as cockles and mussels at home you can simply save the shells; otherwise they are regularly discarded by restaurant kitchens and if you make friends with your local seafood restaurant the staff may be happy to save some for you.

Old shell necklaces and trinkets are a very good source of small shells for jewellery-making, with the advantage

that the shells are already drilled for threading. They're cheap and easy to find at flea markets and jumble sales.

Dust mask

Always wear a mask when sanding shells to avoid inhaling the dust.

Glue

A glue gun is useful for attaching shells quickly and accurately, but epoxy resin glue or PVA (white) glue are also suitable. Epoxy putty comes in two parts that are mixed together just before use. It is a strong adhesive that can be used to fill small shells to take button backs and other fittings.

Goggles

Wear protective goggles when drilling or sanding shells.

File

Use a small file to smooth any rough edges on shells that might catch on skin or clothing.

Ink

To colour shells, inks containing shellac are ideal. They can be mixed or watered down to achieve subtle shades and are waterproof once dry.

Mini-drill

A small electic drill is the most useful tool you can invest in for any kind of shellcraft. The very small bits will enable you to drill tiny holes in the most fragile of shells. Other attachments are available for smoothing surfaces, grinding rough edges and polishing shells until they shimmer.

Reusable putty adhesive

Press shells into a large blob of putty on the work surface to hold them securely while you are drilling them. Use a work surface that won't spoil if the drill goes through.

Ribbons

Choose ribbons with a seaside feel – such as checks and stripes in fresh colours – for shellcraft projects, or use delicate pinks and creams to match the colours of the shells.

Stone-effect beads

Natural-looking beads in a variety of shapes combine well with shells.

Tweezers

A pair of tweezers may be helpful for picking up and positioning tiny shells.

Shells are delicate and brittle so skill and caution are both needed when working with the raw material, so that the shells don't shatter. You could purchase prepared shells from a craft shop.

Shell Techniques

Sanding and Polishing Shells

Amazing results can be achieved by sanding and polishing ordinary shells such as these green mussels. Wear a dust mask and goggles.

1 Using a coarse sanding disc on a mini-drill, remove the outer coating of the shell and smooth down the ridges.

2 Switch to a fine sanding disc to strip the shell down to mother-of-pearl (the shell will now be fragile).

3 Use a woolly mop head to shine the inner body of the shell. To get into the corners, use a conical felt mop.

Drilling and Sawing Shells

A mini-drill can be used to make holes in small shells. The more fragile the shell, the finer the bit should be and the slower the drilling speed.

Secure each shell to the work surface with reusable putty and hold it firmly. The more fragile the shell, the finer the drill bit should be and the slower the speed of the drill. It is best to drill small conch shells through the bottom of the mouth of the shell.

Holes large enough for a nail to pass through can be made in strong, large shells, using a larger drill bit.

Buttons can easily be made from all sorts of shells, as long as there is a means of attaching them. They look especially effective on clothing made from natural fabrics, such as wool and cotton, in neutral colours.

Snail-shell Buttons

you will need
Protective gloves
Epoxy putty
Small snail shells
Small eyelet screws
Wire cutters
File or abrasive paper
Needle and matching button thread

1 Wearing protective gloves, mix together the two parts of the epoxy putty. Push putty into the mouth of each snail shell and fill the spiral recesses on the back of the shell. Smooth the surface with your finger.

2 Press a small eyelet screw into the putty on the back of each shell. If it is too long for the depth of the shell, snip off the end with wire cutters before inserting it.

3 Leave the putty to dry, then file or sand smooth, making sure there are no sharp edges at the mouth of the shell. Sew the shell buttons on to the garment with a needle and matching button thread.

Rainbow cockle shells in pretty, variegated colours are stitched on to a coloured cord to make this simple necklace. The long trimmed ties at the back make it a perfect accessory for beachwear or a backless dress.

Cockle-shell Necklace

you will need

Rainbow cockle (small clam) shells

Coloured cord

Reusable putty adhesive

Mini-drill

File

Stranded embroidery thread (floss)

Embroidery needle

Epoxy resin glue

2 small winkle shells

1 Select an odd number of cockle shells and arrange them around the cord with the largest one in the centre at the front of the necklace.

2 Supporting each shell on a lump of reusable putty adhesive, drill a small hole through the top. File any rough edges smooth.

3 Stitch the shells on to the cord using embroidery thread.

4 Apply epoxy resin glue to the ends of the cord and insert each one into a small winkle shell.

Combine the contemporary look of corrugated cardboard with a dynamic shell arrangement. For the finishing touch, paint the box in pure white, and the result is a seashell box that resembles a meringue-topped cake.

Seashell Jewellery Box

you will need
Selection of seashells
Round corrugated cardboard box
with lid
Glue gun
Paintbrush
White acrylic gesso or paint

1 Sort the seashells into different shapes and sizes. Arrange them on the lid of the box, using some larger shells as the bottom layer of the design.

2 When you are happy with the arrangement, begin to glue the bottom layer on. Glue the outside shells first, and gradually move inwards.

3 Work with the shell forms, building the middle of the design up into a domed shape.

4 Paint the box and the lid white. If you are using acrylic gesso, two coats will give a good matt (flat) covering; ordinary acrylic paint will benefit from an extra coat.

The shell used to make this romantic locket is called a heart cockle because of its shape. It opens naturally down the middle, revealing a chamber large enough to conceal a message or small memento.

Valentine's Locket

●●●●

you will need
Heart cockle shell
Reusable putty adhesive
Mini-drill
Pink stranded embroidery thread (floss)
Embroidery needle
Pleated satin ribbon
Scissors
PVA (white) glue
Small mementoes
Fine silk ribbon

1 Holding the shell steady on a piece of reusable putty adhesive, drill a small hole through the top of each half through which to thread the ribbon.

2 Using pink embroidery thread and an embroidery needle, stitch the words "I love you" inside the pleats of a small piece of pleated satin ribbon.

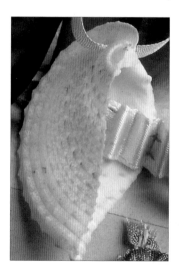

3 Glue one end of the ribbon inside each half of the cockle shell and leave to dry. Tuck the ribbon inside and insert small mementoes such as a lock of hair and a photograph.

4 Close the shell and thread a fine silk ribbon through the holes at the top of the shell. Wrap the ribbon around the shell to hold it closed.

Paper, Card
and Wood

As a raw material, paper is both plentiful and adaptable. Turned into durable papier mâché it can be fashioned into beads, sculptural brooches or earrings, and intricate decoupage shapes make a fascinating decorative treatment for even the smallest items. Wood crops up in jewellery design as beautifully turned beads and bangles, or combined with silver or gold in modern pieces, while on a simpler scale it's ideal for making bright, fun badges.

Wood and wood pulp are the basic source material for the materials used in this chapter. Each material – paper, card and wood – has different qualities that can be exploited by craftspeople.

History

Paper-making

One of the oldest crafts, paper-making has a long and fascinating history. The word 'paper' is derived from the papyrus used in ancient Egypt, Stems of papyrus, which grew abundantly on the banks of the River Nile, were cut and split, then laid at right angles to each other like a woven mat of reeds. This was wetted, then pounded to form a hard, thin sheet and left to dry in the sun.

Modern paper-making techniques using pulped rags were first experimented with in China in AD105 but

Below: Wood is one of the most versatile raw materials that has been appreciated by craftspeople for hundreds of years.

were kept a closely guarded secret for more than 600 years. The technique was later refined by Japanese Buddhist monks. Paper-making spread to Europe and, with the German invention of the printing press in the middle ages, the demand for paper and books greatly increased, Initially the paper-making materials were beaten by hand, but this technique was replaced by a stamping machine. This machine was later replaced by a roller which chopped, pounded and pulverized rags against stone plate, In the early 18th century the French ground wood fine enough to produce cellulose for paper-making. Refined wood pulp, to which chemicals are added, is used for industrially produced paper today.

Above: Cardboard is strong and sturdy, making it an ideal source material for sculptural use.

Today paper is used in so many ways and in so many industries. In an age of mass production the qualities of hand-made paper have an appeal to crafts-people, who can create papers with fibres, flower petals, leaves and any number of found objects embedded in their surface. Paper is manufactured in different grades, with different finishes, colours and qualities.

Cardboard

This basic material has a short industrial history. Cardboard is manufactured from rough wood pulp into a material that is strong and sturdy. These qualities have made it ideal for packaging, model-making and for

mock-ups of furniture and architecture. Its use became especially popular in World War II when resources of other materials were low. Since it had little printing on it, this robust, bland material, which was mostly associated with waste products, was used for crafts: examples of playing cards made from cardboard cigarette boxes, with the suite hand-drawn on them by prisoners of war still exist.

Cardboard production increased with the development of corrugated cardboard. This new material, made from lining papers and fluting papers allowed for a greater number of uses for the basic product. Designers in the 1960s started to explore the creative possibilities of cardboard, with sculptural furniture. However, the fire risk imposed by such a material limits its use in the home to small-scale items, making it a perfect source material for craft items.

Wood

This material has a universal and appealing presence to every culture. In its natural form trees provide shelter, fuel, food, a home to myriad creatures, and produce much of the clean air that we breathe.

Trees have been harvested since man first had the tools to make use of the amazing raw material that they offered. Early people carved wood to make boats, drinking vessels, storage containers and tools, as well as a whole host of other everyday items. Centuries of woodworking tradition have refined the techniques and tools that are used and available to us today. As a constructional material wood is

invaluable, and for its weight it is very strong, making it the ideal source material for use in industry as well as domestically for furniture, housebuilding, and household products.

For master craftsmen, the innate qualities of wood are its appeal. The colour, texture, scent, grain and strength of different tree species make each appropriate for different uses. Since no two pieces of wood are alike, cabinet-makers are skilled at exploiting the natural grain of the wood to best advantage in their piece of work. On a small scale, too, wood can be used to make intricate objects for home accessories, as well as items of adornment.

Right: Découpage is a traditional paper craft that is not difficult to master.

Above: Handmade paper has very appealing qualities for craftspeople. Here a paper collage has been embellished with hand embroidery.

Today's craftspeople are exploiting the natural qualities of paper, cardboard and wood, following the traditions of previous generations of craftspeople and differing world cultures.

Gallery

Today's craftspeople have a host of natural materials with which to work, and a sophisticated range of tools and equipment to use to create their art. Added to this the vast quantity of products available such as paints, varnishes, dye, and ephemera to enhance and embellish the finished product means the range of items that the craftsperson can produce becomes almost limitless.

With current trends in recycling, papercrafts have become all the rage, with papers crafted into papier mâché jewellery, découpage necklaces, rolled paper beads as well as recycled jewel boxes. Cardboard, too, can be pulped and reformed into bracelets and necklace charms, which are decorated with bold and colourful motifs to make them unique and individual items.

Wood is the ideal source material for children's badges as well as crafted jewel boxes.

Below: DECOUPAGE BEADS
Old wooden beads are given a new lease of life when covered with decorative papers and découpage.
Lucinda Ganderton

Below: LEAF COLLAGE
This beautiful design originates with small sheets of white paper cast over leaf shapes, using a small mould and deckle made from two picture frames. The leaf shapes used here are fabric relief forms.
Elizabeth Cousins-Scott

Above: HOUSE OF DOLLS
An unusual display case housing an eccentric collection of dolls, created from buttons, jewels and doll parts, bound together with papier mâché. The dolls are decorated with newspaper collage.
JULIE ARKELL

Above right: ELEGANT CASKETS
Recycled card and paper were used to construct the basic armatures for these caskets. Their elegance is created through a subtle combination of restrained background colours.
CLAIRE ATTRIDGE

Below: PAPER BOWLS
These little bowls are made from layered paper circles that are moulded over fruits while damp. Ribbons are inserted between the paper layers. They are great for holding earrings, or small trinkets.
WENDY CARLTON-DEWHURST

Gorgeous paper is easy to find in specialist stores, but look out for unusual packaging, gift wraps and foils that can be recycled in your jewellery projects, and collect pretty patterns for découpage designs.

Paper and Card Materials

Cardboard

Double-walled corrugated cardboard makes a firm base for papier mâché, but for small items use stiff, thin card. Single-walled corrugated cardboard is flexible; use it to cover stylish boxes.

Foil

Use gold, silver or coloured foil.

Gift wrap

Printed wrapping paper is a good source of découpage images.

Glue

PVA (white) glue is ideal for sticking paper and card. It can also be diluted and used to soak newspaper for papier mâché as an alternative to wallpaper paste. Use strong epoxy resin glue to attach jewellery findings to your finished pieces.

Newspaper

Tear single sheets of old newspaper into thin strips and soak in wallpaper paste or dilute PVA (white) glue for papier mâché. Always protect the work surface.

Paints

Gouache and acrylic paints dry quickly and are easy to use. For brilliant, glossy colour and sparkling metallic effects, use enamel paint.

Papier mâché pulp

You can make papier mâché pulp easily yourself (see page 466) or buy it ready-made from craft suppliers. It is strengthened with a filler such as plaster of Paris and is ideal for building up sculpted shapes that can then be covered with strips of paper ready for decorating.

Primer

Painting papier mâché shapes with one or two coats of white acrylic primer will provide a good surface for decoration.

Sanding sealer/shellac

This toffee-coloured, spirit-based lacquer can be used to seal and strengthen paper and card and to give an antique look to painted finishes.

Varnish

Several coats of glossy acrylic or oil-based varnish protect a painted surface and make colours glow. Crackle varnish is a two-part treatment that gives an antique look and is especially effective with découpage designs. Always follow the manufacturer's instructions.

The equipment needed for working with paper and card is minimal, and you will probably already have nearly everything you need. Some woodworking tools are useful when shaping papier mâché.

Paper and Card Equipment

Abrasive paper
Hard papier mâché can be smoothed by rubbing it down with medium- and fine-grade abrasive paper.

Blender
If you want to make your own papier mâché pulp, whizzing the soaked and boiled paper in a blender produces a smooth texture very easily.

Bowl
Use an old mixing bowl to dilute PVA (white) glue or mix wallpaper paste for papier mâché.

Craft (utility) knife
Replace the blade of a craft knife or scalpel often as paper and card will quickly blunt it. Always use a cutting mat to protect the work surface.

Cutting mat
A self-healing cutting mat is an ideal cutting surface.

Paintbrushes
A selection of artist's brushes is useful for applying glue and smoothing down layers of papier mâché as well as for painting. To paint decorative lines use a coachliner (liner) brush: this has long hairs of uniform length and is designed to hold a lot of paint so that you don't have to keep lifting the brush to reload it.

Pencil and ruler
For tracing templates and marking out designs. Use a metal ruler with a craft knife to cut straight lines. Always work on a cutting mat.

Scissors
Use general household scissors for cutting paper and card. Dressmaking shears will quickly be blunted. A pair of small, sharp-pointed scissors is essential for cutting images accurately.

Sponge
A natural or synthetic sponge can be used to create different paint effects such as stippling, to stick down decoupage motifs and wipe off excess paste, and to apply glazes.

Many different decorative techniques are possible using paper and card: just experiment with the materials that inspire you. Papier mâché and papier mâché pulp are both excellent for sculpting items of jewellery.

Paper and Card Techniques

Papier Mâché Newspaper is most commonly used for papier mâché and is very pliable and strong. For very delicate items you could try using tissue paper, though it is tricky to handle when wet.

1 Tear the newspaper into strips about 2cm/³⁄₄in wide. Tearing with the grain makes it easy to produce regular strips. Dilute PVA (white) glue with water to the consistency of single (light) cream or use fungicide-free wallpaper paste.

2 Use a paintbrush to coat each strip of paper in the glue or paste and press it on to a cardboard base, or into a mould. Use the brush to smooth the paper down and expel any air bubbles.

3 When you have built up the shape, leave to dry completely. Sand the surface smooth if necessary and hide the newsprint with two coats of white acrylic primer before decorating.

Making Papier Mâché Pulp

Prepared pulp can be bought but it's easy to make. You will need:

5 sheets newspaper
60ml/4 tbsp PVA (white) glue
10ml/2 tsp plaster of Paris
10ml/2 tsp linseed oil

Tear the paper into small squares, place in an old saucepan with water to cover and simmer for 30 minutes. Pour into a blender and blend to a pulp. Add the other ingredients and stir vigorously. Pulp can be stored for some weeks in a plastic box.

Working with Papier Mâché Pulp

You can use paper pulp very effectively to build up sculpted forms, simply pushing it into shape with your fingers. Allow plenty of time for the pulp to dry out thoroughly before completing the project.

1 To make a three-dimensional piece, build up the papier mâché pulp on a base such as a cardboard shape. Leave to dry out thoroughly.

2 When the pulp shape is dry and hard, cover it completely with two layers of papier mâché and leave to dry before decorating.

Decoupage Though most often associated with furniture and decorative household items, paper cutouts can be used to enhance many different objects, large or small. Glass, metal, wood and china are all suitable surfaces.

Surface Preparation

Whatever you are decorating, it is vital to have an absolutely smooth surface to achieve a "painted on" look.

1 Sand wood smooth with medium- then fine-grade abrasive paper. Prime and sand again, then apply two coats of paint. If you want to leave the wood grain visible, seal the surface with shellac before decorating.

2 Metal should be scrubbed and coated with red oxide primer to provide a key for paint. If you are using a light-coloured paint, apply one or two coats of white acrylic primer.

Painting Edges

On items such as boxes, painted edges can enhance a decoupage design. Choose a colour that contrasts with the base colour and goes well with the cutout designs. It's advisable to paint lines before adding cutouts, in case of mistakes.

Load a coachliner (liner) brush with acrylic paint diluted with a little water. Holding the brush like a pen, and using the edge of your hand as a support, drag the brush towards you. Use your little finger against the edge to keep your hand steady. Lift the brush gradually when you get near the end of the line so that it doesn't drag over the edge. If you need to reload the brush before reaching the end, overlap the lines a little to ensure continuity.

Tinting Prints

Black and white prints are easily enhanced with delicate colour.

Subtle effects can be achieved using coloured pencils. Start with the lighter areas, working with gentle strokes in one direction. Build up the colour gradually, blending it carefully. Seal tinted prints with sanding sealer and leave to dry before cutting out.

Cutting Out Motifs

Whether you prefer to use a pair of scissors or a craft (utility) knife, the basic principles remain the same. Always use a cutting mat with a craft knife.

1 Cut the excess paper from around the outer edge of the motif using a large pair of scissors.

2 Cut away any background areas within the design, piercing a hole in the centre of the area then cutting outwards to the edge. Cut around the outside edge without leaving any trace of background: it is better to cut slightly inside the edge of the motif.

Gluing Motifs

PVA (white) glue is suitable for decoupage on most surfaces. Dilute the glue with a little water to make it spreadable. A glue stick can be used for very small designs, especially on paper or card (stock).

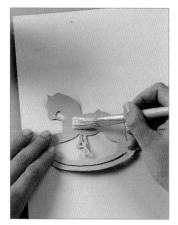

1 Use an artist's brush to paint glue over the back of the motif, thinly covering the entire surface right up to the edges. Alternatively, if the motif has a very intricate design and might be damaged by the brush, you can paint the glue on the base surface, wiping away any excess while still wet after positioning the motif.

2 Lay the cutout gently on the surface. When you are satisfied with its position, press it down gently with your fingers or a barely moistened sponge, starting at the centre and smoothing outwards. When you are working on a small piece you can hold the work up to the light to highlight any air bubbles or areas that have not adhered properly.

3 Lift any edges that have been missed and dab on some more glue if necessary. Leave for a few minutes then gently wipe away excess glue using a damp sponge and leave to dry.

Varnishing

Careful varnishing protects the decoupage, adds depth to the design and completes the illusion that it is a painted surface. Build the varnish up in a series of thin coats, sanding gently between each. Matt (flat) acrylic varnish is easy to apply and dries quickly, but you may like to finish with a few coats of durable oil-based varnish to protect the surface. For an aged effect brush a little thinned raw umber paint over the varnished surface, leave a few minutes, then wipe off with a cloth.

◄ A crackle finish gives an antique look. It can be applied over varnish and consists of two layers: a slow-drying base and a quick-drying top coat that cracks as the first layer dries out. Apply the second coat when the first feels dry but slightly tacky. If no cracks appear as it dries the process can be speeded up by playing a cool hairdryer over the surface. Rub a little artist's oil paint into the cracks to emphasize them: raw umber is the colour most commonly used. Finish with two coats of oil-based varnish.

This glittering star-shaped brooch in papier mâché makes an ideal birthday badge if you decorate it with the appropriate sign of the zodiac: the colourful design used here represents Cancer the Crab.

Star-sign Brooch

you will need

Scrap paper, pencil and scissors (for template)

Corrugated cardboard

Craft (utility) knife

Self-healing cutting mat

Newspaper

PVA (white) glue

Artist's brushes

White acrylic primer

Gouache paints: light blue, yellow, red

Gloss acrylic varnish

Gold enamel paint

Brooch back

Epoxy resin glue

1 Draw a star shape on to scrap paper, cut it out and draw around this shape on to the corrugated cardboard. Now cut out the cardboard star shape. Soak some newspaper in diluted PVA glue, scrunch it up and mound it in the centre of the star.

2 Cover the whole brooch in several layers of newspaper strips soaked in PVA glue. Allow to dry.

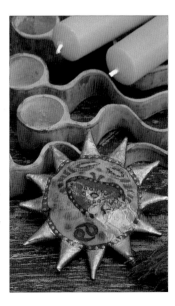

3 Give the brooch a coat of PVA glue, then one of white acrylic primer. Allow to dry, paint on the design and then the clear gloss varnish.

4 Add gold enamel paint details. Finally, fix a brooch back in place using epoxy resin glue.

This quirky little box makes a bold romantic statement. To break the mirror, wrap it in newspaper and hit it with a hammer, then carefully pick out fragments of the shape and size you need to cover the lid.

Mirrored Trinket Box

you will need
Section of poster tube
Cardboard
Pencil
Scissors
Masking tape
Pair of compasses
PVA (white) glue
Newspaper
4 marbles
Artist's brushes
Epoxy resin glue
Chemical metal filler (car-body repair filler)
Mirror fragments
White acrylic primer
Gouache paints
Gloss acrylic varnish
Gold enamel paint

1 Stand the section of tube on a sheet of cardboard and draw round it. Cut out the disc and tape to the tube. Cut out a slightly larger circle for the lid and another 1cm/½in smaller in diameter. Glue the two together. Bend a roll of newspaper into a heart shape and attach to the lid with masking tape. Cover four marbles with tape.

2 Tear some newspaper into strips and brush with PVA glue diluted with water. Cover the box, lid and marbles with several layers of papier mâché. Leave to dry thoroughly. Glue the marbles to the box base using epoxy resin glue. Mix up the filler, spread it over the lid, and carefully push in the mirror fragments.

3 Paint the whole box, except the mirror pieces, with PVA glue. When dry, prime the box with white acrylic primer. Paint the design with gouache.

4 Coat the painted box with several layers of gloss acrylic varnish, and leave to dry. To finish, pick out details of the design in gold enamel.

Use papier mâché to create an unusual summery bracelet, decorated with slices of different citrus fruits. Glints of gold picking out the details on the fruit echo the sparkling gold foil lining inside.

Fruity Bracelet

you will need

Tracing paper, pencil, paper or card (stock) (for template)
Scissors
Thin cardboard
Masking tape
Large hook and eye
Newspaper
PVA (white) glue
Strong clear glue
Artist's brushes
Gold foil (from a chocolate wrapper)
White acrylic primer
Acrylic paints: yellow, red, orange and gold
Gloss acrylic varnish

1 Copy the template at the back of the book, enlarging it to fit your wrist, to make a paper or card template. Use this template to cut the shape out of thin cardboard. Tape a large hook to one end of the cardboard bracelet and a matching eye to the other.

2 Tear newspaper into strips and soak in diluted PVA glue. Cover the cardboard with several layers of papier mâché, covering all the edges neatly. Leave to dry. Use strong, clear glue to stick a sheet of gold foil to the inside of the bracelet. Trim the edges.

3 Prime the outside of the bracelet with a coat of white acrylic primer to smooth the surface. Decorate with slices of citrus fruit using acrylic paints. Add touches of gold paint around the edges, pips and dimples.

4 When the paint is dry, protect with several coats of gloss acrylic varnish.

This lavishly decorated box is a stylish way to present a gift of jewellery. You can use paper ribbon both to cover the box and to tie the chunky bow on top, which is trimmed with a posy of fabric flowers.

Presentation Box

you will need

Scissors

Paper ribbon

Oval cardboard box with lid

PVA (white) glue

Paintbrush

Corrugated cardboard

Pencil

Selection of fabric flowers

1 Cut a piece of paper ribbon long enough to fit around the rim of the box lid, allowing a small overlap. Unfurl, brush with glue and stick in place. Fold and glue the excess ribbon under and above the rim.

2 Place the lid on the corrugated cardboard with the corrugations running straight from end to end. Draw around the edge and cut out the shape. Glue on to the lid to cover the surplus ribbon.

3 Cut two lengths of ribbon each measuring three times the width of the lid. Unfurl, and glue one end of each piece to the lid, tucking the ends under the rim. Tie the other ends together in a large bow. Trim.

4 Put the lid on the box. Measure the distance from the bottom of the box to the lower edge of the lid. Cut a strip of corrugated cardboard to fit this width, long enough to wrap around the box. Glue in place.

5 Cut the fabric flowers and leaves from their wire stalks. Glue on to the box, so that they give the effect of a sheaf of flowers lying on the lid underneath the bow.

Beads made from paper were traditionally used to make bead curtains, but this old technique can also transform good-quality printed paper into colourful abstract designs for beautiful necklaces and bracelets.

Rolled-paper Beads

you will need
Ruler
Pencil
Gift wrap
Scissors
Glue stick or PVA (white) glue
Gloss acrylic varnish
Varnish brush
Thin elastic

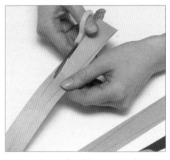

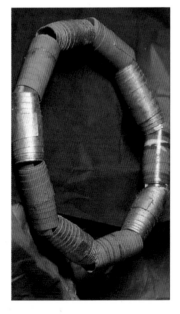

1 Draw a series of 2.5cm/1in-wide strips on the back of a sheet of gift wrap. Now make a mark halfway along one short edge of each strip. Draw lines from the two opposite corners to the marked point, in such a way that you are dividing the strip into long, thin triangles.

2 Cut along the lines on each strip. The central triangle will make a symmetrical bead. Use the right-angled triangles if you want to make conical beads, such as for earrings or the ends of a necklace.

3 Starting at the base of the triangle, roll each strip of paper tightly around a pencil. Make sure the end is correctly aligned with the pencil when you begin so that the bead is symmetrical. After the first turn, apply glue to the wrong side of the paper.

4 Put a little extra glue on the end of the paper triangle and press it down firmly. Leave the bead on the pencil until the glue is dry. The beads can be strengthened and protected with a few coats of acrylic varnish before they are threaded on thin elastic.

This exotic piece of jewellery is made from papier mâché pulp, hand-painted in gorgeous colours and then decorated with artificial gemstones and glass tear-drops.

Winged Cupid Brooch

you will need
Tracing paper
Pencil
Thin card (stock)
Craft (utility) knife
Cutting mat
Papier mâché pulp
Newspaper
PVA (white) glue
White acrylic primer
Artist's brushes
Flat-backed glass gems
Epoxy resin glue
Dressmaker's pin
Eye-hook pins
Gouache paints
Matt (flat) acrylic varnish
Gold enamel paint
Small glass tear-drop beads
Small jump-rings
Round-nosed (snub-nosed) pliers
Brooch back

1 Trace the template from the back of the book, transfer it to card and cut out all of the sections. Cover the card pieces with papier mâché pulp and apply several layers of newspaper strips soaked in PVA glue. Allow to dry completely.

2 Paint with a coat of PVA glue, then with white primer. Glue on the glass gems using epoxy resin glue. Make holes using a pin and insert the eye-hook pins, securing them with epoxy resin glue.

3 Paint on the design with gouache paints. When dry, coat with matt varnish. Leave to dry again, then add gold enamel details.

4 Assemble all the brooch pieces and tear-drop beads, joining them with jump-rings (using the pliers). Glue the brooch back into position.

This little trinket box with its pretty posy of roses is ideal for small pieces of jewellery and adds a feminine touch to a dressing-table. Crackle varnish gives the rose design a lovely antique look.

Decoupage Roses Box

you will need

Small wooden box with lid
Screwdriver
Small paintbrush
White acrylic primer
Fine-grade abrasive paper
Cream emulsion (latex) paint
Artist's acrylic paints in raw umber and gold
Coachliner (liner) brush
Acrylic varnish
Printed rose motifs
Small sharp-pointed scissors
Metal ruler
Pencil
PVA (white) glue
Craft (utility) knife
Crackle varnish
Hairdryer
Raw umber oil paint
Kitchen paper
White spirit (paint thinner)
Oil-based varnish

1 Remove the box lid. Paint the box with a coat of acrylic primer and leave to dry. Lightly sand the surface, then follow with two coats of cream emulsion paint.

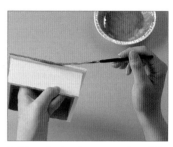

2 Now prepare some antique-effect gold paint by mixing a little raw umber and artist's gold acrylic paint with just a touch of water. Then, very carefully lay your coachliner brush in the gold paint and ensure that the brush is thoroughly covered.

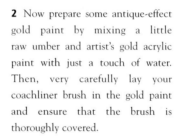

3 Place the brush on one edge of the box rim and drag it along to the end. Now paint all of the edges on the base and lid of your box with gold paint, as described in step 2. Leave until completely dry. Follow with an even coat of acrylic varnish, used to protect the base colour.

4 With small sharp-pointed scissors, cut out the rose-heads, making sure that you choose colours that complement each other. Use different designs for the front and sides.

5 Measure the width and length of the box lid with a ruler to find the centre. Mark this point with a pencil. Dilute some PVA glue with a little water and brush it on to the back of the first rose. Stick it in the centre of the box lid, then add the rest, one at a time, around the central rose until you have a circle.

6 Fit the lid on to the base but don't screw the hinges back on. Apply the designs to the back, front and sides, sticking your motifs over the join (seam) of the lid and base. Leave the box to dry.

◀ **7** Place a metal ruler along the edge of the join over which you have stuck the motif and draw a very sharp craft knife along the join, making sure that you cut really cleanly through the paper. Repeat on the other two sides.

▶

8 Seal the the surface by brushing on 5–10 coats of acrylic varnish. Allow each coat to dry throughly before applying the next.

9 Following the manufacturer's instructions, brush on the first stage of the crackle varnish and leave until slightly tacky to the touch (about 1–2 hours, although this can vary).

10 Brush on the second stage of the crackle varnish, making sure that you have covered all areas. Leave to dry naturally for about 1–2 hours.

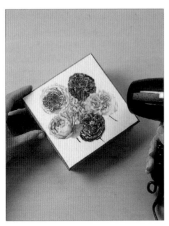

11 If no cracks have appeared, use a hairdryer on its lowest setting and move it over the surface until the cracks begin to appear.

12 Put a tiny amount of raw umber oil paint on to kitchen paper moistened with white spirit and wipe over all surfaces of the box.

13 Take a clean sheet of kitchen paper and wipe off the excess, leaving the paint only in the cracks. Leave to dry overnight. Varnish with two coats of oil-based varnish. Screw the lid and base of the box back together.

Wear one of these jolly badges as a colourful and bold brooch on a plain coat or sweater. Simple to make, these badges are bound to lift your spirits in the morning.

Sun and Moon Badges

you will need

Tracing paper, pencil, card (stock) and scissors (for templates)

5mm/¼in birch plywood sheet

Coping saw or fretsaw

Medium- and fine-grade abrasive paper

White acrylic primer

Artist's brushes

Ccrylic paints: yellow, red and blue

Gloss acrylic varnish

Epoxy resin or hot glue

2 brooch backs

1 Make card templates (size as wished) from those at the back of the book, and draw round them on to the wood. Cut out the shapes with the saw and sand the edges smooth.

2 Paint both sides and all the edges of the shapes with white acrylic primer. When the paint is dry, sand the surfaces lightly until smooth.

3 Paint the fronts of the sun and moon with acrylic paint and add the features and other details. When the paint is dry, add a coat of varnish and leave to dry. Put a thick line of glue on the back of each badge and press the brooch back firmly into the glue.

Wood is an infinitely adaptable material to work with. Chunky wooden beads and bangles make the most of its natural grain and colours, but it's also an ideal base for paint and other applied decorations.

Woodwork Materials and Equipment

Abrasive paper
Small abrasive particles, glued to backing paper, are graded according to their size: the finer the grit, the smoother the finish.

Bradawl/Awl
The sharp point can be twisted into wood without splitting the grain and is used for scribing and piercing guide holes for drilling.

Drill
A hand drill can be used for quickly making small holes in wood to take jewellery fixings. An electric mini-drill is a convenient alternative.

Glue
PVA (white) glue dries clear and is ideal for joining pieces of wood, though for small projects a hot glue gun is fast and convenient. Use strong epoxy resin glue to attach jewellery findings securely.

Paintbrushes
You could use artist's brushes for most jobs, but ideally use a fine decorating brush for primers and undercoats and artist's brushes to decorate small pieces. Varnishing brushes have long, flat bristles to minimize brush marks.

Paints
Acrylic paints are ideal for painting wood. Start with a coat or two of white acrylic primer to give a smooth,

clean surface so that the colours of your design look clear and bright.

Plywood
Birch-faced plywood is smooth and strong and because of its construction will not warp or split. Thin plywood suitable for small projects such as badges is available in small sheets from model and craft suppliers.

Saws
Frame saws are designed for intricate cutting. They work on the pull stroke so blades should always be fitted with the points facing towards the handle.

Coping saw – This is fine for small projects and can be fitted with a range of disposable blades.

Fretsaw – This cuts more deeply than the coping saw as it has a larger frame.

Square
A try square is essential for accurate marking out of right angles.

Varnish
Both acrylic and oil-based varnishes are available in a range of finishes from matt to high gloss. Several thin coats of gloss varnish will make bright paint colours glow like enamels.

Fine details are all-important when you are working on a small scale. Accurate marking out and cutting, meticulous smoothing of the wood, and painstaking surface finishes are the keys to success.

Woodwork Techniques

Transferring Designs

◀ **1** Draw or trace the design and scale it up if necessary by copying it on graph paper of a larger scale or using the enlarging facility on a photocopier. Cut out an accurate template from thin card (stock) and draw around it on the wood using a sharp pencil. For square or rectangular items such as boxes it's essential to check all right angles with a try square when marking out the component parts.

2 Use compasses to draw circles directly on wood. For a motif such as a sun, adjust the compasses and draw an inner circle as a guide for drawing the rays.

Using a Frame Saw

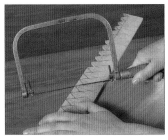

Fret saws and coping saws work on the pull stroke for accurate control. The frame allows the blade to be swivelled for cutting curves. The wood should be clamped so that there is clearance underneath all the lines of the design to move the saw.

If you are cutting out a pierced design, use a hand drill to make a starter hole in each inner section. The removable blade of the saw can then be fed through and re-attached. Saw carefully to the edge of the marked shape and then follow the outline.

Smoothing Surfaces

Many different materials are used to make abrasive papers, generally known as sandpapers. Glasspaper, in medium and fine grades, is suitable for smoothing wood before decorating. Silicon carbide paper is more hard-wearing. Dark grey silicon paper, known as "wet and dry" paper, needs lubricating with water and can be used for fine smoothing of painted and varnished finishes on wood.

Sand all sawn edges until they feel smooth and splinter-free to the touch. Wrap a square of abrasive paper around a wooden or cork sanding block for best results on flat surfaces. Make sure the block is free of defects to avoid scoring the surface of the wood.

For smoothing curved areas wrap a small piece of abrasive paper around your finger, or fold it abrasive side out to get into tight angles.

The sunflower is an enduringly popular image and an effective stylized motif. Simply painted in warm yellows, this cheerful little badge makes a bright decoration for a plain sweater or a denim jacket.

Sunflower Badge

you will need

5mm/¼in birch plywood sheet

Pencil

Pair of compasses

Coping saw or fretsaw

Medium- and fine-grade
abrasive paper

PVA (white) glue

White acrylic primer

Artist's brushes

Acrylic paints: yellow, red,
Chocolate-brown and gold

Gloss acrylic varnish

Brooch back

Epoxy resin glue

1 Draw a circle for the flower-centre on the plywood with the compasses. Draw the petals freehand around the centre. Draw another circle the same size as the centre. Cut out these two shapes with a saw.

2 Sand any rough edges on the flower and sand the edge of the circle to a curve. Glue the circle to the centre of the flower shape using PVA glue. Paint with white primer and allow to dry. Sand lightly.

◄ **3** Paint in the flower details with the acrylic paints. Mix yellow and red to make a golden-yellow for the petals. Paint the centre brown. When dry, add gold dots to the centre. Apply a coat of gloss varnish. Attach the brooch back using epoxy resin glue.

This jolly little shooting star can be decorated as fancifully as you like in brilliant contrasting colours. Use pearlized paint for its tail and add several coats of glossy varnish to make the colours glow.

Shooting Star Badge

you will need
Tracing paper
Pencil
4mm/⅙in birch plywood sheet
Coping saw or fretsaw
Medium- and fine-grade abrasive paper
White acrylic primer
Artist's brushes
Acrylic paints
Water-based pearlized paints
Gloss acrylic varnish
Brooch back
Epoxy resin glue

1 Trace the template at the back of the book and transfer to the plywood. Cut out. Sand all the edges.

2 Paint with a coat of white acrylic primer. When dry, sand lightly and mark the remaining points of the star.

3 Paint on the badge's design in acrylic paints, using pearlized paint for the tail. Protect with several coats of gloss varnish.

4 Glue the brooch back on to the badge using epoxy resin glue.

This attractive little box is easy to construct, but the delicate painting and the raised crab design make it unusual and eye-catching. The lid is decorated with a wavy pattern inspired by the crab's watery home.

Crab Jewel Box

you will need

Coping saw or fret saw

40cm/16in pine slat, 3cm x 8mm/ 1¼ x ⅜in

4mm/⅙in birch plywood sheet

Ruler

Tracing paper, pencil, card (stock) and scissors (for template)

Abrasive paper

Wood glue

Masking tape

Artist's brushes

White acrylic primer

Acrylic paints: blue, gold and red

Matt (flat) acrylic varnish

1 Cut the pine slat into four 10cm/4in lengths. From the plywood cut two rectangles measuring 8 x 10cm/3¼ x 4in for the base and lid insert, and one measuring 11.5 x 10cm/4½ x 4in for the lid. Enlarge the crab template at the back of the book, transfer it to the plywood and cut it out. Remove rough edges with abrasive paper.

2 Assemble the sides of the box and stick with wood glue. Hold the sides in place with masking tape until the glue is completely dry. Glue in the base. Glue the lid insert centrally on to the lid. Sand again to smooth any rough edges.

◀ **3** Paint the box and crab with a coat of white acrylic primer. Sand lightly when dry. Paint the box and the lid in blue, thinned with water and applied with wavy brushstrokes. Paint on the border pattern and stars. Paint the crab in red and pick out details in blue and gold. Finish off with a coat of varnish. When dry, glue the crab firmly on to the lid of the box.

Patterns for some of the projects are given here so you can make templates. The way you copy these may depend on the materials being used, but cutting out a card template and drawing round it is often the best approach.

Templates

Tracing

Unless you have access to a photocopier, you will need to trace the printed pattern before transferring it to a piece of card for cutting out.

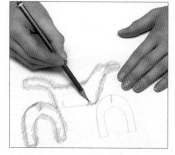

1 Use a pen or pencil to draw over the image. Turn the tracing over on a piece of scrap paper and use a soft pencil to rub over the lines.

3 Lift off the tracing to reveal the design. Go over the lines if necessary before cutting out the template.

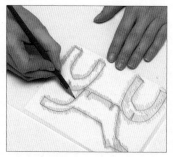

2 Place the tracing, right side up, on a sheet of paper or card (stock). Using a hard pencil, draw firmly over all the lines of the design.

4 When working with fabric, it may be possible to trace the design directly using a fabric pen. Tape the drawing to a light box or window and tape the fabric over it to hold it still while you draw.

Scaling up

You may want to make a template that is larger than the printed design. Scaling up is easily done using a photocopier with an enlarging facility, but failing this you can use graph paper. For very small designs, scaling down may be required.

1 Trace the design and tape the tracing over a sheet of graph paper. Using an appropriate scale, draw the design on a second piece of graph paper, copying the shape from each small square to each larger square.

2 Lay or paste the graph paper template on a sheet of card and cut around the outline.

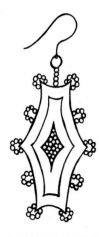
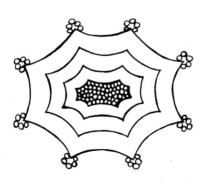

Victorian Earrings and Brooch, p52

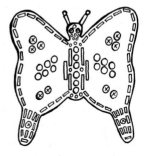

Butterfly Brooch, p53

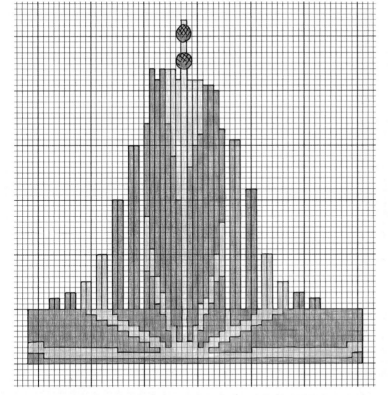

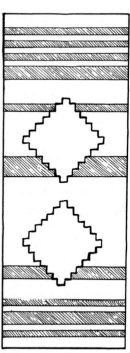

Loom-woven Choker, p64   Repeat line 1 35 times   Woven Bracelet, p50
                                    Repeat line 63 35 times

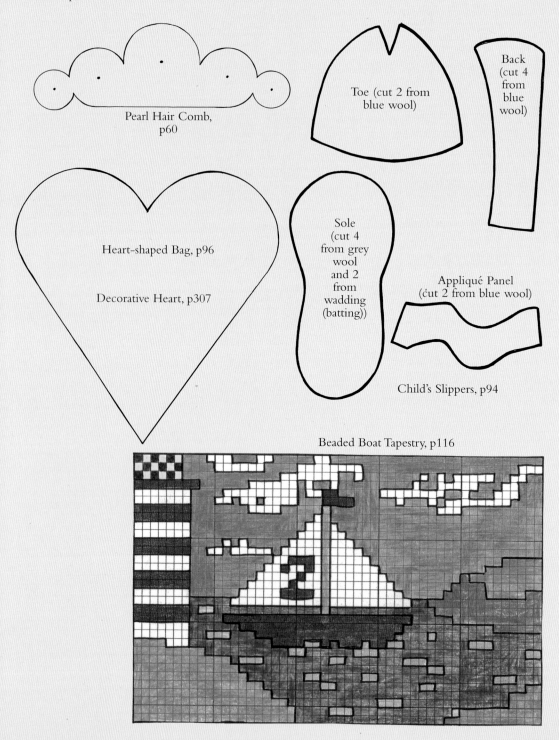

Pearl Hair Comb,
p60

Toe (cut 2 from
blue wool)

Back
(cut 4
from
blue
wool)

Heart-shaped Bag, p96

Decorative Heart, p307

Sole
(cut 4
from grey
wool
and 2
from
wadding
(batting))

Appliqué Panel
(cut 2 from blue wool)

Child's Slippers, p94

Beaded Boat Tapestry, p116

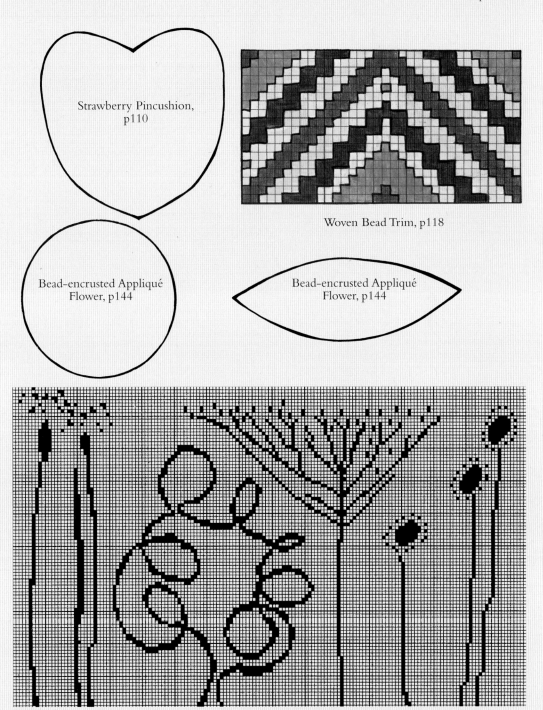

Strawberry Pincushion,
p110

Woven Bead Trim, p118

Bead-encrusted Appliqué
Flower, p144

Bead-encrusted Appliqué
Flower, p144

Needlepoint Photograph Album, p126

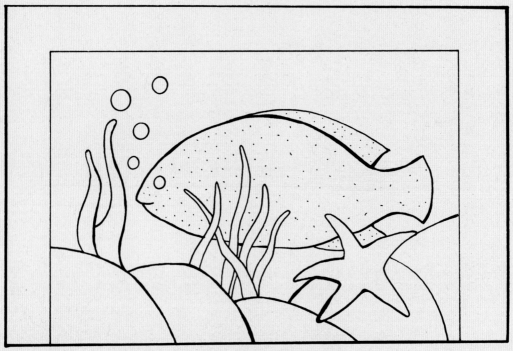

Fish Mosaic Splashback, p160

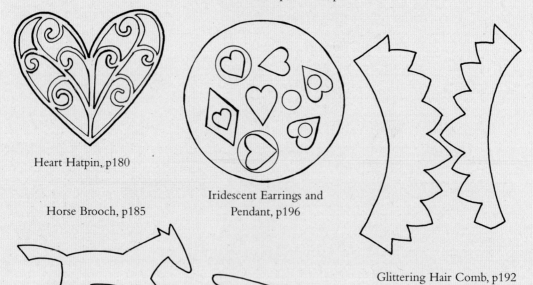

Heart Hatpin, p180

Horse Brooch, p185

Iridescent Earrings and
Pendant, p196

Glittering Hair Comb, p192

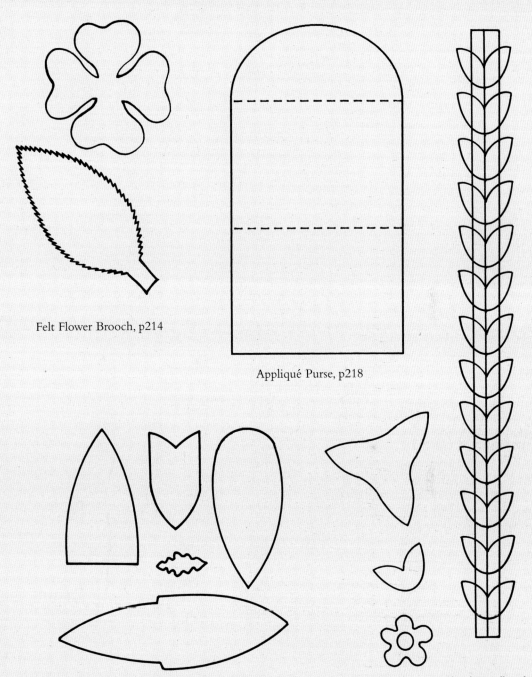

Felt Flower Brooch, p214

Appliqué Purse, p218

Oak-leaf Purse, p242

Floral Headband
and Brooch,
p245

Oak-leaf Hair Clasp and Buttons, p246

Leather Chain Belt, p248

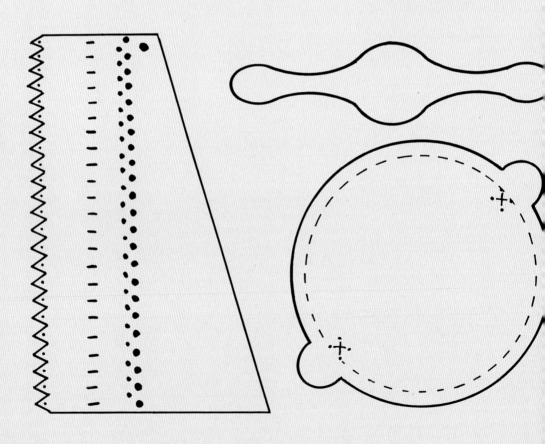

Suede Tassels, p250

Coin Purse, p252

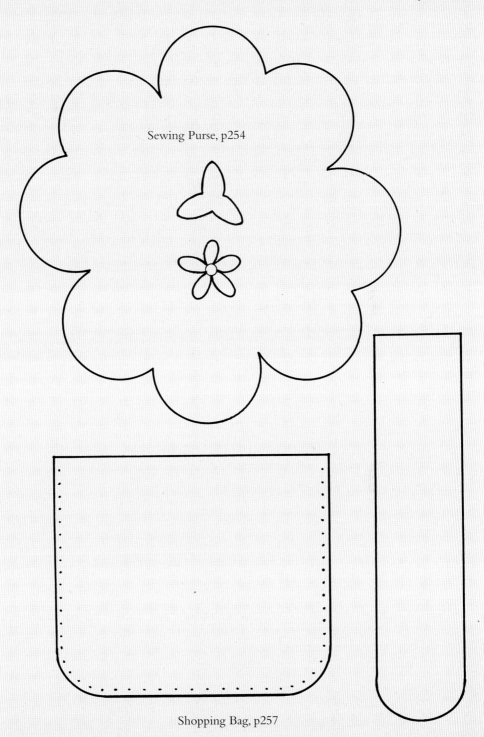

Sewing Purse, p254

Shopping Bag, p257

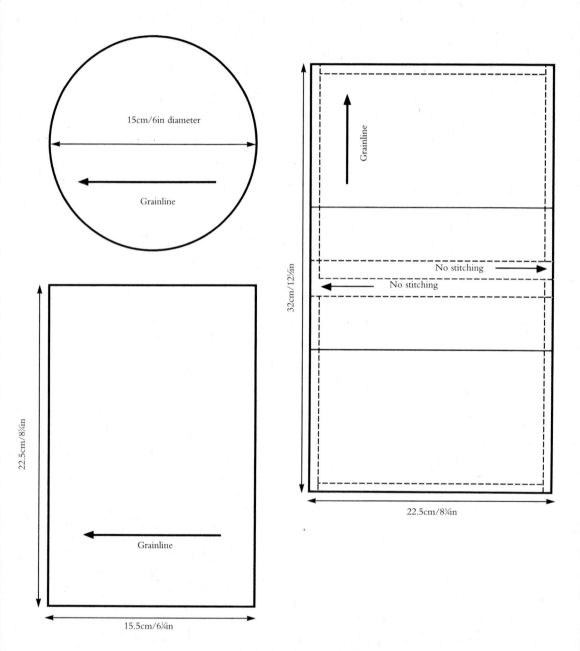

15cm/6in diameter

Grainline

Grainline

32cm/12⅝in

No stitching

No stitching

22.5cm/8¾in

22.5cm/8¾in

Grainline

15.5cm/6¼in

Classic Evening Purse, p311

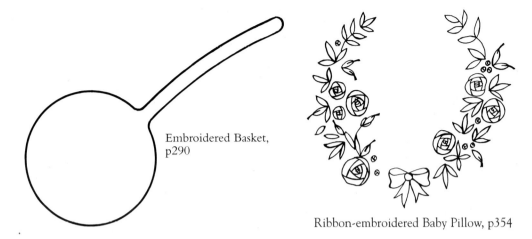

Embroidered Basket,
p290

Ribbon-embroidered Baby Pillow, p354

Two alternative designs are shown here

Bird Lapel Pin, p368

Fishy Cufflinks, p384

Stargazer Earrings, p386

Banded Ring, p382

Flower Pendant,
p390

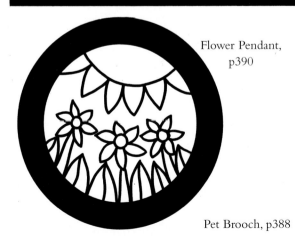

Pet Brooch, p388

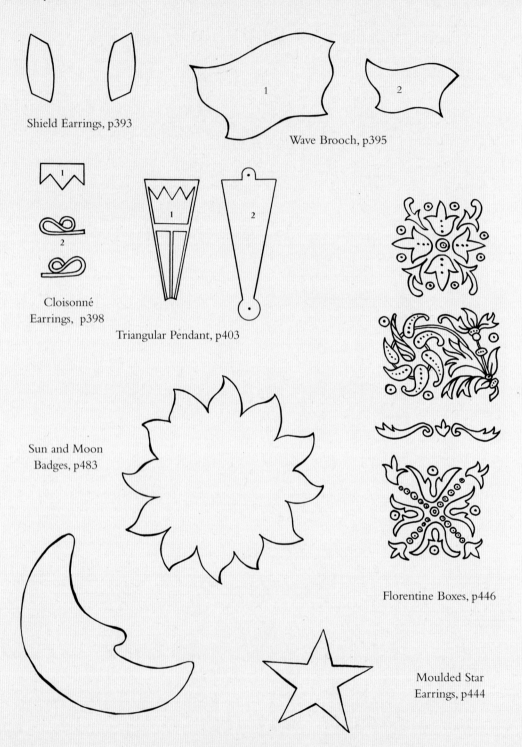

Shield Earrings, p393

Wave Brooch, p395

1

2

Cloisonné
Earrings, p398

1

2

Triangular Pendant, p403

Sun and Moon
Badges, p483

Florentine Boxes, p446

Moulded Star
Earrings, p444

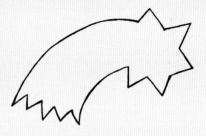

Winged Cupid Brooch, p478

Shooting Star Badge, p488

Fruity Bracelet, p472

Crab Jewel Box, p490

Index

abrasive paper 465, 484
acids 362
adhesives 224, 240
awls 484

baby pillow, ribbon-embroidered 354, 501
backing fabric 224
badges
  blazer badge 182
  shooting star badge 488, 503
  sun and moon badges 483, 502
  sunflower badge 486
bags
  heart-shaped bag 96, 494
  little fringed bag 78–9
  monogrammed bag 70–1
  ribbon evening bag 314–15
  ribbon-embroidered bag 288
  shopping bag 257–8, 499
  textured shoulder bag 238
baking parchment 425
ballet shoes 278
bamboo mats 205
bars 33
basket, embroidered 290, 501
bathroom set 286
baubles 309
bead looms 22
bead trim, woven 118, 495

beading needles 22
beading thread 24
beading wire 24, 30
beadwork 7, 8, 35, 69, 135
  bead chains 30
  bead flowers 31
  bead picot 26
  bead weaving 8, 29
  beads 7, 11, 20
  couching 28
  equipment 22
  findings 32–3
  fringes 26–8
  gallery 16–19
  history 12–15
  needle-woven beading 28
  scallops 28
  wire beading 30
  wrapping 30
beeswax 22
belt, leather chain 248, 498
belt, silver chain 83
bench vices 407
blenders 465
blocks 363
bobbins 170
bookbinding fabric 24
bottle collars, lacy 124

bowls 465
bows 270
boxes
  crab jewel box 490, 503
  decoupage roses box 480–2
  Florentine boxes 446–7, 502
  gift boxes 284–5
  glittering trinket box 98–9
  mirrored trinket box 470
  presentation box 474
  ribbon hat box 303–4
  seashell jewellery box 455
  tinware jewel box 416–17
bracelets 33
  beaded charm bracelet 40
  cord-beaded bracelet 46
  Egyptian bangle 434–5
  felt bracelet 212–13
  fruity bracelet 472, 503
  harlequin bracelet 188–9
  off-loom mesh bracelet 54–5
  spiral bracelets 56–7
  woven bracelet 50, 493
bradawls 484
brass brushes 363
brass screw binders 24
brass shim 406
brayers 425
bronze powder 424
brooches
  butterfly brooch 53, 493
  cloisonné brooch 401–2
  crispy brooch and ring 234–5
  felt flower brooch 214–15, 497
  floral headband and brooch 245, 497
  horse brooch 185–6, 496
  painted tin brooch 412
  pet brooch 388–9, 501
  sparkling starfish brooch 178

spider's web brooch 414–15

star-sign brooch 469

Victorian earrings and brooch 52, 493

wave brooch 305–7, 502

winged Cupid brooch 478, 503

bugle beads 20

buttons 24

acorn buttons 222–3

beaded buttons 81–2

button backs 424

cover buttons 24

multicoloured buttons 370–1

oak-leaf hair clasp and buttons
246–7, 498

snail-shell buttons 453

spider buttons 429

candle-holder, bead 92

candlesticks, beaded wire 74

card 8, 460–1

equipment 465

materials 464

cardboard 460–1, 464

cardboard: gallery 462–3

carded sliver 204

carders 205

centre punches 407

ceramic fibre 362

chandelier, spiralled 90–1

check ribbon 269

choker, loom-woven 64, 493

Christmas beadwork decorations 102

Christmas decorations, ribbon 309–10

clay 8 see also modelling clay;
polymer clay

clay hardeners 424

cloisonné beads 20

coat hangers, ribbon-rose 301–2

collar, lace 208

compasses 170

composite beads 439–40

copper wire 406

cord 24

cord pulls, giant bead 85–6

corsage, French beading 66–7

cotton spheres 24

crab claws 33

craft (utility) knives 22, 205, 240,
425, 465

crystals 20

crystal butterfly 58–9

cufflinks, fishy 384–5, 501

curtain, appliquéd ribbon café 345–6

curtain, ribbon door 330

curtain, simple door 138

cushion trims, beaded 157–8

cushion, basket-weave 350

cushion, golden braid 332

cushion, striped ribbon 336–7

cushion, velvet bolster 146–7

cushions, bead-fringed 155–6

cut-edge craft ribbon 268

cutting mats 465

deck-chair cover 348

decorative heart 307, 494

decoupage 459

cutting out motifs 467

découpage roses box 480–2

gluing motifs 168

painting edges 467

varnishing 468

diamond-impregnated paper 363

double-loop bow 270

drawing pins (thumb tacks) 22

dressmaker's chalk 267

dressmaker's pins 22, 267

drills 451, 484

drop beads 20

drum carders 205

dust masks 451

dyes 170, 204, 241

earrings

cascade earrings 42

cloisonné earrings 398–9, 502

diamond earrings 190

domino hairslide and earrings 226

iridescent earrings and pendant
196–7, 496

Libran earrings 48

marbled earrings 220

moulded star earrings 444, 502

orange-slice earrings 443

plique-à-jour earrings 380

shield earrings 393–4, 502

shimmering earrings 437–8

stargazer earrings 386–7, 501

sun and moon earrings 449

Victorian earrings and brooch 52, 493

wrapped earrings 62–3

embellishments 168

embroidery hoops 22, 170, 224

embroidery scissors 22

embroidery threads (floss) 24, 168, 224

enamel gum solution 362

enamelling 7, 8, 357

acid etching 365

application of enamel 366

equipment 363

finishing 367
gallery 360, 361
history 358
kiln firing 367
materials 362
photo-etching 365
preparation of metal 364
preparing enamel 365
soldering 364
enamels 362
epoxy resin glue 406
equipment 8
beadwork 22
enamelling 363
feltwork 205
machine embroidery 170
metal and wirework 407
paper and card 465
polymer clay 425
ragwork 224
ribbonwork 267
wood 484
etchants 362
eye pins 32

fabric cord 168
fabric dyes 170
fabric markers 22
fabric paints 24
fabrics 24, 168, 224
felt 7, 8, 199, 224
commercial felt 204
self-adhesive felt 168
felt polishing mop 363

felt-tipped pens 24, 240
felteen 204
feltwork 200
equipment 205
gallery 202–3
making felt balls 207
making flat felt 206–7
materials 204
files 363, 407, 451
findings 9, 24, 204, 224
findings: beadwork 32–3
fishing twine 24
florist's tape (stem wrap) 267
floss thread 24
flower, bead-encrusted appliqué
144–5, 495
foil 224, 362, 464
folder, woven ribbon 316–17
frame, flowery 129–30
frame, sequin and bead 122
frames, bead-encrusted 72
fusible bonding web 24

gallery 8
beadwork 16–19
enamelling 360, 361
feltwork 202–3
leatherwork 202, 203
machine embroidery 166–7
metalwork 360, 361
paper, card and wood 462–3
ribbonwork 264–6
shells and clay 422–3
galvanized wire 406

gift wrap 464
giftwrapping, luxurious 280
glass beads 20, 204, 424
glass fibre brush 363
glass gemstones 424
glover's needles 240
glue 170, 267, 406, 424, 451, 464, 484
goggles 451
gold foil beads 372–3
graph paper 22
grosgrain ribbon 268

hair accessories, hooked 228–9
hair clasp and buttons, oak-leaf
246–7, 498
hair clasp, abstract 430
hair comb, glittering 192, 496
hair comb, pearl 60, 494
hairband, geometric 230
hairslide and earrings, domino 226
hammers 407
hand carders 205
hand-wired bow 270
hat, felt 216–17
hat, hooked 236–7
hatpin, embroidered sun 184
hatpin, heart 180, 496
hatpins, beaded 49
head pins 32
headband and brooch, floral 245, 497
headboard, woven ribbon 352–3
headdress, flower and ribbon 321–2
hessian (burlap) 224
history 8
beadwork 12–15
card 460–1
enamelling
feltmaking 200
leatherwork 201
machine embroidery 164–5
metalwork 359
papermaking 460
polymer clay 420–1

rag rugs 201
ribbons 262–3
shells 421
wood 461
hook and eye fasteners 33
hooks 224

ink 451
interfacing 24, 168
invisible thread 168
irons 170

jacket, sunflower-motif 294–5
jacquard ribbon 268–9
jewellery 6–7
  findings 9, 24, 32–3, 204
  ribbon jewellery 296
  wrapped jewellery 232
jewellery wire 424
jug covers, bead-trimmed voile 76–7
jump rings 32

kaolin (ball clay, batwash) 362
kilns 363

lace-edged satin ribbon 269
lampshades 8
  bead pendant light 152
  chunky beaded lampshade 150–1
  fringed lampshade 148–9
  ribbon lantern 338
  rosy lampshade 282
  satin and velvet ribbon shade 340–1
lampwork beads 20

lapel pin, bird 368–9, 501
lavender bottles 306
leather 8, 199, 240
leather needles 240
leather stain 240
leatherwork 201
  dyeing leather 241
  gallery 202, 203
  moulding leather 241
  punching 241
lil pins 24

machine embroidery 8, 163
  equipment 170
  gallery 166–7
  history 164–5
  materials 168
  stabilizers 168, 174–5
  stitch problems 172
  stitches 176–7
  threads 168
  transferring designs 170, 173–4
machine feet 170
machine needles 170
mandrels 363
masking tape 170
materials 8
  beadwork 24
  clay 424
  enamelling 362
  feltwork 204
  machine embroidery 168
  metal and wirework 406

paper and card 464
  ragwork 224
  wood 484
memory wire 30
merrow-edge ribbon 269
metal beads 20
metal scissors 22
metallic leaf 424
metallic ribbon 269
metallic threads 168
metalwork 8, 9, 357
  cutting metal 409
  equipment 407
  finishing edges 409
  gallery 360
  history 359
  materials 406
mica 362
millefiori beads 20, 420, 423
mini-drills 451
mirrors 425
modelling clay 419, 424 *see also*
  polymer clay
  decorating clay 443
  drying clay 443
  mixing clay with colour 443
  mixing clay with hardener 443
  preparing clay 443
modelling tools 425
moiré ribbon 269

natural materials beads 20
necklaces 33
  beaded necklace 194
  burnished bronze necklace 432–3
  Chinese-style necklace 44
  cockle-shell necklace 454
  felt bead necklace 210
  flower pendant 390–1, 501
  furry flower necklace 411
  pearl and crystal necklace 38–9
  striped necklace 377–8
  triangular pendant 403–4, 502

Valentine's locket 456
Venetian necklace 36
needles 22, 170, 205, 240
needlework case, roll-up 318–19
newspaper 464

ombré taffeta ribbon 269
outliner 170
ovens 425

paintbrushes 22, 425, 363, 465, 484
paints 24, 406, 424, 464, 484
palettes 22
paper 7, 8, 168, 459
  découpage 467–8
  equipment 465
  gallery 462–3
  materials 464
  papier mâché 459, 464, 466–7
paper clips (fasteners) 406
pasta machines 425
pastry cutters and moulds 425
pearl beads 20
pencils 465
pens 170
pestle and mortar 363
photograph album, needlepoint 126–7
pickles 362
pillowcase edgings 328–9
pin boards 22
pincushion, Edwardian-style 114
pincushion, strawberry 110–11, 495
pine cone parcels 310
pins 22, 24, 32, 267

pipe cleaners 406
plaid ribbon 269
plastic bags 224
plastic foils 224
plexiglass 425
pliers 22, 407
plywood 484
pocket clips 410
polymer clay 420–1 *see also*
  modelling clay
  clay cane work 427
  complex canes 428
  equipment 425
  flower cane 428
  gallery 422–3
  history 420–1
  jelly roll 427
  making beads 426
  materials 424
  metallic finishes 428
  picture cane 427
  preparing 426
  rolling out 426
  storing in boxes and bags 425
pompom bow 270
pottery beads 20
primer 464
protective clothes 407
pumice powder 362
punches 240, 363
purse, appliquéd 218, 497
purse, classic evening 311–12, 500
purse, coin 252, 498

purse, oak-leaf 243–4
purse, sewing 255–6, 499
putty adhesive 451

quills 363

rags 8, 199, 202
ragwork 201
  backing and finishing 225
  equipment and materials 224
  hooking 225
resists 362
ribbons 7, 8, 24, 261, 268–9, 277,
  327, 451
  equipment 267
  gallery 264–6
  history 262–3
  ribbon bows 270
  ribbon embroidery 275
  ribbon roses 271
  ribbon weaving 272–3
ring, banded 382–3, 501
ring, reptilian 374–6
rocailles 20
rolled-paper beads 476
rolling mills 363
rolling pins 425
rose, stemmed wire-edged 271
rose, stitched ribbon 271
round-nosed (snub-nosed) pliers 22
rulers 22, 170, 465

sanding sealer 464
satin ribbon 269
saws 484
scarf, devoré 100–1
scissors 22, 170, 205, 224, 240, 267, 465
screen, waterfall 131–2
semi-precious stones 20
sequins 20
set squares 170
sewing machines 170
sewing materials 224

sewing needles 170, 205
sewing threads 168, 240, 267
shears 240
sheer ribbon 269
sheet metal 362
shell calottes 33
shellac 464
shells 8, 419, 450–1
  drilling and sawing 452
  gallery 422–3
  history 421
  sanding and polishing 452
shot-effect taffeta ribbon 269
sieves (strainers) 363
silicon carbide (wet and dry) paper 407
silver 7
silver-plated copper wire 406
slippers, child's 94–5, 494
soap flakes 205
solder 362, 406
soldering equipment 363, 407
spacers 33
spheres, glittering bead 108–9
splashback, fish mosaic 160–1, 496
sponges 465
squares 484
stitching 274–5
  machine stitches 176–7
stone-effect beads 451
string 205
stub (floral) wire 267

table decoration set 87–8
table mats, ribbon 292
taffeta ribbon 269
tape 24
tape measures 22, 170, 267
tapestry canvas and wool (yarn) 24
tapestry, beaded boat 116–19, 494
tartan ribbon roses 298–9
tassel, golden 310
tassel, ribbon tassel tie-back 343–4
tassels, beaded 120–1

tassels, silken key 112–13
tassels, suede 250, 498
techniques 8
  beadwork 26–33
  enamelling 364–7
  feltwork 206–7
  machine embroidery 172–7
  metalwork 409
  modelling clay 443
  polymer clay 426–8
  ragwork 225
  ribbonwork 270–3
  shells 452
  stitching 274–5
  wirework 408
  wood 485
templates 170, 493–503
  scaling up 492
  tracing 492
thread 24, 168, 204, 267
throw, beaded 140
throw, ribbon-decorated 334–5
tie-back, ribbon tassel 343–4
tie-backs, chunky bead 104–5
tiger tail 30
tin plate 406
tin snips 407
tools 8
triangles 32
tweezers 22, 363, 451

uncarded fleece 204

vanishing muslin 168

varnish 424, 464, 484
velvet ribbon 269
Venetian glass beads 20

waistcoat, woven ribbon 323–4
wall sconce, beaded 106–7
washing (baking) soda crystals 362
water 362
water-soluble polythene 168
water-soluble stabilizer 168
weaving boards 267
window decoration, glittering 136
window hanging, beaded 142–3
wire 24, 30, 224, 267, 362, 406, 424
wire cutters 22, 267, 407
wire-edged taffeta ribbon 269
wired tape 406
wirework 359, 360
  equipment 407
  making coils 408
  materials 406
  twisting soft wire 408
wood 8, 459, 461
  gallery 462
  materials and equipment 484
  smoothing surfaces 485
  transferring designs 485
  using a frame saw 485
wool threads 168
wound beads 20
woven-edge ribbon 269

zinc sheet 406

510

Acknowledgements

The publisher would like to thank the following people for the projects and photography in this book: (Apologies to any people who may, unintentionally, not be credited.)

OFER ACOO, Spider's Web Brooch p414, Moulded Star Earrings p444, Sun and Moon Earrings p449.

EVELYN BENNETT, Tinware Jewel Box p416.

PENNY BOYLAN, Ribbon Rose Coat Hangers p300.

LISA BROWN, Monogrammed Bag p70, Bead-encrusted Frames p72, Beaded Wire Candlesticks p74, Bead-trimmed Voile Jug Covers p76, Giant Bead Cord-pulls p84, Table Decoration Set p87, Chunky Bead Tie-backs p104, Beaded Wall Sconce p106, Glittering Bead Spheres p108, Strawberry Pincushion p110, Silken Key Tassels p112, Beaded Boat Tapestry p116, Woven Bead Trim p118, Lacy Bottle Covers p124, Simple Door Curtain p138, Beaded Throw p140, Beaded Window Hanging p142, Bead-encrusted Appliqué Flower p144, Beaded Cushion Trims p155, Fish Mosaic Splashback p160, Luxurious Giftwrapping p280, Rosy Lampshade p282, Embroidered Basket p290, Ribbon Evening Bag p314, Pillowcase Edgings p328, Ribbon Door Curtain p330, Ribbon-decorated Throw p334, Striped Ribbon Cushion p336, Ribbon Tassel Tie-back p342, Appliquéd Ribbon Café Curtain p345, Deck-chair Cover p348, Woven Ribbon Headboard p352.

VICTORIA BROWN, Sequin and Bead Frame p122, Lace Collar p208, Felt Bead Necklace p210, Felt Bracelet p212, Felt Flower Brooch p214, Felt Hat p216, Appliquéd Purse 218, Marbled Earrings p220, Acorn Buttons p222.

LOUISE BROWNLOW, Libran Earrings p48, Iridescent Earrings and Pendant p196.

JUDY CLAYTON, Embroidered Sun Hatpin p184.

MARION ELLIOT, Painted Tin Brooches p412, Rolled-paper Beads p476.

SOPHIE EMBLETON, Fruity Bracelet p472.

LUCINDA GANDERTON, Pearl and Crystal Necklace p38, Beaded Charm Bracelet p40, Cascade Earrings p42, Beaded Hatpins p49, Off-loom Mesh Bracelet p54, Crystal Butterfly p58, French Beading Corsage p66, Silver Chain Belt p83, Heart-shaped Bag p96, Edwardian-style Pincushion p114, Ribbon Hat Box p303, Florentine Boxes p446.

DAWN GIULLAS, Pocket Clips p410.

SUSIE JOHNS, Glittering Trinket Box p88.

JILL HANCOCK, Sun and Moon Badges p483, Sunflower Badge p486, Shooting Star Badge p488.

ALISON HARPER, Victorian Earrings and Brooch p52.

ANGELA HARRISON, Wrapped Jewellery p232.

ALISON JENKINS, Glittering Window Decoration p136.

LINDSAY KAUBI, Loom-woven Choker p64.

CHRISTINE KINGDOM, Ballet Shoes p278, Gift Boxes p284, Bathroom Set p286, Ribbon-embroidered Bag p288, Ribbon

Table Mats p292, Sunflower-motif Jacket p294, Ribbon Jewellery p296, Tartan Ribbon Roses p298, Ribbon Christmas Decorations p308, Classic Evening Purse p311, Woven Ribbon Folder p316, Roll-up Needlework Case p318, Flower and Ribbon Headdress p344, Woven Ribbon Waistcoat p347, Golden Braid Cushion p332, Ribbon Lantern p338, Basket-weave Cushion p350, Ribbon-embroidered Baby Pillow p354.

KITCHEN TABLE STUDIOS, Egyptian Bangle p434.

MARY MAGUIRE, Oak-leaf Purse p242, Floral Headband and Brooch p245, Oak-leaf Hair Clasp and Buttons p246, Leather Chain Belt p248, Suede Tassels p250, Coin Purse p252, Sewing Purse p255, Shopping Bag p257, Furry Flower Necklace p411, Spider Buttons p429, Abstract Hair Clasp p430, Burnished Bronze Necklace p432, Shimmering Earrings p436, Composite Beads p439, Snail-shell Buttons p453, Cockle-shell Necklace p454, Valentine's Locket p456.

ABIGAIL MILL, Sparkling Starfish Brooch p56.

JANE MOORE, Banded Ring p382, Fishy Cufflinks p384, Stargazer Earrings p386, Pet Brooch p388, Flower Pendant p390.

DENISE PALMER, Plique-à-jour Earrings p380.

MAGGIE PRYCE, Découpage Roses Box p480.

ALEX RAPHAEL, Multicoloured Buttons p370.

LIZZIE REAKES, Domino Hairslide and Earrings p226, Hooked Hair Accessories p228, Geometric Hairband p230, Crispy Brooch and Ring p234.

KIM ROWLEY, Star-sign Brooch p469, Mirrored Trinket Box p470, Winged Cupid Brooch p478.

RUTH RUSHBY, Bird Lapel Pin p368, Gold Foil Beads p372, Cloisonné Earrings p398, Cloisonné Brooch p400, Triangular Pendant p403.

ISABEL STANLEY, Venetian Necklace p36, Chinese-style Necklace p44, Cord-beaded Bracelet p46, Woven Bracelet p50, Spiral Bracelets p56, Pearl Hair Comb p60, Wrapped Earrings p62, Little Fringed Bag p78, Beaded Buttons p80, Spiral Chandelier p90, Bead Candle-holder p92, Child's Slippers p94, Devoré Scarf p100, Christmas Beadwork Decorations p102, Beaded Tassels p120, Needlepoint Photograph Album p126, Flowery Frame p128, Waterfall Screen p131, Velvet Bolster Cushion p146, Fringed Lampshade p148, Chunky Beaded Lampshade p150,

Bead Pendant Light p152, Bead-fringed Cushions p154, Heart Hatpin p180, Blazer Badge p182, Horse Brooch p185, Harlequin Bracelet p188, "Diamond" Earrings p190, Glittering Hair Comb p192, Beaded Necklace p194, Satin and Velvet Ribbon Shade 340.

JU JU VAIL, Hooked Hat p236, Textured Shoulder Bag p238.

SARAH WILSON, Reptilian Ring p374, Striped Necklace p377, Shield Earrings p392, Wave Brooch p397.

DOROTHY WOOD, Butterfly Brooch p53, Orange-slice Earrings p442.

PHOTOGRAPHY
The publishers would like to thank the following photographers for their work on the featured projects: Karl Adamson, Lisa Brown, Steve Dalton, Nicki Dowey, James Duncan, John Freeman, Michelle Garrett, Janine Hosegood, Tim Imrie, Gloria Nicol, Lizzie Orme, David Parmiter, Debbie Patterson, Lucinda Symons, Debi Treloar, Peter Williams.

This edition is published by Hermes House,
an imprint of Anness Publishing Ltd,
Blaby Road, Wigston, Leicestershire LE18 4SE
Email: info@anness.com
Web: www.hermeshouse.com; www.annesspublishing.com

If you like the images in this book and would like to investigate using them for
publishing, promotions or advertising, please visit our website
www.practicalpictures.com for more information.

Publisher: Joanna Lorenz
Editorial Director: Helen Sudell
Project Editor: Simona Hill
Designer: Nigel Partridge
Editorial Reader: Penelope Goodare
Production Controller: Steve Lang

A CIP catalogue record for this book is available from the British Library

Previously published in two separate volumes, *Create Your Own Jewelry* by Ann Kay and
Complete Beads & Beadwork by Lucinda Ganderton

PUBLISHER'S NOTE
Although the advice and information in this book are believed to be accurate and true
at the time of going to press, neither the authors nor the publisher can accept any legal
responsibility or liability for any errors or omissions that may have been made nor for
any inaccuracies nor for any loss, harm or injury that comes about from following
instructions or advice in this book.

ETHICAL TRADING POLICY
At Anness Publishing we believe that
business should be conducted in an
ethical and ecologically sustainable way,
with respect for the environment and a
proper regard to the replacement of the
natural resources we employ.
As a publisher, we use a lot of wood pulp
to make high-quality paper for printing,
and that wood commonly comes from
spruce trees. We are therefore currently
growing more than 750,000 trees in
three Scottish forest plantations:
Berrymoss (130 hectares/320 acres),
West Touxhill (125 hectares/305 acres)
and Deveron Forest (75 hectares/185
acres). The forests we manage contain
more than 3.5 times the number of trees
employed each year in making paper for
the books we manufacture.
Because of this ongoing ecological
investment programme, you, as our
customer, can have the pleasure and
reassurance of knowing that a tree is
being cultivated on your behalf to
naturally replace the materials used to
make the book you are holding.
Our forestry programme is run in
accordance with the UK Woodland
Assurance Scheme (UKWAS) and will
be certified by the internationally
recognized Forest Stewardship Council
(FSC). The FSC is a non-government
organization dedicated to promoting
responsible management of the world's
forests. Certification ensures forests are
managed in an environmentally
sustainable and socially responsible way.
For further information about this
scheme, go to
www.annesspublishing.com/trees